Android™ Apps

Secrets to Selling Your Android App

Marketing

Jeffrey Hughes

800 East 96th Street,
Indianapolis, Indiana 46240 USA

Android™ Apps Marketing: Secrets to Selling Your Android App

ISBN-13: 978-0-7897-4633-7
ISBN-10: 0-7897-4633-6

The Library of Congress Cataloging-in-Publication data is on file.

Printed in the United States of America

First Printing: September 2010

Trademarks

Warning and Disclaimer

Bulk Sales

Que Publishing offers excellent discounts on this book when ordered in quantity for bulk purchases or special sales. For more information, please contact

U.S. Corporate and Government Sales
1-800-382-3419
corpsales@pearsontechgroup.com

For sales outside of the U.S., please contact

International Sales
international@pearson.com

Associate Publisher
Greg Wiegand

Senior Acquisitions Editor
Katherine Bull

Technical Editor
Gary Bennett

Development Editor
Susan Zahn

Managing Editor
Kristy Hart

Project Editor
Betsy Harris

Copy Editor
Bart Reed

Indexer
Lisa Stumpf

Proofreader
Debbie Williams

Publishing Coordinator
Cindy Teeters

Book Designer
Anne Jones

Compositor
Nonie Ratcliff

CONTENTS AT A GLANCE

TABLE OF CONTENTS

About the Author

Jeffrey Hughes brings more than 18 years of industry passion as a marketer, publisher, and keynote speaker in high technology industries, including such companies as McAfee, Blue Coat Systems, Webroot, and Novell. Hughes is the author of 12 books and numerous trade press articles on marketing and technology topics. He is also the author of the popular book *iPhone and iPad Apps Marketing: Secrets to Selling Your iPhone and iPad Apps* (ISBN: 978-0789744272).

Hughes is the developer and lead instructor for Xcelme's (www.xcelme.com) popular app marketing courses, which have helped scores of developers learn how to market their apps the right way in a highly competitive market.

Hughes is a frequent contributor of articles to popular app sites. He has also been a consultant for a growing number of independent developers and small companies, teaching them how to launch and market their apps as well as offering marketing expertise and consulting services to help their apps gain maximum exposure. Hughes has a B.S. in marketing and a minor in computer science from Brigham Young University. He resides in Scottsdale, Arizona.

Dedication

For my daughters, Laurin and McKenna, who keep me motivated. Here's to your success in everything that you do.

Acknowledgments

I would like to acknowledge senior acquisitions editor Katherine Bull, who approached me with the idea of creating this book and who has guided this project from start to finish with her expert advice and suggestions. I also want to thank Gary Bennett, app developer and instructor extraordinaire, who was one of the first to bring app development courses to the masses via live and recorded webinars.

Thanks also to Susan Zahn, development editor, and Bart Reed, copy editor, who have done a marvelous job editing the entire book. They have made great suggestions and provided great input to the project! I also want to thank Betsy Harris for her speedy and accurate production of the book into its final form. She has worked tirelessly under very tight deadlines and always does a superb job.

Finally, I wish to thank the developers of Android apps across the world! Some of you I have spoken to personally and have included some of your apps as examples in this book. I wish all developers phenomenal success in their app-development projects. We are only at the beginning of this marvelous new journey of mobile computing, which can be likened to the dawn of the Internet in its importance!

We Want to Hear from You!

As the reader of this book, *you* are our most important critic and commentator. We value your opinion and want to know what we're doing right, what we could do better, what areas you'd like to see us publish in, and any other words of wisdom you're willing to pass our way.

As an associate publisher for Que Publishing, I welcome your comments. You can email or write me directly to let me know what you did or didn't like about this book—as well as what we can do to make our books better.

Please note that I cannot help you with technical problems related to the topic of this book. We do have a User Services group, however, where I will forward specific technical questions related to the book.

When you write, please be sure to include this book's title and author as well as your name, email address, and phone number. I will carefully review your comments and share them with the author and editors who worked on the book.

Email: feedback@quepublishing.com

Mail: Greg Wiegand
           Associate Publisher
           Que Publishing
           800 East 96th Street
           Indianapolis, IN 46240 USA

Reader Services

Visit our website and register this book at quepublishing.com/register for convenient access to any updates, downloads, or errata that might be available for this book.

...ssed something remark-...reated and posted apps ...dy pace. The Android ...apps and shows steady ...old rush to sell Android ...want to create) the next ...e dollar signs and want to be a part of this explosive new business opportunity. So do thousands of your friends, all toiling late nights and weekends to strike it rich. Large development companies also want a piece of the action and have teams of pro- grammers cranking out apps as quickly as they can bring them to market. Compounding the problem is the acceler- ated pace of technology. We have moved beyond "Internet time," referring to the incredible speed at which technology advances, to "mobile time," where technology is deployed almost instantly to anyone with a mobile device. This means that consumers have an avalanche of choices when it comes to the technology and content they consume.

What we are seeing on the Android Market, however, is not a new phenomenon. Amazon boasts hundreds of thousands of book titles, most selling perhaps a few copies a month. Only the most publicized and bestselling books make Amazon's Top 100 list on its home page. The fact that the top 100 selling books are on the list helps them sell even more copies. It's self-perpetuating. So, every author aspires to be on that list. In similar fashion, every Android app developer aspires to make it on Google's best selling list, or to be showcased on the Android Market as a featured app. Developers know that making it on those lists will catapult them into realizing dramatically higher sales. How do you increase your chances of getting noticed? Well, doing no marketing is a surefire way *not* to get noticed. Marketing in some form or another is going to raise your chances of success. All apps that have achieved notable success have done so through marketing, either intentionally or unintentionally. These apps have managed to attract the attention of reviewers and capture the imaginations of thousands through positive word of mouth.

Beyond posting your app on Google Android Market, you may be wondering what else is needed to successfully market your Android app. In short, lots! The days of simply posting your app on the Android Market and achieving instant success are long gone. Sure, some developers have hit pay dirt, just like the next Vegas jackpot winner. We all love to read those stories. It's not impossible, but the odds of hitting the jackpot have gone down dramatically. So many apps have been introduced so quickly that it's impossible for any casual observer to keep track of the 200+ apps delivered to the Android Market each day. Once on the market, customers are faced with the challenge of reviewing scores of similar apps, trying to figure out the best one to download. It's a tall order for any app buyer.

How does an independent developer stand out in a sea of apps? How can someone beat the odds in this high-stakes game? The answer is (sort of) simple. Build a great (and I mean great) Android app and devise a stellar marketing plan to capture the hearts and minds of thousands. The execution of these two strategies, however, is not so simple. Many developers rush their apps to market and think the momentum of the Android smartphones and the Android Market will carry them forward. They hope a little luck will be on their side and that they'll get a positive review or get noticed by Google's staff with a mention. But often, they end up with a mediocre app, no reviews, and maybe three of four downloads a day. Then, they consider marketing...as an afterthought.

But, if you have aspirations to make more than a little spending money from your app, then you must follow tried-and-true marketing (and some offbeat) principles to get your app noticed. You must also look at the newer tools of marketing, including social media, to keep your message in front of a very tech-savvy audience. As a developer you need to think about the key areas of marketing before, during, and after your app is created. You need to build your app with a clear objective and have a clearly identified audience who is interested in your solution. You also need to think about pricing and promotions, sales and support, and creating buzz for your app. This is not easy work, but it's absolutely necessary to achieve the results you want to see with your app.

The good news is that the marketing process for Android apps is really no different from marketing any other product; it's just highly compressed in terms of the buying process. The principles are the same, even though some of the marketing tools have expanded dramatically in recent years, especially in the area of mass communication and social media. The steps are also still the same: You develop an app that customers need and want, create a solid marketing message, deliver the message to the right audience, build a following, and develop new apps and upgrades to retain existing customers. Remember that marketing is a *process*, not a one-time event. Marketing also takes hard work and effort. It is not a spectator sport.

When you understand that marketing is a continuum that incorporates these fundamental steps, you will be able to plan and implement them to increase sales success for your Android app. This book will assist you in understanding the necessary marketing steps to increase exposure for your Android app(s), whether you are just starting out as a first-time developer or have created and posted a number of apps for sale. This book assumes you want to move beyond being a casual developer and seller of Android apps to a successful marketer of your own best-selling apps and brand.

1. **Build Your Android App Marketing Plan**

    Marketing doesn't have to be mysterious or complicated. You can quickly gain a greater understanding of marketing processes and make them work for you. You can learn how to generate a solid, reusable marketing plan through the following:

    - The identification and definition of your Android app's unique value and purpose

    - The creation of a powerful, easy-to-remember message for your app

    - The use of the right marketing tools to deliver your message to the right audience at the right time

2. **Deliver Your Marketing Message**

    The timely delivery of the right message to the right audience using the right technology will help set you apart from the competition.

3. **Convert Your Prospects to Customers**

    By following the instructions in this book, you will be able to develop an effective marketing plan. A marketing plan is your guide to converting prospective buyers to becoming customers of your Android apps.

4.   **Reuse Your Marketing Plan**

Marketing is a process that, when followed, brings predictable results. This book provides a valuable overview of basic marketing principles, but also includes the secrets of moving prospective customers from being casual app observers to enthusiastic buyers.

Part I: Your Marketing Message

Everything from naming your app to the text you place on the Android Market (and many other components) contributes to your marketing message. What sets your Android app apart from all your competitors? How can you convey that unique message to your buyers? Let's face it. There are lots of competitors with similar apps. In this part of the book, you'll review steps to help you create a unique message that will distinguish your app from the competition. You'll do this by examining positioning, target audience, competition, and other market conditions. The following chapters are included in Part I of the book:

- **Chapter 1: Your Android App Marketing Strategy: Grand Slam or Base Hits?**

  Learn how messaging works and understand how Android messaging is similar and, in some cases, very different from marketing for other products.

- **Chapter 2: What Makes for a Winning App?**

  What are the key selling points of your app? Can you identify key strengths and competitive advantages to highlight your app? Learn how to distill this essential information.

- **Chapter 3: Identifying Your App's Unique Value**

  Zero in on what matters and create a crisp message that meets some basic criteria and is easy to remember.

- **Chapter 4: Identifying Your Target Audience**

  The best results from your marketing message come when you have targeted a specific audience with a clear message. Learn how to find your target audience.

- **Chapter 5: Building Your App's Total Message**

  An effective app name, a crisp Android Market store message, and a clear and concise website all contribute to your overall marketing message. Choosing not to do some of these things may not impact your sales. Not doing any of them, however, will.

Part II: Delivering Your Message

With a carefully crafted message you are now ready to deliver your message to the right audience and through the right means for maximum exposure and effectiveness. This section provides an overview of the various methods available to reach different audiences and create demand for your Android apps. Demand is created when you help a prospective customer see that you have a solution to their problem or you pique their curiosity with a challenging game or puzzle. The demand for most products is already there; it's just a matter of creating a message that resonates with that audience and gets them to notice your app. The following chapters are included in Part II of this book:

- **Chapter 6: Electronic Word of Mouth**

  Word of mouth is one of the most powerful means of increasing sales of your Android app. Learn how to get people talking about your app.

- **Chapter 7: Using Social Media in Your App Marketing**

  Create a following for your brand and your apps using Facebook, MySpace, Twitter, blogs, and YouTube. LinkedIn is another way to use these newer tools to achieve greater exposure for your app.

- **Chapter 8: Timing Your Marketing Activities**

  When do you want to communicate your message? Often, timing plays a role in how well your marketing message will be received. Learn how to coordinate the delivery of your marketing message for maximum impact and results.

- **Chapter 9: Getting the Word Out About Your App**

  A press release can be a very powerful tool to spread the word about your app, but it has to be written professionally and adhere to very specific guidelines to attract the attention of your audience. Learn the tricks of the trade.

Part III: Pricing Your Android App

A key aspect of marketing your Android app is to carefully set your price. Setting your price is not a trivial matter. Part III of this book walks you through pricing considerations and helps you understand the buyer's mentality and decision-making process. You'll learn how to create promotions and cross-sell your app where possible—another important aspect of pricing. The following chapters are included in Part III:

- **Chapter 10: Pricing Your App**

  Perhaps one of the biggest challenges of developing an Android app is pricing. In this chapter you'll learn how and where to begin to price your app for maximum success.

- **Chapter 11: Conducting an App Pricing Analysis**

  A pricing analysis will help you calculate your breakeven point—that is, how many apps you need to sell to cover your costs and start to make a profit.

- **Chapter 12: Selling Value over Price**

  Some apps will be priced higher than the usual $0.99 or $1.99. Learn how to convey the value of your apps and get the price you're entitled to for all your hard work.

- **Chapter 13: Breaking into the Android Market Top Paid Apps**

  You can do a number of things in an effort to get your app into the top tier of sales. Learn the best tips to reach maximum success on the Android Market.

- **Chapter 14: Level the Playing Field with a Free App**

  Learn the pros and cons to creating a free version of your app to expand your sales. Free apps with a paid app are the trend of the future for Android applications.

- **Chapter 15: The App Pricing Rollercoaster**

  Raising and lowering your price can have an impact on sales, but there is a cost and you'll learn it here.

- **Chapter 16: App Promotions and Cross-Selling**

  Promotions aren't just for your local car dealership. Some promotions can work to sell your Android app. Cross-selling can also work in certain circumstances.

- **Chapter 17: Using Android Analytics**

  Now's the time to let math be your friend. The app analytics discussed in this chapter will help you sell more of your apps. Learn the tools available for Android developers and how to interpret the results to your benefit.

Part IV: Implement a Marketing Plan/Launch Your App

With the right message and the right audience, combined with the right marketing tools and methods, you can create extremely effective marketing campaigns. Part IV of this book walks you through the steps of implementing a marketing campaign and provides a fully developed sample campaign ready for you to implement. The following chapters are included in this part of the book:

- **Chapter 18: Why Have a Marketing Plan?**

  When developers hear about a marketing plan, they usually run the other way. This marketing plan is short, to the point, and effective. You need to have a plan to guide your app to sales success.

- **Chapter 19: Components of an App Marketing Plan**

  Learn the basic components of an Android app marketing plan and how they can be used to help you stay on track during development and launch.

- **Chapter 20: Marketing Essentials**

  Not all marketing plans are designed the same. Learn which types of apps need a certain plan. Also learn what to do if you've already posted your app and you're not seeing great sales.

- **Chapter 21: Twenty-Five Essential Android Marketing Activities**

  Learn the top 25 marketing activities that will help your app achieve maximum exposure and success.

- **Chapter 22: Implementing Your Plan**

  If you have planned for it, your app launch should be an exciting and exhilarating experience. Learn how to get ready for the launch of your Android app.

- **Chapter 23: Android Apps for Corporate Marketing**

  If you are working for a large corporation, you'll want to read this chapter on how to develop apps that help your company with branding. Lots of companies have built free apps for name recognition and brand value alone, while others are charging for them.

Conclusion

So there you have it. Who thought so much could be said about marketing an Android app? Google has created an incredible and growing opportunity for developers around the world to achieve success on the Android Market and other sites that showcase Android apps. Although not without its flaws and complaints, the Android Market has created a tremendous opportunity for individual developers and app companies to build and sell mobile technology for the masses. Here's to your success.

1

Your Android App Marketing Strategy: Grand Slam or Base Hits?

As an Android app developer, you want to strike it rich selling your app to millions of customers—or at least tens of thousands of customers to make your hard work pay off. Other equally ambitious developers hope to achieve a steady income and perhaps write apps full time and leave their other full-time jobs behind. Although these goals are possible, it takes a lot of hard work to achieve such success.

There are several reasons. First, the sheer number of apps for sale on the Android Market has made it a little more difficult to stand out from the crowd. Instead of just a few similar apps in your category, there are likely many vying for the buyer's attention. You are competing against free and paid apps—some brilliantly written and some not even worth giving away. Although not as large as the iTunes App Store, the Android Market it growing considerably, with 70,000 apps at the time of this writing. The Android Market is currently adding about 5,000 apps per month.

Second, the intense pricing pressure causes many developers to start off at a low price or quickly drop their price to $0.99, a figure that makes it extremely difficult to break even, much less make any profit. According to researcher Mobclix (www.mobclix.com), the average price of an app on the Android Market is $4.10 compared to $3.37 on the iTunes App Store.

The sheer number of competing apps may seem daunting; however, these statistics are not presented to be discouraging. Rather, this chapter is designed to point out that the Android Market is maturing very quickly, just like other app markets, and you *have* to develop a solid marketing strategy to realize success. The Android Market is not running on Internet time, it's on mobile time! Your marketing strategy also has to be tuned to work with your buyer.

We've Seen This Before

The Android Market is much like your local supermarket. In the 1980s the average supermarket carried about 7,500 items. Today, that same supermarket carries upwards of 50,000 items! Every vendor is fighting for shelf space so more people will buy its products. Manufacturers want their products positioned at eye level or placed on their own display at the end of an aisle. They are willing to pay extra for this privilege. The supermarket makes its money through high volume turnover of its products. Those items that don't sell well are pushed to the bottom of the shelves or moved to another part of the store.

Amazon.com is no different; vendors are trying to stand out in a very crowded market. Not counting other items, Amazon's bookstore alone boasts well over 250,000 titles. Many authors hope to achieve fame and fortune by landing on the top-100 list on Amazon's book home page. Other authors hope to get their big break by being mentioned on *Oprah*.

The Android Market has exploded from its introduction of less than 500 apps to well over 70,000 apps at the time of this writing. Just like the supermarket vendors, every app developer is vying for that eye-level virtual shelf space, hoping to get top billing so buyers will take a look. They are hoping to get a mention in the "Featured" section of the Android store. Table 1.1 shows the breakout of the different categories of apps available in the Android Market. Approximately 150–250 apps are posted to the store each day! According to Google, almost 1,000 apps per week are submitted for placement on the Android Market. At this pace we could easily see well over 100,000 apps posted to the Android Market by the end of 2010.

Table 1.1   Percentages for the Most Popular Categories in the Android Market

Type of Android App	Percentage of Total Apps
Games	30%
Books	18%
Entertainment	20%
Travel	15%
Education	10%
Other	7%

Source: www.androlib.com

As the Android Market has grown, it has necessitated reconfiguration numerous times to further segment the apps into logical groups where buyers can more easily connect with sellers. Google has improved the search capabilities of the store, added subcategories, and added Top Paid, Top Free, and Featured links, as shown in Figure 1.1. The top paid and free apps are displayed on the home page of the Android Market, along with a Featured section.

Figure 1.1   The Top Paid, Top Free, and Featured links are shown on the left of the Android Market's home page.

 Note

The web-based Android Market only displays a portion of the available Android apps. To view all apps you must use an Android smartphone of your choice.

The Android Market will continue to make improvements to help strengthen and refine the search process and showcase apps in the best way possible. After all, Google has a vested interest in your success. The more apps you sell, the more the company makes. Perhaps more importantly, the more apps that are sold, the stronger the Android brand. Google doesn't publish Android Market sales in its earnings results, but like Apple it is using the store to help build its platform and increase sales of its phones to the masses.

 Note

Someone once said (possibly Rudi Giuliani) that hope is not strategy. Hope is also not a marketing strategy! Posting your app on the Android Market and hoping for the best is not a plan and will more than likely result in mediocre sales from the start.

To create a winning sales and marketing strategy for your app, it's important to understand the dynamics of the Android Market and understand that there are several strategies you can employ. Most developers are trying to knock their app out of the park. They want the grand slam and think anything less is failure. A number of developers give up, thinking there's only two possible outcomes: the big win and no win. But, there are actually three possible outcomes: the Big Win app, the Steady Win app, and the No Win app. All apps fall into one of these three categories. Over time, and without marketing or product updates, all apps will eventually slide from one category to the next one below it.

The Big Win—Grand Slam

The Big Win apps (or Grand Slams) are generally characterized by explosive sales from their launch. Games, by far, make up the majority of the Big Win apps. Why? Because games take advantage of the impulse buy, which occurs directly from an Android smartphone. Games are the most likely apps to be bought on impulse. The impulse buyer doesn't care about reviews. Sometimes a community of people is familiar with a particular development company and they are hungry to purchase its new app. Some companies have made their apps successful by porting an already successful PC or Mac game over to the Android platform.

Big Win apps have been positioned by large development companies with huge followings. Their aim is to achieve quick sales on apps that are priced in the games sweet spot—from $0.99 to $2.99. At these price points, the impulse buyers are looking for something to occupy their time. The longevity of this type of app may be short, lasting only a few weeks or months. Then the same company releases another

app and focuses its attention on that. Some winning apps are designed in such a
way to bring the customer back over and over again with multiple levels of play.
One of the most popular game apps, providing 120 levels of play, is *Robo Defense*,
shown in Figure 1.2. *Robo Defense* provides at least 30 minutes of play per level, and
the makers of the game have developed a very strong community of users who
keep the game in the spotlight.

Figure 1.2   *Robo Defense* has done a very good job keeping customers engaged with
an enormous number of play levels (120 total if you figure 40 levels of play with three
different maps).

Another common element for Big Win games is that they are usually simplistic in
their premise. The masses of Android users purchase games that are easy to learn.
Low on learning, high on enjoyment is the rule of thumb for the quick win Big Win
games. The typical game buyer doesn't want to learn tons of rules to a new game
and instead wants to understand the point of the app immediately.

The Big Win apps can also come from independent developers. However, the big
wins for independent developers are happening less and less often due to the number of games on the Android Market and because game quality is going up while
the time to market is going down. Larger companies have the development staff
that can bring apps to market more quickly without sacrificing quality. It simply
takes an independent developer longer to create a high-powered, high-quality game
app. Once a following is created and the app is updated frequently, you will continue to attract customers, as has been the case with the *Bejeweled* app, which is
shown in Figure 1.3.

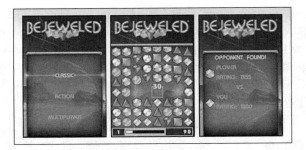

Figure 1.3   Positive reviews and sales continue to roll in for the infamous *Bejeweled* app.

The last characteristic of these apps is that they often get a big break from the press as being an app to look at. Tom Clancy achieved remarkable success with his book *The Hunt for Red October* when Ronald Reagan praised the book after he read it while on vacation. After Reagan's comments, sales of that book skyrocketed. If an Android app gets a lucky break from a major news agency, it can serve as the catalyst to get sales moving in a big way. Word of mouth takes it from there.

Another app that falls into this category is shown in Figure 1.4. This app has achieved solid success. *Car Locator* continues to stay on the bestseller list due to its simple navigation and huge following.

Figure 1.4   *Car Locator* has achieved Big Win success with well over 1.3 million downloads.

The Steady Win—Base Hits

The next category of Android apps is the Steady Win, also known as "base hit apps." This category may be overlooked by some app developers who focus solely on the Big Win. The majority of new Android apps land in this category, even if the developer has intentions of its app making it into the Big Win group. These apps rely on Android app reviews, positive blog posts, and making it onto the Android Market's "wall of fame," where the app is placed in the "New and Noteworthy" or "Staff

Picks" section for a time. These placements are definitely helpful and will boost sales noticeably while you remain on the list.

These apps also rely on good old-fashioned, consistent marketing. The revenue of this type of app can be more predictable when the seller understands what marketing activities work for them. With a good app, the right marketing mix, and product updates, your app can achieve success on the Android Market. It may not be multi-million dollar success, but it can be decent. It may be enough to compel you to write multiple apps, build a brand, and truly make a business out of your efforts.

Some apps that have achieved solid success that are not necessarily Android games are shown in Figure 1.5 and Figure 1.6. These apps have been achieving a steady revenue stream for their developers, albeit not at the $10,000+ per month level. They have strong value propositions and the products resonate with their intended audience. These apps are focused on getting healthy and saving money, topics that interest almost everyone.

Figure 1.5   *Piggy Bank* is an app that allows you to track how well you are doing quitting smoking by rewarding yourself with money each time you avoid the bad habit.

Figure 1.6   *Racing for Cardio Trainer* is an app that simulates a full virtual race, with a voice telling you exactly how far behind or ahead you are.

Because most apps fall into the category of Steady Win, the bulk of this book is focused on helping you achieve ongoing success through a complete marketing approach. These apps generally command a higher selling price and can have more predictable revenue streams. Independent developers will most likely be playing in this category whether they realize it or not.

The No Win—Strikeout

Sadly, a large number of apps on the Android Market are DOA. After working months and months or paying someone else to write your app, you post the app to the Android Market and anxiously await its review and placement on the store. The app is posted and your expectations soar! You can see the checks rolling in from Google. You've already bought the swimming pool (think *Christmas Vacation*). Then, you wait. You check your sales stats. A few sales here, a few sales there.... What has happened? Where are all my buyers? What happened to the 2,000 downloads overnight? You thought people would be breaking down the doors to get at this new app. You are discouraged and think you've wasted your time. You've probably thought about dropping your price. Surely there must be something wrong with the Android Market to cause this.

Sometimes, even very well written apps end up unnoticed and ignored. An app that sees no sales or just one or two a day is not going to cut it when you're trying to reach your breakeven point. Some apps become inactive and are no longer for sale on the Android Market. So, what do you do when you find yourself in this predicament, where your app is not doing well at all? It's time for a total app makeover. Ask yourself the following questions, and be brutally honest:

- **Is there really a market for my app?** Did you come up with your app idea while sitting around with a bunch of friends and thought you had stumbled onto something that was incredible? Or did you do some solid competitive research to see if there were similar apps already posted, especially in the Free category? Nothing wrong with creating a competing app if you can make it better, but it *has* to be better! Often, whenever we think we have a great idea, we need to really analyze whether it's viable or not. Ask some family, friends, or co-workers if they would be willing to pay for such an app. Find out if you have a market (and its potential size) for your app before you start coding or launch into an expensive project with a developer.

- **Is my app extremely well written?** A number of apps on the Android Market are poorly written. They have bugs, or some of the features don't work. This is a surefire way to get a one-star rating on the Android Market by a disgruntled buyer. Even at $0.99 people will take the time to point out on the customer reviews that your app is crap or not worth the money. One of the outcomes of competition is that prices

fall and quality goes up. Customers expect an app to work just as well at
$0.99 as they do at $29.99.

- **Have I done any marketing?** As I will mention time and time again in
  this book, marketing is not posting your app to the Android Market.
  You've had your app approved by Google, and that's a great accomplish-
  ment, but now the second half of your work starts. Selling Android
  apps is not a passive activity if you intend to make money at it. A few
  other questions to consider: Does your app's icon convey what it does?
  Icons that don't convey what the apps do, or at least what category they
  are in, will cause you to miss a marketing opportunity. Does the name
  of your app communicate the value of your app or help tell the story of
  what it does? Does your web copy match your product website in terms
  of crisp, well-written content? All of these things combined help you to
  tell the story of your app and communicate its value. Figure 1.7 shows a
  sample icon that does a good job of communicating its app's value.
  Color Pop allows the user to turn images into grayscale and then color
  specific sections of the photo, as shown in the icon's graphic. This app is
  similar to Color Splash and the child eating a lollipop in color helps
  illustrate the point of the app.

Figure 1.7   This icon communicates very nicely what the app does. This is an important part of your overall marketing strategy.

Taken together these three components are the pillars of your app's success, as
shown in Figure 1.8. Failure to address all three of these areas well means the likelihood of your app succeeding in the market is slim. I know there are stories of some
apps seemingly not addressing these areas and yet achieving wild success. However,
there are always examples of people achieving success in books or movies that, for
some odd reason, defy all understanding.

The same goes for Android apps. But, even the successful Android apps that achieve
(perhaps) undeserving success have done at least two of these three things right.
They definitely have a market, regardless of how stupid or pointless the app may be.
The developers may claim to have done no marketing, but word of mouth (a form
of marketing) has propelled them to success. There is always an explanation for
why an app is not successful, but finding it sometimes takes a little digging.

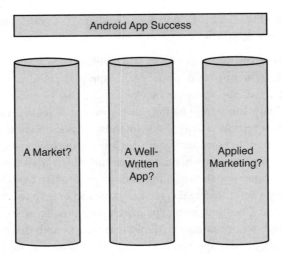

Figure 1.8 Three pillars of Android app success: a market, a well-written app, and focused marketing.

If you decide that your old app should rest in peace, at least you have a better understanding of what you can do the next time around to help you achieve success. Don't kid yourself on the answer to any of these questions. If you truly believe you have a great idea for an app and you've done your homework, then go for it. If you have a written a great app and know it without a doubt, then apply some marketing and get those sales moving.

Benefits/Drawbacks of the Big Win and Steady Win Strategies

The Android Market is not a perfect democratic society and never will be. No matter how many changes Google makes to the Android Market, there will always be unhappy participants. So, you can whine about what's wrong or you can figure out how to work the system to your best advantage. Table 1.2 illustrates the advantages and disadvantages of the Big Win strategy. It is not for the faint of heart. Table 1.3 shows the advantages and disadvantages of the Steady Win strategy. Again, it's more likely you'll end up in this category than in the Big Win category.

If you haven't started developing your Android app, you are at an important decision-making point. Making a strategy decision now will help you make important marketing decisions as you get closer to launch. Having clear (and realistic) expectations of where your app will be positioned in the Android Market gives your app purpose and will help you avoid the No Win bucket.

Table 1.2   Big Win Advantages/Disadvantages

Big Win Advantages	Big Win Disadvantages
You can make lots of money quickly.	Customers expect high quality at a crazy low price, such as $0.99.
Apps are delivered quickly to market.	The development team is usually required to get the app created quickly. Time is of the essence.
Games are extremely popular with this strategy.	The market is extremely competitive and very fickle.
You can charge a low price to attract customers to the app quickly.	Customers are highly price sensitive, promotions have limited impact, and there's no flexibility in pricing.

Table 1.3   Steady Win Advantages/Disadvantages

Steady Win Advantages	Steady Win Disadvantages
You make money slowly but more predictably.	Developers get discouraged easily and don't see their efforts through to success.
Apps build a customer following with repeat business for add-ons.	You must build updates on a frequent basis and respond quickly to customer feedback.
Almost any app can participate in the Steady Win category.	Games are a challenge here because of their short lifespan. Developers must build in add-ons to keep the audience coming back.
Apps can move into the Top 100 (or other categories) with consistent marketing.	Income drops off dramatically if steps are not taken to keep the consumer in front of the app. Marketing is a full-time job.

Summary

Android apps fall into one of three categories: Big Wins, Steady Wins, and No Wins. The Big Win is what most independent developers tend to go after. However, they would be wise to look closely at the Steady Wins category of selling because this affords the best opportunity for most developers. Good marketing can make the difference between no revenue (No Wins) and steady revenue (Steady Wins).

Decide now what your Android selling strategy is going to be—you'll have an easier time defining a marketing plan and sticking with it. It will save you a lot of heart-burn, too, if you look realistically at your app and its market and set realistic expectations for success. Don't get me wrong, I want you to be wildly successful in selling your app. I hope you hit a grand slam into the parking lot, but I also want you to realize that it's hard work to get there. Even getting base hits is hard work, but they are more likely, especially when you apply some marketing to your efforts.

For those of you who think you've got an app lost in the No Win bin, it's never too late! You can resurrect your app from the No Win status to the Steady Wins status as long as your app is well written, has a strong premise, and gets some marketing. Are you prepared to rewrite a poorly written app? Does your app really have sales appeal? If so, then roll up your sleeves, put your marketing hat on, and keep reading.

2

What Makes for a Winning App?

Everyone is searching for ideas to build the next winning Android app. Although there is no single formula for building a successful-selling Android app, a number of things can and must be done to achieve success. Without covering the basics, your app is likely to languish on the Android Market with minimal sales. Some very good apps have been posted to the Android Market that have not sold as well as they should have, and this is usually because not much marketing has been applied to the project. Unless you stage a large event to launch your app and get it started with strong momentum, or your app gets featured on the home page of the Android Market, you may find yourself in this situation.

Keep in mind that marketing is not a single event but a continuous process of aligning your message with your buyer and delivering your message over and over again so that your audience absorbs it and acts on it. Think about marketing in terms of other products you buy. How often do you see the same commercial on TV? How many times have you seen the same email ads or banner ads? Either you start out with a following and/or do something significant to get people's attention, or you have to get the word out.

In this chapter, we walk through some of the key elements of a winning app. If you are just starting development of your app, you are at a good point to evaluate whether the app you are building has these characteristics. If you are in mid development or have completed your app, then use this chapter as a benchmark to assess how well you stack up in each of these areas. It's never too late to go back and retrofit your app. Updates are one of the keys to a successful app, as you'll read in this chapter.

Build Something Unique

The best way to come upon a unique idea for an app is to rely on your own personal experience and identify where you see a need. This is easier said than done, because most of us go along and may not think about how we could improve our lives with a new technology solution. You have to make a conscious effort to envision new ways of doing things. You can start by considering the following questions:

- **What are your favorite hobbies?** Is there anything about those hobbies that could be improved by applying an app solution to the problem? (Hobbies can be anything that you enjoy: gardening, stamp collecting, coin collecting, photography, genealogy, scrapbooking, cooking, antiques, and so on.)

- **What sports do you play?** Is there a particular technique that you have learned playing a sport that would be helpful to others? (Some examples include a better golf swing, ways to hit a ball better, how to be a better right fielder, how to swim faster, how to prepare for the triathlon or Ironman competition, better tennis tips, and so on.) Could your practice, training, or actual performance benefit from tracking it through an Android app?

- **What line of work are you in?** Is there anything in your line of work that could benefit from the use of an Android app? (Examples include sales tools, materials and construction calculators, financial and insurance aids, and so on.)

- **What challenges do you face in your life?** Is there an app that could help someone cope with a handicap or other illness? (Think about soothing apps, mental health apps, physical health apps, stress coping apps, and so on.)

- **What are your least favorite chores?** Is there an app that could help someone with bill paying, gift buying, and so on?

- **What daily activity takes you the most time to complete?** Is there an app that could help people speed up that activity?

- **What childhood games did you enjoy playing?** Could that game (or a variation of that game) make a great game app?

We're all trying to build a better mousetrap. With each passing day, it becomes more difficult to build a completely new and unique app. As I mentioned before, whenever you come up with an idea for an Android app, the first thing you should do is a search in the Android Market or any Android app website for that type of app. The chances are pretty good that you will find some or many apps that are close to what you have thought about building. For example, let's take a topic such as knitting. You think you've got a great idea to develop an Android app that helps one learn how to knit. So, let's check the Android Market for knitting apps. An example of one knitting app from our search is shown in Figure 2.1.

Figure 2.1   Our search of knitting apps reveals multiple knitting-related apps and one of them is shown here. Who would have thought?

However, on close inspection of the knitting apps in the list, some apps help you count stitches, and some of the apps actually teach you how to knit, cross-stitch, and weave. So, when you perform a search for your particular app idea, be sure to look more closely at the group of apps that you see and dissect them into separate groups to get an idea of exactly how many apps you are competing against. In this example, although it looks like quite a few apps at first glance, it's more like one or two that closely match your goal of teaching someone how to knit.

It's a little more difficult to do this type of analysis for game apps because there are so many similar apps with so many variations. You can do a more targeted search by using Cyrket's App website (www.cyrket.com) and targeted category searches, as shown in Figure 2.2. If you are searching on card games, you can select "games" as the main category and then search on "most popular" or "number of downloads" as the subcategory. This will help narrow down the number of apps, but it's still a very large number to sift through.

Figure 2.2 Search for similar games on Cyrket using subcategories to narrow down the search results.

 Note

At the time of this writing, finding Android apps on the Android Market alone is very limited. You can search other Android app websites, such as Cyrket, that do a good job organizing new apps and providing reviews, or you can search apps on any Android phone itself.

Although you may not land on an original idea, it is possible to build an app that improves on what's already out there. The chances are very good that you will find a number of functions missing from a competitor's app. As mentioned before, if you can narrow down the top competitive apps to just a few, go ahead and spend a few dollars to download some of them and see what features they have and what they lack.

List the key features of the competitive apps as well as features that the available apps are lacking. You will start to see a pattern in terms of base features that this type of app must have to be viable in the market. Then you can look at what features you can add that will make your app a whole lot better.

Deliver New Features

Winning apps require frequent feature updates. If you don't keep the app updated, your audience will lose interest in your app and will quit coming to your product website. You must look at your app as a dynamic product. Your app should be architected in such a way that you can easily add enhancements and updates.

Some developers have adopted the idea that they will increase their sales by doing an upgrade as fast as they can push it through. Figure 2.3 shows a snapshot of the first page of the Social Networking category of the Android Market if you search by the default (most recent) apps. If you click a number of these apps, you'll notice that some of them are updates to existing apps. Depending on the category, this percentage may be 30% or higher.

Figure 2.3   Some developers use frequent updates to keep their app refreshed and in front of their customers.

Each update also helps you address customer comments/suggestions/complaints and keeps your relationship with your customers intact. You can use each update to comment on how you are addressing customer recommendations and how you are listening to your customers. This helps you build a following of loyal users because they know they are being heard by you and you are addressing their concerns and suggestions.

Note

If you have bugs that need to be resolved, these should be fixed right away. Do not wait because your customers may become discouraged and give you bad reviews. They may also comment on other blog posts, suggesting your app is not worth the money.

Tie Your App into Trends and News

Trends are always occurring around the world; look no further than the Internet or cable news stations for ideas. Here are some trend ideas to help you get your thought process moving:

- **Going green**—Look for opportunities in this space on how someone can use an Android app to make a difference in the world. How about an app that helps you drive more economically or an app designed to reduce your cost of heating or cooling? An example of such an app is shown in Figure 2.4, as shown on Androlib (www.androlib.com), and it capitalizes on the very popular "green" trend. Other green areas you could consider include how to save water, make your own cleaning supplies, composting, recycling, walking and biking instead of driving, and so on.

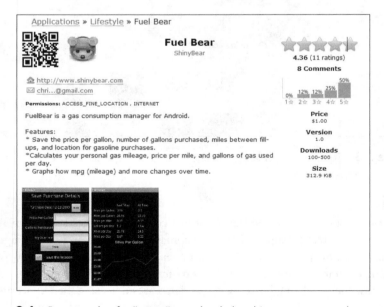

Figure 2.4   An example of a "green" app that helps drivers save gas and money by tracking their mileage and gas usage, as shown on Androlib, a popular Android app website.

- **Eating healthy**—A lot of money is spent each year by consumers who want to eat better, feel better, and live longer. This is a long-term trend that has lots of growth opportunity. Apps to consider for this area might be meal planners and the nutritional value of fruits, vegetables, and so on. Contact publishers of health books and ask if they would like to partner with you to write a healthy Android app to be included with every book sale for free. You could also contact health food product companies with the same idea. An example of these types of eating healthy apps is shown in Figure 2.5 from Androlib.

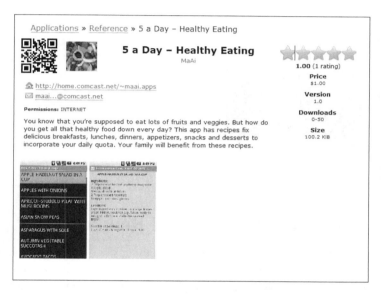

Figure 2.5 Eating healthy is a strong trend, and many apps could be created for this category.

- **Fashion**—Fashion trends are always popular, and you can look to design all kinds of apps around them. One idea is an app that helps someone dress with clothes that match. (Dare I say that men need this type of app more than women? Children and teens could use it as well.) Another idea is an app that allows someone to get the latest updates in fashion trends—for example, which accessories (such as hats and boots) are in or out this year?

- **Home décor and design**—This is a huge trend because people want to make their homes comfortable through quick projects and full renovations. There are tons of ideas for developing apps that help someone get organized, landscape an old rundown backyard, create a new look with paint and other inexpensive supplies, and so on. An example of a land-scaping app is shown in Figure 2.6 from Androlib.

Figure 2.6   An app that helps you landscape your home's exterior utilizing a database of numerous plants and how to care for them.

Tie Your App into Seasons and Holidays

Another way to come up with a winning app is to look at seasons and holidays for ideas. The only problem with seasonal apps is, well, they are seasonal. You'll see a burst of sales for apps tied to a particular holiday or season and then sales will drop off dramatically after it has passed. One strategy is to create multiple apps for different holidays so you are focusing on selling apps all year long. This means, however, that you will have to apply your marketing efforts to selling your brand with some specific holiday sales campaigns for each app during its holiday.

Seasonal apps can do better because a season can last for a number of months. There are apps for all seasons. Figure 2.7 shows one for summer.

Games, however, can transcend all seasons and do well with consistent marketing. Games such as downhill skiing, shown in Figure 2.8, can do well all year long if they are fun and exciting.

Figure 2.7 Seasonal apps can be sold for longer periods of time and can sell well all year, depending on the app.

Figure 2.8 Games, even if they are seasonal, can do well all year long when marketed well.

Tie Your App to Part of a Wider Solution

Perhaps the most popular category of apps is that of social networking–related apps. Any time there is a powerful and well-known Internet application such as Facebook, Twitter, MySpace, LinkedIn, and others, there is an opportunity for you to create an ancillary app to one of these (and many more) Web 2.0 technologies. Look for ways to add value to these applications and you may be able to create a blockbuster app that people will purchase to help them use these other technologies. Figure 2.9 shows a clever app that can aid Facebook users in updating their status. Figure 2.10 is another example that helps you use Twitter from your Android phone.

Figure 2.9   Look to create apps that add value to Web 2.0 technologies.

Figure 2.10   Twitter and many other social networking sites lend themselves well to creating add-on apps.

App Created from Other Platforms

Provided you have the rights to a PC or Mac application, you can develop the application for the Android. Many successful games were originally developed from the success of PC- or Mac-based games. If you happen to like computer games, you can always check with the developer/publisher of that game to see if they would like to collaborate on building a similar game for the Android.

Note

Always be careful of copyrighted games. Never duplicate an existing PC/Mac game for the Android without obtaining complete written permission from the owner of that game to build the app.

One of the most successful games in smartphone history—*Bejeweled*—is shown in Figure 2.11. The company already had a strong following from its successful computer game business and therefore had a natural progression to the Android app.

Figure 2.11   Building a game from a successful PC/Mac game can help you achieve huge success.

Summary

A winning app requires some real planning and thinking. Although there is no single formula for creating a blockbuster app, winning apps must be sufficiently unique, and you must be able to create a message that will generate huge interest. Hitting on a completely unique idea for an app is fairly difficult, although not impossible. If you are having difficulty coming up with a great new idea, look to improve an existing app out there. Download some of your competition's apps and see what features they offer and which they lack.

A successful app must also have frequent feature updates. Use the updates as an opportunity to broadcast your message to your existing audience and to new buyers. Marketing is not a single event but a series of activities that persuade the potential buyer to take a look at your app and then buy it. Rather than looking at doing a single press release, look for opportunities to make multiple announcements to keep your app in front of your market.

3

Identifying Your App's Unique Value

In this chapter you will learn the criteria and steps required to develop a unique selling proposition, including details on understanding your application's unique qualities, strengths, weaknesses, and competitive selling points. Working through these steps will provide you a messaging platform that you will use through all of your marketing programs.

What is really meant by marketing? To many developers, marketing typically means two things: advertising and selling. However, marketing is really much more. Marketing is the process by which you convert a prospect into a buying customer. In its most basic progression, your potential buyer first learns that you understand his needs and that you have a solution to his problem. This is accomplished through many different means of messaging that will be covered throughout this book. For many non-game apps, the solution to a buyer's problem can be fairly straightforward.

If you sell a calculator app, for example, your solution is geared toward someone who wants a tool to perform calculations of some type. This buyer knows what he wants and goes looking for it on the Android Market or other Android app sites. Your job as a marketer of your app is to make sure your app is among those the buyer reviews.

If a buyer is looking for a tennis game, he is going to search the Android app websites for tennis games (of which there are a number). He will enter "tennis games" or something similar in the search. A list of tennis games will then come up for review. If the buyer has no particular type of game in mind, his decision will be much more spontaneous and your challenge to stand out from all the other games across the Android markets is more complicated. Your goal is to connect with the buyer at some minimal level, enough so that your prospect will read more about your app. This trust leads to a more in-depth review of your app. This whole process can take place in a split second.

Once a prospect trusts you, you can then lead him through the steps to purchasing your app. Depending on the app, you may lead him through these steps rather quickly, or he may spend some time trying to make a decision about several similar apps. Figure 3.1 shows the buying process, which happens very fast for some buyers and slower for others.

Your App Marketing Cycle

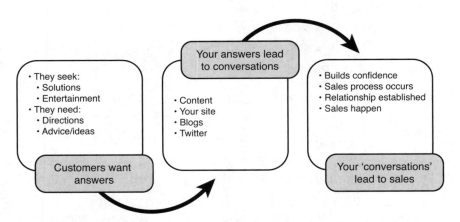

Figure 3.1   The buying process includes awareness, connection, trust, and purchase decision. Buyers of any product, including Android apps, go through this decision process, although usually at an accelerated pace.

To guarantee a successful marketing effort of your app, start by taking a look at the bigger picture and analyzing your Android app as a whole in relation to the following key points:

- Who are your possible customers?
- Who is your competition?

The (crisp and concise) answers to these questions are what help you define your app's unique value to your buying audience. Although you have probably heard this idea before, your unique value has also been defined as identifying your unique competitive advantage. The term "unique selling proposition" or "unique value proposition" is also used frequently. That's general marketing speak for identifying what's really cool about your product or service and conveying that to your audience in a concise, easy-to-understand message.

In the Android app world, you have to identify the unique functionality of your app and communicate that value to your audience. The trick to creating a powerful unique selling proposition is to boil down into in a few words an identifying point that embodies your app's unique value. Your unique selling proposition must answer the question as to why anyone should buy your app over all the other similar apps in the Android Market to choose from. This assumes that your app *has* unique value, something we'll talk about later in this chapter.

 Note

Having a clear and concise selling proposition will help you differentiate your app from the competition. With so many competing apps on the Android Market, you must do everything you can to maintain an edge against the competition. Your app, plain and simple, must stand out.

The Four Questions

You need to answer four questions to help you define your app's unique value and create a unique selling proposition. The answers to these questions become the pillars of your marketing efforts and should be incorporated into your overall marketing plan for maximum success:

- Who are your competitors?
- What are the key features of your Android app?
- What are the benefits of your Android app?
- What is unique about your app?

Note

Your marketing message matters now more than ever. With more than 70,000 Android apps for sale, you must do everything you can to stand out. Your message will be seen on your own website, on the Google Android Market (and other Android app sites) description area for your app, and other promotions you may create. Take some time to do this right!

The rest of this chapter is devoted to helping you ask and answer the four questions.

Who Are Your Competitors?

Competition in any business can be defined as "the effort of two or more parties acting independently to secure the business of a third party by offering the most favorable terms" (see http://en.wikipedia.org/wiki/Competition). Competition gives consumers greater selection and better products at better prices. It is important to understand that competition should not be viewed as a bad thing. Competition establishes a market and creates interest in your Android app. Although it is possible to open a new business and truly offer a niche service (meaning that you have entered a new market without any direct competitors), it rarely happens in today's business environment. The same holds true for apps on the Android Market.

Understanding your competition is one of the most critical, yet misunderstood, aspects of marketing and applies to Android app marketing just as well as it does to marketing anything else. Even if you have not started developing your Android app, you should survey the Android Market and look at the competition to see what you're up against. Do you think you've thought of the perfect Android app? Check the Android Market (and other Android app sites) to see what has already been built in that category. I can almost guarantee that there is a similar app to what you are building or plan to build.

Chances are there are many competitors out there with the same or similar applications. This is not said to discourage you but to emphasize the point that you must take a close look at the competition. Not too long ago (relatively speaking) Hyundai entered the U.S. car market. They no doubt surveyed the competition to determine what they were up against. They had a very large hill to climb. They built their business and marketing plans and executed on them and have been quite successful by any measure. A quick scan of the market for apps to help you name your baby, for example, reveals more than ten apps on this topic, as shown Figure 3.2.

You can also be guaranteed that if you do create a truly unique application and your app shows signs of success, you will not be the only one offering that app for very long. Other people and companies emulate success. Rather than fearing the competition, learn to understand your competitors to leverage their successes and note their failures. Competitive reviews should also be viewed as an ongoing task—new competition will enter your market, and if you do not keep a watchful eye on your competitors, you will allow others to displace you.

Figure 3.2   A search of the Android app market will help you identify similar apps that may be your competition.

 Note

> Your competition can be leveraged to aid your marketing efforts. There's no shame in "copying" a good idea, especially if it works. You can be assured that your competitors will be watching you closely, too.

Meaningful differences in your Android app compared to that of your competitors should be created and communicated to your target buyer via multiple avenues, several of which will be discussed in this book. These channels include your web messaging, features and benefits copy on the Android Market with other Android app sites, product design graphics, icon colors, advertising, and other promotion media, including marketing campaigns and even spokespersons.

Intuitively (or based on research and/or trial and error) you believe that your app will succeed. You believe this because you are doing something different from some or all of your competitors. The first marketing test of any business, small or large, is to understand how you are unique when compared to your competitors. For example, you may be selling a financial app that offers some unique features you think nobody else can match. So perhaps you focus your message on communicating that your app has a highly complex financial formula that is so handy to have on the Android. This special feature will resonate with some customers and separate you from your competitors.

Identifying Your Competition

There are two types of competitors: direct and indirect. A direct competitor could be considered anyone who offers the exact app you provide to the same target audience. So, in the previous example of applications that help you name your baby, there are at least ten that do the same thing. An indirect competitor is someone who offers a similar app but targets a different audience. For example, if you look at the Games category on the Android Market you will see thousands of games. Some are geared toward younger kids, as shown in Figure 3.3, whereas others are clearly geared toward a male audience. Regardless, they may be your competitor, especially if someone is just looking for any game to play.

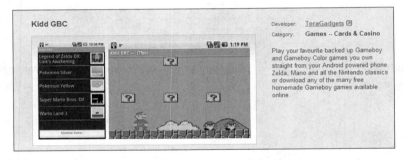

Figure 3.3   Indirect competition can come from a category where your app resides on the Android Market.

Identifying your direct competitors is important as you finalize your decision about your app's unique messaging. It reduces risk, time, required resources, and expense when planning a marketing strategy. It may be more profitable to carefully target a specific segment of a category where the odds of success are greatest. Thus, posting an app and focusing your animal-related app on residential customers who spend a lot of money on their pets can be a very good marketing approach. Figure 3.4 illustrates an Android app that is focused on pets and dog training in particular.

Finding your competitors takes some effort. Because the number of apps is so great, the easiest way to search for your competitors is to go into the Android Market (www.android.com/market) or other popular Android app sites or on your

Android-enabled phone and do a search. You can search by unique category (Games, Lifestyle, Entertainment, and so on) for paid or free apps. Search for your app type by starting with the Arcade & Action category if you are searching for games on the Android Market site. This will give you broad results for apps that might be similar to yours, as illustrated by searching Androlib.com in Figure 3.5.

Figure 3.4   This app has been targeted to dog owners around the world.

Figure 3.5   Start your competitive search by using the Arcade & Action category and scrolling through the available game apps in this category.

The following example in Figure 3.6 shows the results of doing a search on Android apps by selecting the Lifestyle category. Given that the list is short, you can quickly see all the apps that are top selling and pertain to this topic. The Android Market is currently not particularly advanced in its searching capabilities. Other Android app sites offer the ability to search by app names or topics more easily.

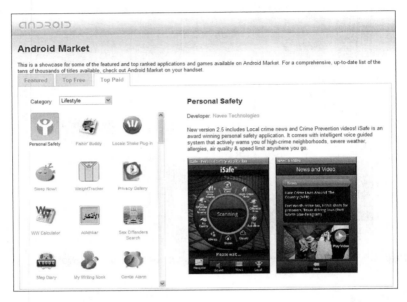

Figure 3.6   Select the closest category for the type of app you are looking for. This will help you narrow down your search.

Now let's look at the games category again. There are, of course, thousands upon thousands of games in nearly every category in the store. So, you will need to be very specific about the type of games you want to identify in your competitive exercise. In the following example, we are searching for competitive battleship games. The best way to find these apps is to first select the category Games and then type in the keyword **battleship**. Figure 3.7 displays the results using the Androlib website. Selecting the See All button reveals three pages of battleship-related apps. You can then scan through them to see which ones most closely approximate the app you have written or intend to write.

 Note

The Android Market does not display the number of pages for the app type you search on. Most of us are used to seeing "Page 1 of 10" in search results, for example. The Android Market simply lets you scroll down to view the apps. The reason for this perhaps is to give all apps a more level playing field when it comes to being found. As searches go, most of us quit after two or three pages. If we see that we are only on page 2 of 10, we may be inclined to give up at that point. If we don't know how many pages there are left, we may keep clicking to the next page. This is only the author's supposition.

Figure 3.7   Searching for battleship games using the Games category and specific keywords.

Learning from Your Competition

Once you've determined your key competitors, build out a small list on a spreadsheet to make some notes about their features and other noteworthy items. You can also use the list to track the competition on an ongoing basis. Table A.1 in Appendix A, "Competitive Worksheet," shows a sample worksheet that can be built in Excel to help you gather your data. Try to narrow your list down to two or three apps that most closely resemble what your app does or will do.

Spend time reviewing the competition's written description of their apps on the Android Market or on other Android app websites. Be sure to review their apps' graphics and, most importantly, the customer reviews. The customer reviews reveal a lot about an app. People tend to talk about what they liked and what they think is missing in an app or what could make it better. No reviews either means that the app is very new or it has not sold too well. You can get an idea about how well an app is selling by the number of reviews posted. An example of an app review is shown in Figure 3.8.

★★★★★	*by Brian the 4/30/2010*
Love the show, Love this game, can be frustrating, but very addictiting, a must buy.	
★★★★★	*by Shari the 4/26/2010*
This is a great game....	
★★★★★	*by Jeremy the 4/25/2010*
Fun game to play	
★★★★★	*by Jerred the 4/21/2010*
it was fun but repetitive	
★★★★★	*by Allen the 4/20/2010*
I think its pretty fun will on my phone for awhile	

Figure 3.8   The more reviews, the more sales an app is experiencing.

Sometimes it may be necessary to purchase an app to understand its full capability and assess its features. Competitors in every product area routinely purchase each other's products to understand their strengths and weaknesses, especially in the software industry. Software companies have dedicated labs, for example, where they do nothing but test their competitors' products in an effort to improve their marketing and positioning of their own products.

 Note

Keep in mind that I am never suggesting that you steal someone else's proprietary work. You are trying to understand how you can improve your own app and build a better app than what's currently out there. This is perfectly legal and within the bounds of ethical behavior.

Once you have narrowed down your list to the most likely competitors, ask yourself the following questions as you do some competitive Android app reconnaissance. The answers to these questions will help you make some important marketing and development decisions:

- What unique features does your competitor's app have that yours doesn't?

- How do the graphics look compared to your app?

- What claims does the competitor make about its app? Is it the only Android app to utilize such and such feature?

- Does the app appear to have multiple updates?

- Is the competitor's marketing message consistent?

- Does the competitor have a strong, compelling offer?

- What do you like or not like about the overall presentation of materials?

Maybe you've borrowed a good app idea from some other source and are attempting to build a successful business around it. Every buyer expects multiple options, and many of the apps look very much alike. However, if you examine the more successful apps, you'll notice that they tend to emphasize and promote something special or unique. It may be better graphics or higher sound quality. Some developers undoubtedly borrowed their ideas from other companies (for instance, Electronic Arts sets a high bar with its game apps) or others they've dealt with, or promotions they have noticed, and so on. Successful developers always find ways to make their apps stand out from the crowd or at least stand out from the crowd in their immediate niche area.

What Are the Key Features of Your Android App?

Features are "descriptions" of your Android app (for example, four levels of play, real-time play, easy user interface, works offline and online, and so on). When you review your app against the competition, you'll want to look at all the quantifiable features the other apps offer as compared to your own. You can use the chart found in Appendix A to build a comparative list. Utility applications on the Android Market, such as financial calculators and other scientific apps, tend to lean toward feature explanations in their product descriptions. Feature descriptions on the Android Market work best when they are in a bulleted list so that the buyer can quickly scan the list for what he is looking for. Keep the list short and relevant. Long lists get ignored, but a short list of features (five to ten items) will get read more readily. An example of an app from the Android Market with a feature list is shown in Figure 3.9.

 Note

Be sure to review the free apps in your category as well. If you are building an app that does not have any more features or functionality than a free app, the chances are slim that you will see sales success with your app. People love free but are willing to pay for value, and it's your job to convey your app's value!

Figure 3.9 A financial calculator with a short feature list enables buyers to quickly scan for functions they are looking for in a calculator.

Once you have determined your app's key features, you want to also think in terms of the benefits those features will provide your buyers. Don't make the buyers figure it out for themselves. You can help them to "connect the dots" by clearly articulating the benefits of each feature, as explained in the next section.

What Are the Benefits of Your Android App?

Benefits are the "advantages" users receive from using your app (for example, experience hours of fun, feel better today, live healthier, feel less stress, lose weight faster, achieve a cleaner, brighter smile, and so on). A benefit is a powerful way to help you sell your product. Many marketers and Android app sellers overlook this very powerful marketing concept when describing their apps on the Android Market. When you link a benefit with a feature, you are helping the buyer see the whole story about your app. When we buy a car, for example, we go into a dealer showroom and start to look around. A particular car attracts our attention. It could be its color or its sleek or sporty look. On the window is a sticker that lists a bunch of features. The salespeople will answer your questions about all the features, but what they really want is for you to experience the car's benefits. They want you to feel good about the car, which is why they always ask if you want to take it out for a test drive. They know that if they can get you to experience the "feel" of the car, its performance, its quiet ride, its new smell, its "benefits," they are more likely to get your business. Obviously buying a car is a much bigger decision than buying an Android app, but in this highly competitive Android market, you want to take every opportunity to reach the potential buyer of your app at both levels: features and benefits.

Notice as you read reviews of each Android app on the Android Market that people tend to discuss their feelings about the app in terms of its benefits ("Most fun I've had in a long time!" or "This game is so addicting I can't put it down"). Notice the reviews shown in Figure 3.10. The writers focus on how much they love the app and its useful features. Whether the app developer has consciously intended to make this connection with his audience is in many cases coincidental, but one thing is certain: All successful apps connect with their audience through features and benefits. Therefore, if you want to increase the chances of your success selling your app, you must make these connections happen with your buyer.

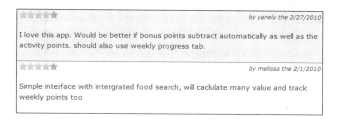

Figure 3.10   Android market product reviews tend to reflect how the buyer feels about an app in terms of its benefits.

What's Unique About Your App?

How is your app different? Can you express it in terms of a concise statement? This forms the basis for all your advertising, promotions, communications, and other marketing activities. Is your difference something that your buyers can appreciate so that they'll prefer or even seek out your app rather than your competitors'? In order to successfully market his or her app, every developer needs to focus on what's special and different about it.

To determine the unique qualities of your app, write down your answers to the following questions:

1. Which words or phrases best describe what your Android app offers your customers?

    For example, educational assistance, financial problem solving, health answers, lifestyle, fitness ideas, entertainment, and so on.

2. What qualities do you think will attract customers to your app?

   For example, incredible graphics, crisp sounds, amazing music, fast action, and so on.

3. What qualities do you think will keep your customers coming back?

   For example, attention to detail, evolving new features, consistently challenging games, frequent updates, and so on.

4. Did your responses to questions 2 and 3 reiterate what you had indicated initially for number 1?

   If you answered no, where is the mismatch? Perhaps you don't fully understand the unique qualities of your app yet or you are not sure about your customers' purchasing habits. Spend some time carefully working on this section until you come up with responses for questions 2 and 3 that fully support question 1.

As an example, we are going to be selling an educational app on the Android Market. We are in the design stages of our app and want to make sure that we are producing an app that is unique in the market. We need to determine the app's unique qualities so that our message is strong and clear to our buyers. We have created the following responses to each of these questions. The application for our example is an education assistance app geared toward high school students to help them prepare for the SAT test.

Here is what we have come up with for our example:

Question 1: What words or phrase best describe our app?

Answer: Premier SAT Preparation

In three short words we have described the quality of our app, the type of app, and our implied audience. You will be able to do the same for your app. A basketball game app can be juiced up by calling it "Blazin' Basketball Pro." A less exciting calculator app can be brought to life by calling it "Genius Calc." You get the idea....

Question 2: What unique characteristics will attract customers to our app?

Answer: Complete SAT Prep (Math, Critical Reading, Science, and Writing)

The answer to question 2 supports question 1. We can call our app "Premier" because we have a complete solution. Not only do we have math and critical reading practice tests but we also include the newer writing component of the SAT. We provide test-taking advice, tips, and tricks.

Question 3: What qualities of our app will keep customers coming back?

Answer: Download frequent updates for the latest SAT test exams.

The app provides frequent updates to help high school students stay up on the latest material so they can be better prepared for their SAT test.

Question 4: Did the responses to questions 2 and 3 reiterate what we had indicated initially for question 1?

Answer: The app's descriptions found in answers 2 and 3 support statement 1 as being a complete SAT preparation app and the fact that you can download frequent updates.

The idea of this exercise is to identify a clear statement of value about our app. When you provide solid answers to questions 2 and 3 that support question 1, you are well on your way to understanding and defining your app's unique value. This information will be tremendously valuable to you in your other marketing efforts, as discussed later in this book.

Summary

Successful marketing of your Android app requires you to determine your app's unique value and be able to boil down a clear, concise message for it. You gather this information by going to the Android Market and reviewing competing apps to identify their strengths and weaknesses. How can you build a better app if you don't know what's already available? Understanding your app's unique value is the first step to building a foundation by which you can market your app.

Understanding your app's unique value will also come in very handy as you prepare to write your press release and design your web and Android Market verbiage. With a clear value proposition for your app, you can confidently promote your app to communities across the Internet.

Identifying Your
Target Audience

As you learned in the previous chapter, identifying your app's unique message is one of the keys to successful marketing. Now it's time to take a look at your target market so you can carefully focus your message to the right audience. Some app developers think it doesn't really matter if they identify their target market. As long as their app is on the Android Market, it will take care of itself. They think the right people will find their app regardless of what they do, especially if they get selected in the "Featured" category. You will definitely see a spike in sales while your app remains in that category. But, when your app is no longer getting top billing, your sales will drop off, and you'll be back to trying to figure out how to market your app. Therefore, identifying your target market does matter.

As shown in Figure 4.1, there are two ways to focus on driving awareness to your Android app. The first way is on the Android Market itself or other Android app sites by specifying relevant keywords for searches and deploying other techniques to make your app stand out. The second way is by driving traffic to your own product website and then convincing visitors to go to the Android Market to buy your app. You will have more influence on driving traffic to your own site than on driving it to the Android Market. Both of these areas are discussed in greater detail in other parts of this book. However, the focus of this chapter is on identifying the target audience for your app—a vital step to achieving sales success. This will also save you time and money if your marketing efforts are aligned more closely with your most likely buyer.

Two Ways to Find Your App

Android App Searches

- Power search
- Keywords specified by you in your app name or description
- Be included on one of the Android Market's Featured areas

Product Website Searches

- SEO activities
- Keywords specified by you
- Advertising
- Press releases
- Blog posts
- Reviews

Figure 4.1   There are two ways to drive interest in your Android apps: Android app site search and product website searches.

You will have a general idea of who will buy your app simply by the type of app you develop. If you are developing an investing app you know your market will be investors. However, there are many categories of investors. Some are risk averse, and they will be looking for an app to suit their conservative investing needs. Other investors are interested in highly risky stock options trading and will want an app to help them make options buy/sell decisions. Games, of course, have all kinds of categories. Some games are focused on children, whereas others target the male teen market. Some games may appeal to a general audience but have as their core audience a specific demographic.

Do you know precisely who your buyer is? Do you know how many apps your audience typically buys each year? These points help you identify your target buyer.

What about other customers who you might provide this app to? What is the lifestyle information (recreational/entertainment activities, buying habits, cultural practices, and so on) for this target buyer? This type of information can help you in two very important ways. First, it can help you make changes to your Android app to better match what your customers likely want. Second, it can tell you how to best reach your customers through search engine optimization (SEO), advertising, promotions, marketing campaigns, and so on.

 Note

A company that sells Android golf games knows that its typical customer is a golf nut. But it also knows that its buyer is a sports fan. Therefore, if the company can build a game realistic enough to be used by professional athletes, it will have a convincing story about its quality to tell. It can also benefit by using athletes as spokespersons in its reviews and advertising, and by placing advertisements in sports magazines where its customers are likely to see them.

Refining Your Audience

How can you refine your understanding of your customer base to help with marketing planning? You should examine this question from two angles:

- **Segmenting the market**—Dividing the existing market up into sections or segments that may become new niches for your Android app sales

- **Targeted marketing**—Identifying the heavy users of your app so you can direct your marketing efforts more precisely to them for repeat business

Segmenting Your Market

Another way to help focus your app's unique value is to take some time to segment your market. This exercise enables you to understand further whom you are selling to and what kind of concise message you can deliver to them. If the universe of all potential buyers is your "market," then the market can be divided into segments based on any number of factors.

For example, you might analyze your customers by age group and find that you sell (or will sell) most of your apps to people aged 18 to 34. You might segment them by family size and find that you sell most of your products to single men. You might divide them up by economic status and find that you sell most products to people with an annual income of about $30,000 to $65,000. Or you might divide them up by interests and find that you sell most of your apps to people who are avid fishermen or sports enthusiasts.

 Note

> Many independent developers stop after segmenting their market once, thinking they have enough information to be able to identify and communicate with their most likely customers. However, larger, more successful app development companies will attempt to push on further to find out even more information about their customers' lifestyles, values, life stage, and other demographic and psychographic variables.

Let's define some terms that you will come across as you segment your Android app market. Obviously other segments could be mentioned as well, but these are some of the most common:

- *Demographics* refer to age, sex, income, education, race, marital status, size of household, geographic location, and profession. An understanding of demographics will help you define your marketing message and define a suitable marketing plan. Every app will cater to at least one of these components.

- *Lifestyle* refers to the collective choice of hobbies, recreational pursuits, entertainment, vacations, and other non–work time pursuits. Some apps are strictly for fun and should be positioned in the appropriate category on the Android Market. Other apps are health-related and therefore should be placed into this category on the Android Market.

- *Belief and value systems* include religious, political, nationalistic, and cultural beliefs and values. Some refer to theses characteristics as *psychographics*. These types of apps include religious topics, sermons, speeches (political and religious), and so on.

- *Life stage* refers to the chronological benchmarking of people's lives at different ages (pre-teens, teenagers, empty-nesters, and so on). Many games can be classified in this category, but other apps such as health and fitness apps fit this scheme as well.

The Android Market requires you to segment your market to some degree when you specify the category in which to place your app. Think very carefully about the category you select for your app. This can impact your sales dramatically if someone does a search on the Android Market by category and does not find your app where it logically should reside. Some apps and their category placement are clear cut, such as games. As a developer you know when you post your game app to the Android Market that you will select one of the Games categories in which to post it. You can specify that the game is a "Card & Casino" game, as shown in Figure 4.2. Other apps are not as simple to categorize. Perhaps you have written an app that helps someone locate a friend. The app could be placed in the Navigation category, or it could be placed in the Social Networking category. Still, someone else may have developed an app that is educational as well as entertaining. Their app could go in the Entertainment or Education category. The best category for your app is where you believe your buyers would most likely search on it.

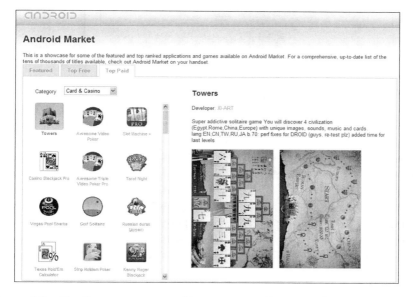

Figure 4.2   The Games category enables you to specify some subcategories to help direct the buyer to your app.

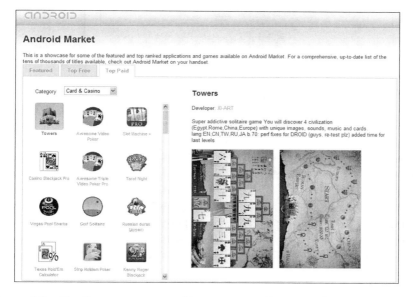 *Note*

If you are struggling to figure out to which category to post your app, ask your friends which location they would naturally search on the Android Market for such an app. Ask 15–20 people to get a good sample. A clear trend should emerge of one category over another. If you feel that your app is in the wrong category after posting, you can always change it at any time by going to the Android Market, logging in, and editing your app's profile information.

A list of Android Market categories is shown in Figure 4.3. From the Android Market store you will add your apps and select a primary category in which to place your app. Because the Games category is so large, the Android Market has multiple subcategories for this section.

Figure 4.3   Android Market allows you to add new Android apps and select a primary category for your app. Selecting the right category for your app will help you to segment your market.

How can you find out more about your potential Android app customers? The most effective means is through some level of market research. Larger companies segment their markets by conducting extensive market research projects, consisting of several rounds of exploratory research. They do customer and product data collection. Professional researchers gather the following data from users of similar products:

- Number and timing of purchases
- Reasons for purchases
- Consumers' attitudes about various product attributes
- Importance of the product to the lifestyle of the consumer

But, how can you find out more about your customers with budget and time constraints? What can an independent Android app developer do to segment his market? Read the reviews posted on the Android Market (and other Android app review sites) to gather valuable information on what customers like and don't like about your competitors' apps. Customer reviews are brutally honest with both praise and criticism. The comments will help you gain an understanding of how people perceive the app, its audience, and overall satisfaction. Obviously the average of the reviews (based on the five star rating) indicates the overall impression of the customer base. Hopefully you will have at least more positive reviews than negative reviews. A predominantly high number of positive reviews indicates strong acceptance of the app. This also means that the app is resonating with a particular market segment. There will always be a few complainers who give the app a one-star rating, but if the majority of reviews are single star then there is reason for concern. An example of an app receiving good reviews is shown in Figure 4.4. The next example, displayed in Figure 4.5, shows an app with a high number of negative reviews.

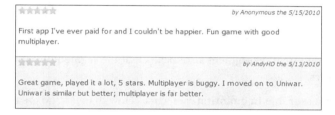

Figure 4.4   An example of an app with generally positive reviews. Read the customer comments on apps that are similar to yours with the idea of understanding what types of customers are buying this app. This will help you segment your market and see what customers like about the app.

Figure 4.5   An example of an app with a poor review.

 Note

If an app is receiving mixed reviews, meaning the number of positive reviews is roughly equal to the number of negative reviews, you should read the reviews very carefully—they usually indicate that the app is hitting a part of the target market but leaving the other part unsatisfied. The reviews always indicate what feature or features are missing from the app.

The customers will indicate why the app is not doing well. Comments such as "App is not worth the money" or "App works very slowly" indicate that the app is poorly written or designed and obviously not really resonating with any market segment.

 Note

If you have multiple apps in your brand, you could have different target audiences based on the types of apps you have developed. For example, you may have developed game apps for children and teens—two markets that you would segment differently based on their needs. If you are selling a single app, you should look to target only one segment. Spillover into other segments is always a nice benefit, but you should focus on one market segment for best results.

Picking Your Market Segment

Picking the right market segment also means that the segment has the following characteristics:

- **It is measurable in quantitative terms.** (How many? Who are they?) If you are developing a game app, try to figure out the potential size of your market. You can estimate your market by doing an Internet search and gathering some general statistics on its overall size. But trying to figure out your market segment size is difficult. You're better off determining who it is. For example, your game market may be young women, 13–17, who are followers of the latest movie sensation.

- **It is substantial enough to generate planned sales volume through planned marketing activities.** One thing is certain: You must have a market large enough to generate sufficient sales. If you develop an app that has a market that constitutes just a few thousand, you may have a difficult time reaching them. The biggest reason is that there is no way to know how many potential buyers in that small market own an Android phone. There must be enough target buyers on a frequent-enough basis to sustain your company sales, spending, and profits from month to month.

You should also examine other important factors around targeting that could affect your app's success:

- **Strength of competitors to attract your targeted buyers away from your app**—How loyal are your customers? Could they be easily persuaded to switch to a competitor based on its marketing efforts (better pricing, better graphics, other advantages)?

- **Similarity of competitive apps in the buyers' minds**—If the customer sees little difference between your app and a competitor's, you will have a problem.

- **Rate of new app introductions by competitors**—If innovation is the key to success in your market and you are asleep at the wheel, the competition will eventually overtake you.

Targeting Your Market

Perhaps the driving force behind targeted marketing or "segmentation" is the need to satisfy and keep those consumers who really love your apps. Even large Android development companies have embraced targeted marketing, continuing to refine and target their product offerings to different buyer groups.

Marketers of most products know that 20% of your buyers consume 80% of product volume. If you could identify the buyers who make up that key 20% and focus efforts on finding others like them, you could sell much more product with much less effort. Why? *Because you're not spending your marketing efforts convincing buyers they need your application—your efforts are spent targeting the potential buyers who already need your application.* You just need to convince them that you are different (and better) than the competition.

 Note

Targeting existing buyers of similar apps is a great way to expand your business because they don't need to be convinced to purchase your apps. They are already looking for an app like yours. You have already done the heavy lifting and made buyers out of them.

The "heavy users" of your app can be thought of as a market "niche" that you should attempt to dominate. *Targeted marketing means targeting, communicating with, selling to, and obtaining feedback from the heaviest users of your business's Android application.* For example, if your market is a specific set of gamers who only like a particular type of game, you've got to make sure that your app and marketing message are spot on with that group.

If you have developed a health-related Android app, who will be the most likely buyer—the patient or the caregiver? If the app is a reference to various health symptoms, it's probably targeted to someone who needs to know more about the health issue. If the app is geared toward giving treatment options, it may be targeted to a health care worker. Savvy Android marketers will recognize the best market for their apps and provide appropriate messaging to their particular audience (or, in other words, the "heavy users" of the apps).

The other important point here is that once you have identified your target market, keep them coming back for additional applications. Every customer win should be cared for so that you can sell them additional apps or other products from your own website. Smart developers not only plan to sell one app but a series of apps to the same customer. In an effort to build their brand, some developers also sell other items on their product websites, including hats and t-shirts. This is not to build another income stream but to help establish a brand and keep their customers coming back to their site. Don't be a one-hit wonder. Think longer term and get to know your market segment well. In turn, it will treat you well.

 Note

A number of developers are creating their game apps in such a way that they are constantly updating them to generate customer interest. Their strategy has been to first attract a following to their apps and then constantly release updates to keep the customers coming back. This accomplishes a couple things. First, it keeps the customers engaged in using the apps, because a lot of app buyers tend to get bored rather quickly. Second, it gives the app developers another opportunity to go out with a press release announcing the new version, which helps drive sales on a continuous basis.

Summary

Market segmentation is a necessity when you're selling an Android app. Segmentation starts when you post your app on the Android Market through the categorization required by the store. Some developers are not sure what category their app should be placed in and should seek the opinions of others for help. Game developers can use one or two subcategories to help them segment their game within a very large market.

Beyond the Android Market segmentation, as a developer, you must also look at and understand your market from a demographic perspective. This will help you craft the right message—one that enables your audience to understand what your app does. What gender mostly uses your app? If it's a motocross app, your most likely buyer is a male teenager, although female teenagers might buy it, too. If you've developed a lifestyle app, your buyer might be a hobbyist or a professional player of some sort. Knowing your market is important. You don't want to waste time and money trying to advertise and market to an audience that doesn't care about your app.

Building Your App's Total Message

5

Some people think marketing your Android app consists of doing a little advertising and a press release. Actually, marketing your app, especially if you want to see steady and consistent sales on the Android Market, requires that you do a number of things consistently well. I call this group of activities creating your app's "total message," and it includes every aspect of your marketing effort—from how you name your app and the icons and graphics you display, to the wording on your product website and the Android Market. Table 5.1 lists the components of the "total message" for your app. Check each category and give yourself a grade that reflects your progress in each area.

Table 5.1 Grading How Well You Are Doing Creating Your App's Total Message	
Marketing Component	My Grade (Haven't Started, Not Bad, Pretty Good, Very Good)
Descriptive app name	
Polished app icon	
Descriptive written content for Android Market	
Crisp product website	

All the activities listed in the table are a means of communication and can help you convey the value of your app and its unique qualities to your buyers. You're not going to fail by not doing them, but your odds of success are much higher than if you sit back and do nothing. The more complete your total message, the more likely people will like what they see on your product website or the Android Market and then buy your app. When people visit the Android Market, they are either simply browsing or are searching for a specific type of app.

People who are the browsing type are usually looking for an app to pass the time. They may be looking for an action game or a puzzle or some other app for entertainment. Perhaps they are looking for an app to keep their kids occupied, but they're not sure which app. Most browsing shoppers will start their search by looking at the Featured category. Other buyers come to the store looking for a specific solution to a problem. It could be a student looking for help with homework or preparing for the SAT exam. It could be a businessman looking for an app to help him in his sales job or to better manage his finances. Or it could be a mom looking to get more daily activities organized.

Regardless of the app they seek, buyers will be presented with pages of apps in that category. So, even when they have found the category they want, they still have to wade through hundreds of apps. Regardless, if you can make your app stand out, it's more likely that visitors will stop and take a look at your app. That's the first step in getting them to buy! If you can't get someone to stop and look at your app, your sales will disappoint. Take a look at the apps in Figure 5.1. Note the ones that catch your attention and ask yourself why these particular apps made you stop and look.

Most people visiting the Android Market are first attracted to the colorful icons. It's simply easier to scan the pages on their phone looking at the graphics to see if one of them is of interest rather than reading every description. Most buyers will scan the screen looking for an icon that grabs their attention. If an icon looks interesting, most people will read the name of the app and its category and then decide whether to click on it or not. Some apps do a better job conveying their value than others. Can you find the icons shown in Figure 5.2 that do the best job conveying what their product does?

Figure 5.1 Which apps attract your attention and why? Understanding a buyer's thought process will help you devise ways to attract sales.

Figure 5.2 Some icons do a better job than others in instantaneously conveying what the app is about.

If visitors to the Android Market like an icon and the name of the app, they will click on the link for more information. When delivered to your Android Market product page, they will be drawn to the graphics you have on your storefront. They will review the graphics on your product page to get a quick idea of what your app does. And, finally, if they like what they see, they will read, in more detail, the full text description about the app. If your app is a game, they are going to look at the description to figure out how the game is played.

If the premise of the game is simple and buyers like the graphics, they will be more influenced to buy your app. They will make a buying decision. If the app is free (or a "lite" version), they will decide whether they want to download it and try it out. If the app is priced, they will decide whether they want to spend the money to download it. An example of the app buyer's decision progression is shown in Figure 5.3.

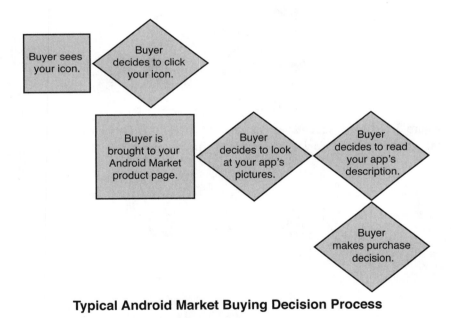

Typical Android Market Buying Decision Process

Figure 5.3   The decision process of a visitor on the Android Market starts visually then moves to the app's written description.

Note

Your goal as a marketer is to visually and textually anticipate and answer the buyers' questions and concerns, helping them to make an informed decision and convince them that your app is the right one for them. By addressing all the points covered in this chapter, you are making it easier for buyers to decide on getting your app. You are connecting the dots in their mind. Not doing some of these things does not mean sales failure for your app. However, why not cover all your bases and improve your chances of sales success?

Choose an Effective App Name

An effective Android app name can help increase your sales because the buyer does not have to invest as much effort to understand what your app does. The more you make buyers work to understand what you are selling, the more likely they will go somewhere else to get their "questions" answered faster. This is not to say that all apps will fail if they don't have a descriptive name. However, if your app is a non-game app such as a utility, financial calculator, or weight loss tool, you can improve your results by describing what the app does in the name.

You can use several words in your app name to be creative and also describe what the app does. For example, if you have written a calorie-counting app, you could call it something like *Melt-Away Pounds (Calorie Counter)*. From the name the buyer can immediately understand what the app does. Figure 5.4 shows an example of an app that combines a clever name with a description of what the app does. Notice that the icon, along with the title, gives you an immediate impression of the app's purpose. You know instantly that the app is a medical reference app directed to the healthcare community. This type of naming works very well on the Android Market for educational and utility-focused apps.

Figure 5.4   An example of a combined naming approach with the product name first, followed by a brief description.

Game apps have much more latitude in their naming options. You are only limited by your imagination and what you think will resonate with your target market. Remember your target market from Chapter 4? If you can focus on a catchy or memorable name that will resonate with your target audience, you can establish a stronger following for your app. There are many categories of games, and this can help you to determine the best type of name for you app. If your game is educational, you'll probably want to name your app more descriptively, as in *High School Math Blitz I: Algebra I and II Refresher* or *High School Math Blitz II: Geometry and Trig Refresher*. Figure 5.5 shows a game app in the Games category that is cleverly and memorably named. Figure 5.6 shows a game app in the Arcade and Action category that also has a name that resonates instantly with the viewer.

Figure 5.5   This game app has a catchy name that is clever and memorable (at least in the author's opinion).

Figure 5.6   App names for games can be geared toward your audience age and gender for maximum sales impact.

Other games are more seasonal and are named for a particular holiday. So, usually the holiday is the first part of the name followed by the type of game. Again, the reader can get an instant picture of what the game is about. The holiday games are impulse buys attracting a buyer's attention for only a short time. Many developers have a collection of games for different holidays to keep their sales rotating around each month of the year. A seasonal example is shown in Figure 5.7.

Basic App Naming

You should consider a number of ways to approach naming your app. First, if you plan to develop a series of apps under a brand name, think of app names that are flexible and will support your overall brand. If you are developing a series of science apps for high school students, your brand may be called "Science Man" and your apps will start with your brand connected with a dash (for example, *Science Man – Chemistry* or *Science Man – Physics*).

Figure 5.7   Seasonal games are named for the holiday and the type of game.

You can use roman numerals for some apps names, such as *Crazy Flips I* and *Crazy Flips II*, or you can choose names such as *MyStory – The Prequel* or *MyStory – The Sequel*. Other general naming rules include the following:

- Make sure your app name is easy to pronounce and spell. You want your app to be easy to remember from a word-of-mouth standpoint. You also want your app to be easily searchable in the Android Market. Apps with difficult spellings may be hard to locate in the store.

- Beware of app names that might mean something else in a foreign language. *Nova* comes to mind.

- Be sure to check on trademarks and other reserved names. For example, Freeverse, Inc., has the rights to use the name *Flick NBA* for their basketball app. Although there are other basketball apps for sale on the Android Market, they cannot use "NBA" in their name.

- Stick to names that don't offend any group of people. Offensive app names may appeal to some buyers, but you'll narrow your audience considerably with that approach.

- Check for domain availability for your app name. With so many domains registered, this may be difficult, but it helps to have the same domain name as your app. If you are building a brand and developing a number of apps, you should register the domain name for your brand first.

Note

While researching your app name, you can go to many different domain registration sites to check availability for your domain. Site such as GoDaddy.com and Register.com are just two of hundreds of sites that can help you.

Get Creative

If you're having trouble coming up with a good app name, you can follow some simple strategies to help you move the process along. Write down answers to the following questions and list as many ideas as come to mind. Then focus on the question where the best answers come to mind. This is most likely where you're going to find the best name for your app.

- What does your app do? (Calculates net worth, organizes coupons, tabulates investments, and so on.)

- What is your app's benefit to the consumer? (Makes a busy working mom's life easier, helps students get better grades, teaches teens how to drive safely, and so on.)

- What will happen for the buyer? (Feel better, look better, run faster, become smarter, and so on.)

- What are the key features of your app? (Ten levels of play, zoom and pan functionality, 150 inputs, 3D graphics, enhanced sound, and so on.)

- How is your app different from competing apps? (Only app to have a certain functionality, multiplay features, and so on.)

- What makes your app unique? (Voted #1 by *MyApp* magazine.)

- Can your app play off a mainstream word or phrase already in use? (If it's a photo utility, use the word *Photo* in the app name, for example. A good example of playing off of other products for a product name is shown in Figure 5.8).

Search for Synonyms

If you've found a few words that might work for your app name, you can also check for synonyms to see if there are any similar words that might work even better for your app name. You can use the thesaurus in Microsoft Word to get started with

Figure 5.8   The app *Face Melter* plays off of the ubiquitous success of Photoshop.

similar words, or you can go to one of many thesaurus websites, such as www.the-saurus.com. This site provides a multitude of synonyms for almost any known word and also provides a handy synonym map showing similar words branching off the root word you have entered.

Use Google to Help

If your app is a game, you can get lots of ideas by simply Googling a particular topic for ideas. For example, if your app is a road racing game, you can get lots of ideas by going to Google and typing in **road racing**. You will find an unlimited list of ideas. Some other topics that might help you in your search are listed here. Simply go to Google and type them in:

- Stars and planets (games, science, astrology apps)
- Finance and money (financial, education, utilities apps)
- Sports players and teams (sports, health and fitness, education apps)
- Cartoon characters (games, other apps)
- Presidents of countries (education, books, other apps)
- Travel (navigation, education, books, other apps)

- Shows and entertainment (entertainment, other apps)

- Fitness training (health, fitness, education, other apps)

- Children's books (books, games, education, other apps)

- Electronics and computers (games, sports, education, other apps)

- Music and musical instruments (games, music, books, other apps)

Select and Test Your App Names

Once you have selected the three names you like the best, run them by family and friends to see which one gets the highest vote. You've got to ask more than one or two people, though. Try to ask at least ten people which name they like the best and why. It's important to understand which name triggered the best response so you can continue to develop your marketing approach by knowing what resonates with your buyers.

Android Market Text: Lighten It Up

In this mobile society, people are reading less when it comes to their communications. Attention spans are short, and with the crush of information thrown at us each day, there is limited time to listen to each seller's message and review buying options. Hence, we see the 15-second commercial and the massive popularity of Twitter. When buyers take the time to read the text for your app on the Android Market, they are interested in downloading it.

Most people will not make the investment in time to read your words unless they have more than a casual interest in your app. So, you've gotten them this far in the process, you need to make the most of your words. Figure 5.9 illustrates a good balance of text and white space, helping the reader to understand quickly the benefits of the app. There is no exact science to achieve perfect content. However, the rule of "less is more" works best. Here are ten suggestions for your Android Market text to help you captivate your reader's attention:

- List any promotions, discounts, sales events at the top of the text to meet the demands of any of your impulse buyers. Use asterisks to call out a sale or noteworthy review or event.

- Post solid magazine, newspaper, or other leading reviews of your app next to the top of the text to reinforce the value of your app from the start. Testimonials, especially from well-known publications, can influence your sales.

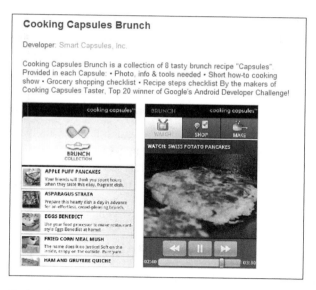

Figure 5.9   Android app example with good balance of text.

- Describe what your app does in a few quick sentences. The reader wants to know right away!

- Talk about the benefits of your app towards the top of the page (feel better today, hours of fun, lose weight fast, learn this skill now, improve your health, and so on).

- Use short paragraphs to describe your app. Two to three sentences work well. Avoid big blocks of paragraphs. Most app buyers will skim through the text and won't read it completely.

- Use bullets to describe your features. Bullets help lead the reader through the key points of your app, and readers are accustomed to going through bulleted lists.

- Include a note to have the buyer look at your other apps as well if you have them up on the Android Market.

- Include a "What's New" section describing the latest updates (if it is an updated app, of course).

- List any updates that are coming up in a "What's Coming" section.

- Review your text periodically to make sure it's still reading the way you like. Sometimes, rereading text after a few days or weeks helps us to see things in a different light. Have someone else take a look at the text to make sure it's on message.

 Note

There is an exception to the short text rule, and that's in the book category. Sometimes it helps to include a compelling paragraph from the book. Whenever the reader might be interested in seeing an excerpt, go ahead and include it. The Android Market does provide an ample allowance.

Make Graphics Your Focal Point

The phrase "A picture is worth a thousand words" is well-suited to the Android Market and selling your Android app. Good graphics help sell your product. Spend time to ensure that your graphics showcase your app in the best possible way. It is possible, for example, to turn your graphics horizontally for a different look rather than showing the pictures of your app vertically. You can showcase your app with a mix of vertical and horizontal photos. The examples shown in Figures 5.10 and 5.11 demonstrate good use of photos and graphics for apps.

Figure 5.10 This example of a photo editing app shows the use of a crisp photo as part of its description.

Figure 5.11   This app makes use of the positioning of graphics to show different angles of the game.

 Note

Some developers only post one or two photos of their app on the Android Market. This is a big mistake. The Android Market allows you to post up to five photos of your app, and you should use every last one of them. To not use all five photos is like being given 30 seconds to do a TV commercial and only using 20 seconds. Use every last tool at your disposal to display you app in its best light.

Make Your App's Icon Pop

Another very important aspect of building a solid marketing message is selecting an icon that helps convey the meaning of your app. The easier it is to see visually what your app is about, the easier someone can make a decision to take a closer look at it. For example, if your app is a utility-related app, select a graphic that conveys the type of utility this app provides. Figure 5.12 shows a good example of an icon that clearly conveys what the app can do for the buyer. Adding a few descriptive words to the icon can also strengthen the visual message.

Virtual Table Tennis
3D

Figure 5.12   The most effective app icons clearly show a connection with the app's function.

 Note

If you've had your app posted for a few months and you're not seeing as many sales as you like, change out your icon for a new one. People get accustomed to seeing the same icon over and over again and may pass right over it. If you post a new icon, you'll attract new buyers.

Another great use of the icon is to post a promotion using part of the icon. Let's say you've decided to have a 50% off sale for a holiday weekend. You can modify the bottom of your icon or the top-right/left corner to announce your sale.

Build a Simple, Clean Product Website

Your product website should be similar in look and feel to your Android Market product page. A carryover between the two sites will help build buyer confidence in your app and show that you are serious about your business. A sloppy website with broken links does not inspire confidence when a buyer is seeking more information about your apps. This does not mean that you have to spend a fortune on your site, but it must look clean and simple. This means that your home page should have graphics and showcase your app just like the Android Market. For more information on the specifics of your website, see Chapter 6, "Electronic Word of Mouth." For now, let's focus on the website message.

You may be building your own website, or perhaps you've hired someone to help you out. Either way, chances are you will be the one coming up with the messaging for your site. It is imperative that you learn to write well and convey the value of your app (or apps) to your reader. Obviously, web copy will vary in style, readability level, and length, depending on the type of apps you are selling. The sole purpose of your site is to make sales, and your web copy should reflect that. Persuasion, clear product descriptions, and rationale for buying will all be important. On the other hand, a website for games may well have short copy that needs to be extremely well written to keep your viewers interested and willing to click around.

 Note

Android apps can be purchased from the Android Market on your mobile phone or from any website showcasing the apps. So, the job of your app product website is not only to instruct and inform potential buyers but to persuade them to click and buy your app.

Who Is Your Audience?

Outstanding web copy helps your website get visitors. You owe it to yourself and your buyers to attend to the words used, and a good place to start is to analyze who your target audience is. For more information on identifying your target audience, see Chapter 4. You need to understand what your audience wants to read. If you have a younger audience, then gear the content and writing style to a younger clientele. If you are selling a scientific app, you will want to write to that audience using terms and phrases that resonate with them.

Make your visitors feel good about your app—this is the key to drawing them back on a regular basis. Your website can include tips and tricks, frequently asked questions (FAQs), and occasional promotions to keep visitors interested in returning.

Developing Great Web Copy

There are lots of different rules and recommendations about how to write good web copy, but the bottom line is that you want to write copy in such a way that it pulls in your visitors. You want to create a statement at the top of your site that clearly identifies what your apps do. Don't make the visitor to your site hunt around trying to figure this out. People will click away in seconds if they don't find a clear explanation of your apps. When you write the content for your website, your goal is to get your visitors to learn about your apps and want to click on the Buy Now button that takes them over to the Android Market.

The best advice is to make your writing interesting. Look at some other sites that sell apps similar to yours and get some ideas. There's nothing wrong with seeing how others are building their websites, especially if they are on the top sellers lists on the Android Market. It almost goes without saying, but I'll mention it anyway: You've got to make sure your content is spellchecked and grammatically correct. Failure to do even the simple things will make you come off as amateurish. If you lack experience in this area, consider hiring a professional copy editor.

If people think your website looks sloppy, they naturally think your app will be equally poor. Nothing says "careless" quicker than a spelling error. Use active voice style and keep your tone friendly, informative, and snappy. Keep the visitors' interest! Make your copy compelling if you want them to keep coming back. An example of a well-written home page for an app is shown in Figure 5.13. Here are some other important tips:

- Your content should quickly describe your app at the top of the page.

- Your web content should be as entertaining as possible. Be sure to have a gallery of pictures showcasing your app.

- The website should inform your visitor as to what your app can do.

- You must educate your visitors with FAQs and videos. Always have a YouTube video demonstrating your app.

- Your website must convince your visitor to buy. Always have a prominent Buy Now button configured to take your buyer directly to your app on the Android Market.

Figure 5.13   Compelling web copy will keep your visitors' interest and help lead them to the Android Market to purchase your app.

Make Your Content User Friendly

According to web design experts, most web viewers scan web pages rather than read them word for word. If you adhere to certain web content principles, you're more likely to have success in keeping your visitors and convincing them to click over to the Android Market. Here are some guidelines to follow:

- Use highlighted keywords (hypertext links serve as one form of highlighting; typeface variations and color are others).

- Create meaningful subheadings (not "clever" ones).

- Use bulleted lists (such as this one, but not too long), just like on the Android Market.

- Write short paragraphs (your readers will skip over any additional ideas if they are not caught by the first few words in the paragraph).

- Use the inverted pyramid style, starting with the conclusion first then going into more detail as the reader progresses through the text.

Mastering your web content will help you achieve greater sales of your app. Remember to update your site whenever you update your app. You want to list new features you have added to the app and anything else that might be of interest to your reader. See Figure 5.14 for an example of how you can showcase your app's updates on your website. This site is light and easy to read.

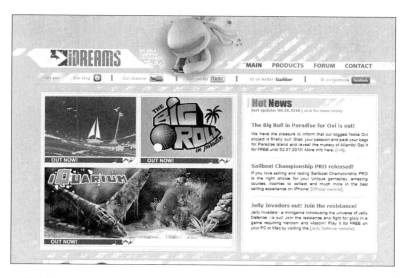

Figure 5.14   Keep your web site updated frequently with the latest features, tips, and promotions. Always have your Buy Now button prominently displayed on your home page.

Strive for Immediate Positive Reviews

There is nothing like getting a good reference. Whether we realize it or not, we all tend to listen to what other people say about things and, in part, we base our buying decisions on what others have said. How many times have you asked a friend whether he or she liked a certain movie? If your friend told you the movie was terrible, chances are you would go to another movie. However, if you read a positive review online or in the paper from a so-called movie expert, you might be inclined to go anyway, regardless of your friend's experience. You may place more stock in what you read than what you have heard from your friend because you judge the movie critic to possibly be a better source of information. On the other hand, what if the movie critic gave another movie a thumbs down, but ten of your friends raved about it and said you must go see it. The chances are pretty good that you would go see the movie despite what the critic has said. In this case, you were probably swayed by what the majority said about the movie.

What about the last time you went out to dinner and asked for someone's advice on finding a good restaurant? Again, if this person raved about a certain place, you would most likely go and give it a try. Other people's opinions about a product or service make a difference for many app buyers. We want to trust what we hear and read about products. It makes us feel safer if we see that others have made a similar purchase and have good things to say about it.

You may be wondering whether reviews really matter for a $0.99 app, or a $2.99 app for that matter. If you are a game developer and trying to get a big win (see Chapter 1, "Your Android App Marketing Strategy: Grand Slam or Base Hits?"), then reviews aren't going to matter too much. Most impulse buys are done straight from the Android device, and buyers aren't going to the Android Market to read what people are saying. However, if your app is in the "steady wins" category (again, see Chapter 1), then reviews do matter. The buyer has more time to look at your app, read a few reviews, and get a general idea of what the majority of the people think about your app. A preponderance of good reviews makes a potential buyer feel good about the purchase. A preponderance of bad reviews is a cause for concern in a buyer's mind, and some will be inclined to look elsewhere for a similar app without the poor reviews.

However, can one really trust the customer reviews posted for each app? Well, yes and no. Google requires any reviews to be written by buyers of the app. The Android Market has definitely made the review process more democratic. However, many app developers would like the ability to respond to the review postings—something that Google has yet to allow on the Android Market.

 Note

If an app does not show any reviews, it means one of two things: either the app has just been posted (or an update has just been released) and it's too early for any reviews to be posted, or the app has languished with no buyers and has not received any reviews. An app that is selling extremely well will generally have many reviews (in the hundreds or sometimes thousands).

If you don't have any reviews yet, you can use some of your free Android Market promotion codes to give to friends to download your app and post a review for you. Ask them to give an honest assessment of the app and post some credible comments. If you've written a great app, you will get some great comments. Glowing reviews that go over the top to point out how good the app is are suspect. A lot of readers can tell whether or not such reviews are authentic. Obviously, having some customer reviews is better than none. Sometimes you have to get things moving along, and having a few family members and friends comment on your app can be helpful as long as they have used the app and are completely honest in their comments.

Summary

Marketing your Android app requires much more than just a press release and a few emails to family and friends. For best results, you need to build a total app message. Your message starts with giving your app an accurate and powerful name that will stick in the minds of your buyers, making it easy for them to pass along the app name to others. Next, you must have an app icon that helps your marketing efforts by its descriptiveness graphically or by including the name of your app. Your icon, combined with the app name, helps a buyer instantly understand what your app does and its value. Having a nondescriptive icon means your buyer has to dig a little deeper to understand your app. The more you can help a buyer "connect the dots," the more likely you are to get the sale.

Another part of your total app message is your Android Market and product website text. Light and airy is the best approach because most buyers are not going to invest a lot time reading text. Remember to post prominent reviews in your text and state a few key benefits of your app, along with some bullet points to describe key features on the Android Market. You can always go into more detail about your app on your product website in an FAQ section or in a users guide. You want to strike a balance between conveying the strengths of the app and overwhelming the reader with content.

6

Electronic Word of Mouth

One of the biggest challenges for any developer is figuring out the best marketing strategy, tools, and techniques to successfully sell Android apps on the Android Market. Your app, for example, may already be posted on the Android Market and you are experiencing moderate sales success. Now you're looking for what else you can do from a marketing standpoint to influence even more downloads. Or you may be getting ready to launch your app and you want to learn what you can do to get people excited about your app and start sales off strong.

This chapter covers the ways that you can achieve exposure for your app with ideas on how you can generate electronic word of mouth, gain positive reviews, implement a solid marketing plan, and generate demand.

Creating Electronic Word of Mouth

As mentioned many times in this book, getting your app approved for sale on the Android Market is only the first step (and probably the easiest) in the selling process. It takes a special mix of marketing activities to get your app noticed and to produce consistent sales success. Each marketing activity discussed in this chapter, when well executed, will contribute to more downloads of your app. Simply rewording your app's top description on the Android Market, for example, may result in an increase of 10–25 downloads per day if your original wording did not get right to the point. An example of a crisp introductory sentence is shown in Figure 6.1.

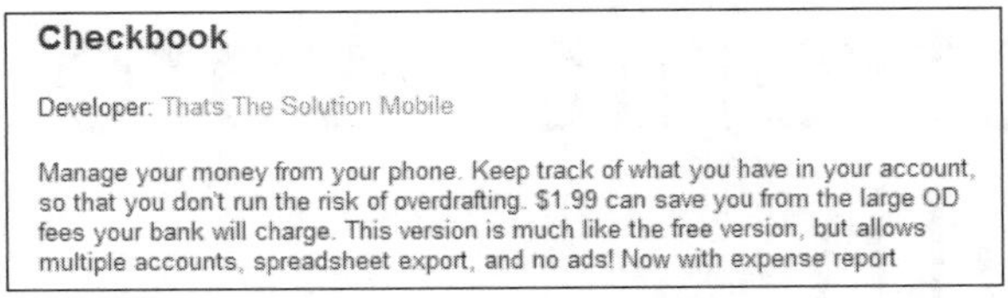

Checkbook

Developer: Thats The Solution Mobile

Manage your money from your phone. Keep track of what you have in your account, so that you don't run the risk of overdrafting. $1.99 can save you from the large OD fees your bank will charge. This version is much like the free version, but allows multiple accounts, spreadsheet export, and no ads! Now with expense report

Figure 6.1   Having a crisp, to the point, introductory description is vital to your selling success and can help you increase your current app sales.

Adding a more descriptive app icon that speaks better to what your app does may result in 25–35 more downloads per day. An example of a great app icon is shown in Figure 6.2.

iFood Assistant by Kraft

Figure 6.2   Having a recognizable and understandable app icon is critical to getting customers to click your app for more details.

Improving the app graphics displayed on the Android Market will help you increase your downloads by some percentage as well. An example of crisp and clear graphics is shown in Figure 6.3. Each one of these seemingly small marketing activities will also help you build positive word of mouth.

Figure 6.3   Clear and easy-to-understand graphics can help instantly convey the purpose and value of your app to Android Market visitors who quickly scan the store for interesting apps.

Word of mouth (or word of *mouse*, as they say in the Internet world) is one of the most powerful methods of getting your message out about your app. Word of mouth is all about building momentum for your app and getting everyone, especially key influencers, to talk about your app and help generate buzz. Some apps start off sales slowly and then gain momentum over time as they get noticed through various marketing activities. With consistent marketing, you can increase the momentum of sales and even help your app become a bestseller.

 Note

For an Android app to become a bestseller, it has to have certain characteristics: It should be well written, have broad applicability and market reach, and be appropriately priced. Not all apps will fit all these criteria. In fact, only a small percentage of apps on the Android Market meet such high criteria. Some Android apps will be good sellers, but not bestsellers because their market may be limited or their applicability is focused on a narrow solution. This is partly why game apps are so popular. They have broad appeal and the audience tends to be quite large. This is also why there are so many game apps for sale on the Android Market. You can make a lot of money selling games if you hit on the right app, but your competition is extremely tough as well.

Word of mouth is a reputation-based form of marketing. If used properly, this form of marketing can be an extremely powerful way to get your app noticed and increase sales. It can take some time to get the ball rolling, so don't be discouraged if your app hasn't achieved momentum in the first few weeks of sales. Word-of-mouth marketing is probably the most powerful marketing tool you have if used the right way and if given enough time.

A good, useful, or cool Android app will prompt your buyers to recommend the app to others through email, blogs, or personal conversations. Earning a good reputation for your app is hard work. Your good reputation, however, can be extremely effective in helping you sell more apps and when you release follow-on apps to your user community.

In contrast, a bad reputation can be damaging to your overall app sales and a bad customer experience can result in additional loss of sales opportunities if word gets too far around. Negative experiences prompt people to tell others their opinion about using your app, and sometimes they write about their disappointment on the Android Market app reviews.

 Note

You will always have a few people who write negative responses to your app. There's no getting around it. Sometimes people purchase an app thinking it does one thing and then they discover it doesn't do what they thought. They then become upset and write a negative review. People even write negative reviews for free apps! However, as long as your ratio of positive reviews is much greater than your negative reviews (10 to 1 or so), your sales will not be impacted too much.

Positive External Reviews

Sometimes a developer is lucky in that his or her app gets a positive review by an Android app review site. That review gets picked up by a blogger or other news agency and it can be off to the races in app sales. If you're not fortunate enough to get such a review, you have to "prime the pump" to help increase the likelihood that your app will have the same sales outcome over time. This means you can't rely on getting a lucky break by a reviewer just stumbling upon your app. Instead you have to employ other techniques to get the word out about your app and get reviewers to notice you. Don't ever give up on getting reviews from as many sources as possible. Try to obtain write-ups in several magazines and websites that would be interested in showcasing your particular app because it's topical to them.

Note

Your strategy for obtaining reviews for your app should be to contact as many Android app review sites as possible that are likely to review your app. Do not submit a non-game app to a game review site because it will simply get ignored. Seek out sites that give you the best chance for a review for your type of app. Utilize any and every contact you may have at these review sites to get your app noticed and reviewed.

Seek out other venues to get reviews of your app. For example, if you have an app that helps people learn how to garden, look for web and print publications that are focused on gardening and make a few inquiries to see if they would be interested in reviewing your app for an article. You'll be surprised how many publications will be interested in doing such a story. The reason is simple. Publications are always looking for topics that would be of interest to their readers. The Android is gaining momentum, even for those readers outside of the traditional tech world, and the Android and apps that are germane to their interests carry strong interest. You will probably have to arrange a call to demo the app for the editor or writer of the publication if they don't have an Android, but it is well worth the effort, and you circumvent the long lines at the traditional review sites.

A truly successful marketing campaign requires that you have a coordinated presentation of your message and offer for your buying audience. You will want to engage in multiple marketing "touch points" to get the word out, such as blogs, product reviews, and other social media tools. All of these delivery options presented to your prospects in a coordinated (or at least steady) fashion will lead them to purchase your app. In short, you have to develop a following for your app. As mentioned before, sometimes the pickup for an app is fast (usually involving a bit of luck) and other times the sales momentum takes more effort on your part. If you have a truly well-written app and it's not getting the downloads you deserve, it's time to roll out a marketing plan and use the ideas presented in this book to make more sales happen.

Coordinated Marketing Effort

The first step is to make sure that all your marketing content uses your newly created unique message, as discussed in Chapter 1, "Your Android App Marketing Strategy: Grand Slam or Base Hits?" Marketing content means every written word and every graphic you use to convey the value of your app. This includes content for your product website, videos on YouTube, product descriptions, blog entries, and so on.

If, for example, you have decided to focus your message on the fact that your new game app offers the fastest action play around, then all your marketing materials will have the same messaging to emphasize fast action play of your new game app. You will want to make sure the following items are updated to carry your new app's message:

- **Icon**—Carefully evaluate your app's icon to ensure that the graphic describes your app and conveys the value of your app. This is tougher than it sounds and requires you to spend some serious time on the creation of this key graphic. If you are concerned that your logo may not convey what your app does, you may want to consider developing another graphic or adding text to the graphic that gives the app's name.

- **Website**—All content on your website should express, convey, and highlight your unique message (for example, fast action play), thus leaving no doubt in the minds of your customers as to the key values of your app. If you are selling a game app, then focus on the levels of play or other benefits of your game as you have identified from Chapter 3, "Identifying Your App's Unique Value."

- **Android Market app page**—All your content and graphics displayed on the Android Market will help direct readers to your app's key values and encourage them make a buying decision concerning your app. The first few sentences on your Android Market page that describe your app are crucial. Make sure you get right to the heart of what your app does and the value it provides in the first two sentences. If someone is interested in knowing more, he will click on the "More" link to open up the description for more details.

- **Email templates**—If you send out emails, make sure your template (the header, footer, text) are updated with your unique message (text, graphics, design, and so on).

- **Signature**—Be sure that your email signature (personal email, product website email) includes your app's name and website. Each time you send out an email, the recipient will see this small advertisement in the email.

- **Other delivery methods**—Videos, Twitter profiles, and such should all contribute to driving your app's marketing message, as discussed in more detail later in this chapter.

Generating Demand

Demand generation is the process of delivering your app's marketing message to the most receptive audience and getting them to respond by reviewing and/or purchasing your app. Somehow, somewhere your app has to get in front of the people most likely to buy it. You can sit back and hope they find it, or you can take some steps to help the buyer "connect the dots," as they say. There are many options to choose from when it comes to creating demand for your Android app. The challenge is that every program you implement costs something: time and/or money.

Not every program is always worth the investment for every type of app. For example, does it make sense to rent an email list to promote your app if you don't already have a list? I believe it's generally not a good use of your marketing funds to rent an email list to generate demand for a couple reasons. First, it's difficult to target your specific buyer with a list. Second, the expense will eat considerably into your profits, especially if it's a lower-priced game app.

Now, does it make sense to build your own email list from your product website? Absolutely! Your product website should have a box on your home page for people to opt in and subscribe to receive product updates, newsletters, new app announcements, and so on from you. Your own email list will become very targeted and specific to your type of app buyer, much more so than trying to buy a list from a broker. Over time you will have a very valuable email list that is highly relevant to your marketing efforts.

Reaching Interested Buyers

There are many possible avenues to obtain buyers for your Android app. Utilizing the different sources outlined in this chapter will assist you in creating a large and targeted approach to leverage when rolling out your new Android app. Here are several other time-tested realities as you deploy your demand-generation plan:

- All app buyers are not created equal. In fact, 80% of repeat business for your apps will come from 20% of your customer base. Take special care of this 20%! You do this by knowing who they are and keeping them updated on every aspect of your product and its future plans.

- The most important download you ever get from a customer is the second download. Why? Because a second-time buyer is at least twice as likely to buy again as a first-time buyer.

- Maximizing direct mail and email success depends first on the lists you use and second on the offer you write.

- Time limit offers, particularly those that give a specific date, outperform offers with no time limit practically every time.

- Free gift offers, particularly where the gift appeals to self-interest, outperform discount offers consistently.

- Sweepstakes offers, particularly in conjunction with impulse purchases, can increase order volumes by 55% or more.

- People buy benefits, not features, but in the case of an Android app, features matter.

- The longer you can keep someone reading your website or Android Market description, the better your chances of success.

Choosing the Right Delivery Methods

It may seem like there are limitless possibilities to reach your audience; therefore, choosing the right delivery methods can maximize your marketing dollars and allow you to grow your sales faster and hopefully beyond your expectations. To begin determining which delivery methods would be best for your app, consider the following questions:

- Where does your target audience go to obtain information? (Examples include online forums, product websites, and blogs.)

- How does your target audience make purchase decisions for your type of app?

- Is interest in your type of app driven by certain websites?

Three Key Areas

In today's very competitive app marketplace, a marketing strategy that ensures a consistent approach to offering your Android app in a way that will outsell the competition and keep your costs down is critical. However, in concert with defining a marketing strategy, you must also have a well-defined methodology—a week-to-week plan for implementing your strategy. After you've completed the necessary steps to define your app's unique selling points and have created a solid marketing message, it is time to deliver that message to your targeted audience. There are three distinct methods (and many derivative methods) that you can use to deliver your app marketing message to your audience. We will take a look at examples and ideas in each of these areas:

- Direct marketing for your app

- Promoting your app

- Establishing a community

Direct Marketing for Your App

Direct marketing includes mailing and emailing.

Direct Mail

Although certainly not a new marketing concept, there are some areas where direct mail marketing may be of benefit to you. Direct mail includes postcards, flyers, or letters mailed directly to a potential buyer, reviewer, or trade show group. Direct mail has pros and cons just like any marketing medium and must be evaluated in the context of your particular app.

Pros

First, the pros of using direct mail:

- Direct mail can be persistent, meaning that if you send out a postcard mailing, the recipients may put it on their desk and read it several times before deciding what to do with it. You may get multiple opportunities for them to pick up the postcard and act on it.

- Getting a reader to look at your ad more than once is obviously a very positive thing and can be cost effective if it leads to the desired behavior.

Cons

We have to look at the cons also:

- Direct mail is expensive and difficult to track response rates. Postcards are generally the least expensive route, with letters being the most expensive. A postcard printed in four colors front and back will cost you around 50 to 65 cents (including postage) for an average mailing of 1,000. An envelope, letter, and postage could easily cost you $1 per recipient to send out.

- Your app will have to be priced much higher to absorb the cost of sending out a mailing. I don't recommend doing a letter mailing for your app under any circumstance. It's just too costly and you won't see the return on your investment in terms of app sales downloads.

Now, before you dismiss postcards completely, there are a few possibilities that you should consider in your marketing plan. First, if you plan to attend trade shows where you have the opportunity to showcase your app, you can print off 50–100 postcards inexpensively by using a site such as www.vistaprint.com. It's always a good idea to have something printed to hand out to remind people how and where to get your app. Second, as you solicit reviewers for your app, you can send the reviewer (or reviewing company) a postcard showcasing your app. This just might nudge them to take a look at your app in the sea of apps they have to review. Sending the reviewer a postcard will help you to stand out in the crowded field.

 Note

Getting a reviewer or industry expert to review your app is much like getting a company to notice your resume. Most employers want you to submit your resume electronically for tracking and filtering purposes. However, it does- n't hurt in some cases to also send them a printed resume to increase the likelihood that you'll get noticed by the hiring manager. Similarly, your app is vying for attention in a very crowded field and you want to stand out. Sending a postcard to a reviewer gives your app that little edge that might make the difference between getting noticed or ignored.

Another use of direct mail is to do a promotion for your new app via a monthly newsletter or a targeted piece designed specifically for a campaign. If you can locate a newsletter that might be willing to carry the announcement of your app, this is the best approach. I would be willing to bet that very few Android developers have tried this approach yet. It is crucial to always create a compelling call to action and a strong offer whenever you use this type of approach. You must give your audience a reason to respond. Direct mail generally nets a 1%–3% response rate.

Email

Email is generally the most inexpensive form of mass marketing to reach large audiences and with somewhat predictable results. Industry averages say that emails have an open rate of 20%, and then 5% will click through to your website. Like reg- ular snail mail, email also has it pros and cons.

Pros

The pros of email include the following:

- Email is great for building relationships and keeping your app buyers up to date with offers, information, and newsletters.

- Some email campaigns can generate a 5%–10% response rate, with additional tracking options to fine tune your messaging, such as tracking click-through rates on links embedded within the email.

- You can quickly adjust and tweak your message or call-to-action quickly based on response rates.

- Email also allows the audience to respond to the offer immediately by directing responses to your specific landing page on your website or to the Android Market.

- Email can be used to easily send promotional codes or invite users to join a registration-based community.

Cons

Again, we must also consider the cons:

- In recent surveys, email is declining in terms of use by younger users who prefer other means of communication through newer social media tools.

- Email is easily deletable, and with so much spam many email users may ignore or not even receive your message.

- It's difficult to attract the attention of app buyers if they don't check email often. You need to go where the users are, which is on their Android or Android tablet. The next section on advertising goes into details on how to capitalize on this emerging trend.

> **Note**
>
> Email can be used to reach out to your contacts on a consistent basis, but it's important to send relevant and timely information to avoid boring and annoying your readers. Direct marketing success is dependent on a well-maintained database of current buyers with valid email addresses.

> **Note**
>
> The best list you can ever have is the one you build organically over time with customers and such who want to be contacted with information about your Android app. Start now with this goal, but remember it takes time and patience.

Promoting Your App

Advertising your app is another way to increase sales and get the word out about your app. Advertising can also be effective to build your overall brand image if you are part of a larger development company and have the budget, time, and money. For most independent developers, effective advertising requires thinking more creatively and constructively about how to get the word out about their apps. Think in terms of getting free advertising where your app has some appeal and a reporter or writer is interested in giving your app some press.

Your App in Traditional Media (Newspapers, Radio, TV)

You might think it's crazy to pursue these options, but let's look at a few ways you can get free press on TV or in your newspaper. You have to approach this from the standpoint that newspapers and local television stations are always looking for stories that will be of strong interest to their reading or viewing audience. If your application is newsworthy or could fit into one of their columns or news segments, then you've got a shot at getting some free publicity for your app. Naturally, if you have a very narrow type of application, you'll have to look harder for a way to pitch your app to the press.

Newspapers

The good old-fashioned printed newspaper is still alive (for now) and it's actually a great medium to help you gain exposure for your app. Keep in mind that if your story runs in newsprint, it will also run in the online edition of the paper in most cases. There are many opportunities to reach out to editors and writers to pitch your story, and reaching them has never been easier because they all post their email address at the end of their columns.

The best approach is to take a look at your local paper and see which categories would fit for your particular app. Most papers have a technology section, so you at least have one category to focus on. Larger papers will also have other sections that fit more closely to your particular type of app. You can approach all reporters/editors in any category you think might be a fit. Don't worry if you contact the wrong person. He or she will usually forward your message to the right person or will respond with a contact for the right person. Table 6.1 shows certain app categories and how they correspond to the sections of your local paper.

Table 6.1   The Various App Categories and How They Line Up with the Sections of Your Local Newspaper

Android App Types	Sections of Local Newspaper
Games	Sports, Technology, Entertainment
Lifestyle	Lifestyle, Technology, Entertainment
Health	Health & Fitness, Technology
Plants & Gardening	Home & Garden, Technology
Navigation	Travel, Technology
Education	Education, Technology
Finance	Financial, Technology

These steps will help get the media to review your app:

1. Match your type of app with the right section of your local newspaper.

2. Take note of all the articles written and find the email addresses of the section's editor and some of the writers.

3. Draft an email with a catchy headline about the value of your app. For example, if you have a gardening and houseplant app, you could contact the home and garden editor of your local paper and say something like this in your email:

Subject Line: New Android App Helps Owners Keep Their Gardens Alive!

Dear Editor (use his or her real name),

I have recently completed this exciting new Android app that allows an Android user to take care of their gardens with clear pictures, descriptions, and tips for many garden varieties across the U.S. and Canada. Because of your coverage of home and garden topics, I feel this app would be of great interest to you and your readers. I would be happy to provide you with a free copy of this app and give you a demonstration of its benefits. I look forward to hearing your response!

Kind Regards,

Your Name

Your Phone Number

You will find articles written for your local paper on Android apps for most major cities. Simply go to your newspaper's website and type **android apps** into the search box. This search of the *Arizona Republic*'s website (www.azcentral.com), for example, revealed many articles, such as the one shown in Figure 6.4. The creators of this app received free press, and this article was syndicated in other papers across the country as well.

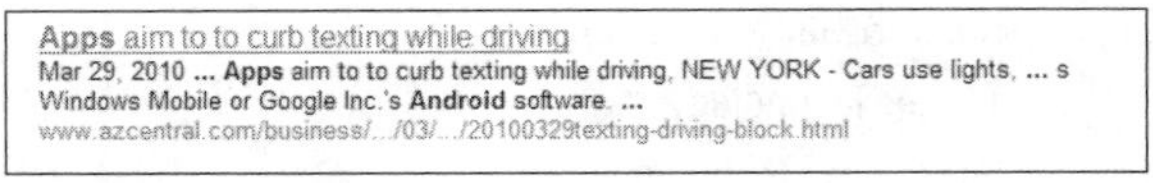
Apps aim to to curb texting while driving
Mar 29, 2010 ... **Apps** aim to to curb texting while driving, NEW YORK - Cars use lights, ... s Windows Mobile or Google Inc.'s **Android** software. ...
www.azcentral.com/business/.../03/.../20100329texting-driving-block.html

Figure 6.4 An example of a local app getting coverage in the *Arizona Republic*.

Once an article is published by one newspaper, it may be picked up by other papers across the country, depending on the interest or importance of the app. Sometimes, even a very large paper such as *USAToday* will pick up a story from another paper. Getting newspaper coverage for your app can help you create the momentum your app needs to build strong sales.

Radio and TV Advertising

Radio and TV advertising might also be effective in some circumstances. Many entrepreneurs believe that radio and TV advertising are beyond their means. Although this may be true for national TV slots and national advertising, which is usually out of the entrepreneur's price range, appearing on local stations or on smaller cable television stations can sometimes be free. For example, if a local station does a technology show once a week, you might be able to get on it to demo or discuss your app. There are also a number of local (city-owned) stations that may want to do a focus story on Android apps targeting a broad base of users from their audience. For example, some stations may do a piece specifically focusing on a smaller market for the busy sales rep or the stressed commuter or perhaps a health segment. Again you can reach out to your local station and pitch the idea that they do a story around a topic that just happens to match the very app you've written.

The best way to reach a reporter is to go to the station's local website. On most sites you will find a link to the reporters, and they are usually listed by categories such as News, Weather, Sports, Entertainment, and so on. When you click their biographies, an email address is usually provided so you can contact them. Use the same email approach from earlier in the newspaper description to reach out to these reporters.

Radio is the last area you may want to explore. Radio is more difficult because you will have to explain your app rather than show your app. Radio is also very broad in its reach and so part of your listening audience may not own an Android phone or

an Android tablet. Some radio shows have technology segments once a week, usually at slower times such as Saturday mornings. You can do a little digging on a
radio station's website to look at its programming schedule to see if there might be
an opportunity for you.

 Note

The ease with which you're able to get a story written about your app often
depends on your app and current events. Don't give up easily. It takes persistence. It's free advertising and can mean the difference between your
app selling okay and selling extremely well.

Advertising Your Apps

First, there is a difference between marketing and advertising, and it's important to
understand the distinction. The premise of this book is how to market your
Android apps, which is a process that includes multiple steps. Part of the marketing
process includes a single component known as advertising. *Advertising*, in the
Android sense, is concerned with the placement of ads on the Android and
Android tablet itself to either help sell your app or to generate revenue selling other
apps or products. A developer can make money selling his app to interested buyers
or by selling space on his app to host other ads.

Typically, a developer who wants to make money selling ad space on his app will
provide a free app to encourage thousands of downloads. He will carry ads on his
app with the hope that the Android user will click one of the hosted ads. Each click
pays the owner of the free app a percentage of the revenue generated for each ad.
Therefore, developers of free apps are incented to develop the very best apps possible to achieve huge volumes of downloads, thus increasing the potential that someone will click through on one of the hosted ads.

At least six major vendors are vying for ad revenue in the Android ad market. Two
such companies have taken center stage in early 2010, namely AdMob and Mobclix.
Both are considered dominant players in this space. There's no doubt that mobile
advertising is big business and getting bigger every month. Analysts peg the market
to grow to $1.3B by 2013, up from $68M in 2010. Just like any type of advertising,
it's important to determine how effective it might be for your particular needs in
selling your app. In most cases the shotgun advertising approach does not work and
you end up spending a lot of money and don't reach your target audience. Mobile
advertising is certainly more targeted (to mobile users), but the challenge is reaching your type of app buyer. Just because someone has an Android or Android tablet
does not mean that person is your target audience. So, you have to understand

whether the service you intend to use can target very specific users interested in your app. The other large consideration is whether to give your app away for free and try to make money by generating ad revenue. A full discussion of this option can be found in Chapter 10, "Pricing Your App."

 Note

If you choose to use a company to advertise your app, always start off with a small test before going too far and spending too much money. Just like Google AdWords, you can set your budget low to test things out and evaluate your success.

In the next sections we take a look at a few of the major players in the mobile ad provider market.

AdMob

AdMob is being acquired by Google. The following list runs down several important points about AdMob:

- AdMob offers pay-per-click (CPC) advertising on thousands of mobile websites and Android apps for Android developers. You decide how much to pay per click through AdMob's auction-based pricing system. The minimum amount to start an ad campaign is $50.

- AdMob allows you to target your ads to Android and iPod touch users only, so that you pay for clicks from users who can download your app. Your ads will appear on mobile websites and inside other Android apps. You can also target your ads to specific geographical locations. However, as mentioned earlier, be careful and do a small test. Just because someone has an Android or Android tablet does not mean that person is interested in your type of app.

- AdMob's free Download Tracking tool tells you how many downloads of your app were driven by each of your ads, helping you to optimize your ad spending.

- You can also choose to serve AdMob ads inside your app. You can use AdMob's Download Exchange—a free way to drive downloads of your app. When you show ads for other apps inside your app, free ads for your app are shown inside other apps.

- If you have more than one app, you can use AdMob House Ads to show ads for your app inside your other apps—another free way to cross-promote your apps.

- AdMob provides free, real-time reporting to help you monitor your campaigns, optimize performance, and manage costs.

Mobclix

Mobclix is another ad platform that provides analytics and monetization through advertising and distribution for application developers. The company provides a mobile ad exchange as well. App developers can use the Mobclix platform to choose from 20 ad networks, including Google AdSense for Android, Yahoo! Mobile Publishers, and many others. App developers sign up with their ad inventory and then ad networks bid for the spots on their apps.

Quattro Wireless

Quattro Wireless (recently acquired by Apple) is another leading global mobile advertising company that allows advertisers and publishers to reach their target audiences across mobile web, application, and video platforms. Its platform allows dynamic targeting technology to optimize every ad impression. However, Apple has announced the iAd advertising platform for the iPhone/iPad market. It is going to be a very closed solution for Apple advertising only.

Paid Search

Google, Yahoo!, and other search engines provide the capability to perform a paid search to locate your product website. Be very careful when employing any type of paid search because it will dramatically eat into your profits. You are basically paying for potential customers to click over to your site when they do a Google (or Yahoo!) search for your products or services. When they perform a search, your website will appear in the "paid" listings section of these search engines. When a user clicks over to your website, you are charged a fee for each click through.

There are pros and cons to using paid placement programs. The benefit is that you can get immediate exposure to your product website. The downside is that anyone can click through to your site just "kicking tires" and can cost you a lot of money every month with perhaps few new sales. You can place caps on how much you want to spend each month for clicks on your website. This all depends on your budget.

If your app is priced between $0.99 and $1.99, paid search is probably not worth the bother because your cost for click-throughs will be very high when compared to the price of your app. The challenge with paid search is that it's going to direct traffic to your product website. You then have to get the visitor to click over to the Android Market or other Android app site to purchase your app. The odds of this happening drop dramatically for this two-step process. Again, you will be disappointed when your credit card is charged a bundle for click-throughs and your sales have not grown much. An example of a developer using paid search is shown in Figure 6.5.

Android Mobile Security   Sponsored link
www.Good.com/Android   Manage and Secure **Android** Devices w/ Good for Enterprise–Learn More!

Figure 6.5   Paid search can be very expensive for low-cost apps. The app shown in this example is selling for $2.99 on the Android Market.

There is some value to using paid search initially when you are building your overall brand as an Android app developer. So, from the standpoint of driving awareness about your products and services, paid search can help you initially to gain traffic to your website and showcase products/services in front of potential customers. Having this mindset is better than hoping to achieve sales from paid search. But, be sure to experiment slowly and optimize keywords at the lowest possible cost per click.

I recommend that you view AdWords (and similar programs) as a way to drive immediate attention to your website because you have not established the site with organic traffic. As you optimize your site over time to appear higher in the search rankings, you should depend less and less on paid search for web placement. See Chapter 7, "Using Social Media in Your App Marketing," to learn how to increase your web traffic.

 Note

An online presence for your business is an absolute must! Some app developers think they can get by without a website. You can't! Your customers can only go to two places to find your app: the Android Market and the Internet. If they go first to the Internet to look up whatever they are looking for, you want to be included in the search results to answer their need. But, do this as cost effectively as you can. Many books and articles are available on the subject of search engine optimization (SEO). However, this topic goes well beyond the scope of this book.

Online Advertising

With the prevalence of Internet users today, online advertising has become increasingly effective because that's where the buyers are. Online advertising includes placing company information, products, descriptions of your apps, and so on, in online listings, including Android app directories. These listings can be free, but you can often upgrade your presence if you determine the site drives traffic to your business. Banner ads, skyscrapers, or other graphic advertisement can be a great way to drive traffic to your product website. Look at costs on the many app review sites available.

The goal behind online campaigns is to drive traffic to your website or a specific landing page of your website. Look to place banners ads and paid listings on websites where folks who might be looking for your app would likely visit. Remember that you are paying for the exposure and click-through rates to your website. You must have a compelling offer to entice the click-through to convert to a lead.

 Note

Advertising in online communities allows you to get your app some exposure very quickly, but a better way to get online exposure is by getting someone to write a review of your app and post it to his or her site. Seek out local newspapers as well to write you a review, especially if your paper has a technology section.

Advertising in *online* review sites is also possible but will cost you more money. Many of the big name brands will use ad space on popular Android app review sites.

Building a Community

Your customers should be your biggest fans—and you should treat them well to keep them coming back as well as recommending and using your apps. Maintaining an accurate user list or having a way to reach out to your customers is imperative to a successful customer-retention program. Selling to an existing customer is far easier and less expensive than obtaining a new one.

Create targeted email campaigns, leveraging your list to do the following:

- Feature app promotions you may offer
- Supply software updates
- Provide cross-sell opportunities with other apps you may implement
- Offer answers to common app questions
- Server up tips and secret features of your app
- Show leader boards for high scores if you are selling a game.

Treating your customers as if they're valued will guarantee a loyal customer base for years to come. Establishing registration-based communities allows you to maintain contact with your database on a frequent basis. Having customers register for a blog (RSS feed) is another great way to build your list.

Another way to build a sense of community is to tie your app from the user to the developer by allowing interaction or communication from the users. Some apps lend themselves well to developing this type of community. Look carefully at your app and consider ways that you can create a strong sense of community. The more you can interact with your buyers, the more likely they will be to come back and buy more of your upgrades or other apps from you. For example, for certain game apps, you can create a leader board. The top three to five leaders can submit their scores to your app website, thus drawing people over to your site and creating a sense of community.

One company has developed an app that helps you quiz yourself on science questions. You can then compare your scores against those in the user community to see how well you rank. This type of interaction with the outside user base helps establish a strong sense of community and links back to the company website, as well as gives the user a sense that a real person is answering questions and giving personal advice. An example of this clever idea is shown in Figure 6.6.

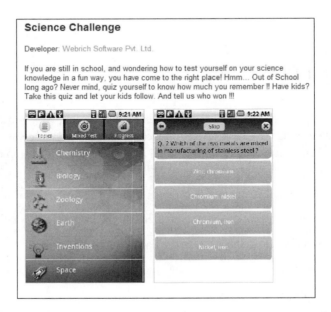

Figure 6.6 You can build a strong sense of community when you provide a link between the user of an app and the developer.

Summary

The Internet and its myriad tools have made it possible for independent developers to gain significant exposure for their apps while managing their unique budgets. Using the right marketing techniques, independent developers can build their brands and gain exposure for their apps in ways unheard of just a few years ago. The challenge for independent developers is to determine which tools will have the most impact for their particular apps.

Generating positive press and positive word of mouth takes hard work. For developers who are aggressive, there are many opportunities to get the word out about their apps. There are still many opportunities to garner free press through newspapers, TV, and radio if you are willing to contact editors and reporters and pitch the idea behind your app. Be willing to give them a free copy and be ready to demo the app, answer questions, and even help write the article if necessary. Free press in a newspaper means that the article will be posted online. Once online, the story about your app can be syndicated across many media outlets. Bottom line: You must achieve momentum to get your app sales moving.

7

Using Social Media in Your App Marketing

When you hear the term social media, what comes to mind? You're probably thinking of Facebook, MySpace, Twitter, Digg, YouTube, and many other websites that enable you to interact within a community of users. But social media is much more. It also includes blogs, RSS feeds, LinkedIn, del.icio.us, StumbleUpon, and other social marketing activities we will discuss in this chapter.

One of the biggest mistakes developers make is thinking that using social media will generate leads and sales of their apps. In reality, social media sites are more about creating relationships with a community of users and potential buyers. Eventually, the community will become buyers if you've gone about your relationship building in the right way. In order to be successful with social media, you must establish yourself as a respected participant in your area of interest and earn the respect of that community. This takes time and steady work.

In this chapter you will learn about the different forms of social media marketing and how they can improve your effort to reach your target market. Some apps, such as games, lend themselves well to the social media approach because younger age groups tend to play the games and also tend to be consumers of social media advertising and marketing.

Harnessing the power of social media does afford app marketers the ability to reach large audiences of groups that share common interests. The great benefit of social media is that they are typically free for you to sign up. Within minutes you can register an account and be logged on to a social media site. There are thousands of sites you could join, but remember that social media sites are like being at a party. You can only be a part of a few conversations to really be effective. Jumping from conversation to conversation at a party is not effective, and the same holds true for social media sites. You simply won't have the time to devote to more than a few of them on any consistent basis.

 Note

Choose your user ID with some care. If you are required to use your name, then use your real first name. If you are asked to create a fictitious user ID that will show up when you post comments, blogs posts, reviews, and so on, then choose a user ID that will help your brand and your app. If your company is Apps R Us, then try to use "appsrus" for your user ID. Always be thinking of how to extend your brand or your app's name wherever you can.

Registering for social media sites may be free, but that's where free ends. There is a cost as far as your time. It takes time to develop a following in social media, and it takes time to establish a presence. So, even though you may get online and registered quickly, the real work comes when you want to get established among your community. You have to earn the respect of others in the community by visiting and commenting on different posts, adding value to conversations, and answering questions where you can provide insight.

The activities of social media will open up opportunities for you to talk about your apps after you build a relationship with your readers. If you barge into an online community with the expectation that you can tout your app, you will be in for a surprise. Other members of the community will recognize your intent and will either call you out on your posts or ignore them. You must earn the right of being a part of the community without outward attempts to cash in. Longer term, your results will be positive as you make new connections, establish yourself on the Web, and reap new sales of your app.

Here are some ideas to help get you get started using social media to establish a presence in your community and become a positive influence:

- **Start soon to establish a presence.** You cannot launch an app and hope to be known in your community a day or week later if you have never visited or made a single posting before. Building up contacts and friends takes time in the real world, and it's the same online. If you have not done so already, sign up for a few sites such as Facebook, Twitter, and Android and Android tablet app blogs that pertain to your type of app. Do this before you even start coding your app, if possible, and you'll be ahead of the game.

- **Actively participate.** In order to be seen, you have to post comments on a regular basis. Join groups and discussions that are focused on your type of app. Be helpful in your posts with information that others will find valuable. After you have become established, you can begin to talk about your app if you have posted it to the Android Market. If you haven't posted your app, you'll want to be careful about how much information you disclose so your idea doesn't get copied in full. Chances are very good that someone is developing a similar app anyway, but not exactly like yours.

- **Pitch bloggers and influencers.** Over time you will have a greater degree of comfort asking bloggers to discuss your app in one of their blog posts. This is one of the fruits of having a relationship with people on the Web. An influential blogger can help your sales tremendously if his or her blog is widely read or the post is picked up by other bloggers. If your blog post is mentioned by Digg, for example, you could see sales of your app skyrocket.

- **Write an article or two about your area of expertise.** If your area of expertise is jewelry making, then write an article offering tips and advice about jewelry making. If your expertise is finance, then give people some good financial advice with no strings attached. People love articles framed around "Ten Tips" or "Five Reasons Why...." These types of titles pique our curiosity and we want to read more. At the bottom of your article you can post your contact information, your product website, and maybe the link to your app if you're lucky. Always ask the editor of the publication what you are allowed to post at the end of your article.

- **Offer to write a guest blog.** Once you get to know a few bloggers and have established a rapport with them, you can approach them about writing a guest post for their blog. Many bloggers will agree to let you do this. Why? Because, often they are looking for ideas and ways to beef up their blog posts. Having a guest blogger gives their blog a shot in the arm and creates additional interest from their readers.

Selecting Your Social Media Tools

The first step to selecting the right social media tools is to understand where your audience is and how they communicate online. In other words, don't just sign up for a bunch of social media sites thinking you'll do a little marketing of your app without first understanding where your buyers are and how they exchange information. If you have developed a really cool app for bowlers, you can do a search on different social media sites to see how many bowling fans there are in any given community. A search for bowling fans on Facebook, for example, reveals multiple fan groups. One fan group is shown in Figure 7.1.

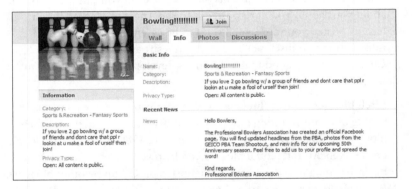

Figure 7.1   A search for bowling fans on Facebook reveals multiple groups, one of them quite large.

You can review groups for any topic of app that you are trying to market. However, many groups listed on Facebook are very small, sometimes 10–100, and that usually means there's not a large enough community on that particular site to really do any effective marketing. You want to locate audiences of several thousand in order to be effective. This means you have a strong community of similar users on the same site, and this can work well for your marketing efforts.

 Note

Locating and joining a group that corresponds to your app does not mean you start spamming the group about your app! Join the groups so you can see what people are talking about and how you might join in and provide value to the conversation.

Using Facebook

Facebook has become an extremely powerful tool for creating a community and attracting users from a social perspective. In fact, Facebook has some 400+ million registered users and is still growing. It has such a large collection of users that it simply can't be ignored. You won't reach all of them, but your goal is to do the best you can to reach your market of interested users and buyers. Need more encouragement? Here are some more reasons why you can't ignore Facebook as part of your marketing plan:

- Of the 400 million users, roughly 100 million are from the U.S.

- Half of the registered users log in daily to Facebook.

- Your app-buying audience is on Facebook.

- More than 65 million users access Facebook from their mobile devices.

- Ten million members become fans of Fan Pages each day.

Using Facebook, you want to accomplish a couple things. First, you want to be found by people who are interested in buying your Android apps. Second, you want to connect with these potential customers and establish a relationship with them. You can use Facebook to create a business page for your app within a few minutes. You can start to build your page by going to www.facebook.com/pages/create.php and filling in the details, as shown in Figure 7.2.

Figure 7.2 Facebook's main screen for creating a business page for your Android app.

Once you have given your fan page a name, you can fill in a description of your app as well as add videos and photos of your app. Of course, one of the links you want to add to your site is a link to the app on the Android Market. This is critical! You can get the URL to your app on the Android Market by going directly to your app, highlighting the URL in your browser, and copying it via the right-click menu. You will see a dropdown option: Copy Link. You can copy the link and then paste it into your fan page. An example of accessing your direct URL link is shown in Figure 7.3.

Figure 7.3   Obtaining the direct web link for your app's URL on the Android Market is done by going to your app on the market, clicking the link in the browser, and then right-clicking with your mouse to copy it.

Once you have completed all the details for your page, you can then invite your friends to become fans of your business (app) page. This will help you to initiate the viral marketing process for your app. When people join your Fan Page, it's published in their newsfeed for all their friends to read, thus further helping the word to get out about your app. An example of the ever popular *Fishin' 2 Go* app with its Facebook fan page is shown in Figure 7.4.

Figure 7.4   The Fishin' 2 Go Android app has many thousands of fans who read up on the latest buzz around this extremely successful app.

Facebook also offers advertising based on click-through activity. You can create an ad for your app's page and target the ad to a very specific subset of people, thus generating huge amounts of traffic to your page. Be careful, though. Just like with Google AdWords, you can set your own budget and spend lots of money on people clicking through. So, go slowly and see if the results generate sales of your app. It's one thing to get traffic to your site, but you need to convert them into buying customers, too.

 Note

Obviously entire books are written on the subject of Facebook and how to utilize the power of this enormous social site. The important point to remember here is that you should consider using Facebook to help you market your Android and Android tablet apps because it's inexpensive and easy to get started. Just like your own product website, Facebook is another extension of the Android Market for driving interest and buyers to your app. The more accessible your app is to your buying audience, the more you will sell.

Using Twitter

Twitter has burst on to the media scene in just the past several years and should also be considered a valuable tool in marketing Android and Android tablet apps. Because Twitter only allows you to send 140 character messages, you must be very concise in your posts. Twitter is meant to allow you to communicate a short message to whole group of people at the same time. You can also communicate privately to a single person or a small group of people. You can use Twitter to accomplish a number of marketing objectives including:

- **Create a following for a soon-to-be-launched app.** Use your name to sign up for Twitter and then search for other Twitter users who are or might be interested in your type of app. At appropriate points in the conversation insert your own comments (Tweets) and start to contribute to the conversation. You'll be surprised how quickly others will start to follow you. At some point you can mention the app you are working on. Remember, contribute first and then talk about what you're doing. There's definitely a protocol to using Twitter successfully, just like any social media.

- **Help maintain a sense of community.** If you have already launched your app, you can put the Twitter logo on your personal website and invite others to follow you on Twitter. This allows you to keep in touch with users of your app and keeps interest alive. You can also add the Twitter logo to other social media sites you join.

- **Forward other relevant posts to your followers.** When you do a press release, be sure to Tweet out to your followers with a link to your announcement. Ask your followers to do you a favor and re-Tweet the post to their followers. This will help you spread the word about your app, and this helps you establish a sense of community with like-minded users of your app.

- **Drive traffic to your site.** Once you have a large enough following, you can use Twitter to drive people to your product website and directly to the Android Market to review your latest app. You can also make app updates with your improved graphics, sounds, and so on available.

- **Post comments or questions about your app.** One of the best ways to communicate to your followers that you are working on a fix or an enhancement to your app is to Tweet about it. This will help get conversations going about your app.

Twitter allows you to create a personal account or a business account with less delineation. If you already have a personal account on Twitter, keep that account for personal communications. You can set up a separate account for your brand or your app. It doesn't hurt, though, to Tweet about your app to family and friends. If you plan to build multiple Android and Android tablet apps, then you should create a Twitter ID that is inclusive of your brand, such AndroidAppsGuy or some name that will describe your company rather than a single app. An example of the Twitter account-creation page is shown in Figure 7.5.

Just like any social network site, setting up your account is the easy part. Building your contacts happens over time. You can do a search for different people who might have interest in your app and begin to follow them. To follow people, you simply click their Twitter icon and then click Follow. In many cases when you follow someone, that person will also follow you back.

 Note

There are whole books on how to make the best use of Twitter. However, the important thing to remember from an app marketing perspective is that this tool is at your disposal to assist you in marketing your apps. Twitter is helpful when you want to communicate short messages to your audience, either to ask a question or to direct them to take a look at your app.

Figure 7.5   Creating a Twitter account for your Android and Android tablet brand/app can be done in minutes.

Using Blogs

Blogging has been around for some time now and is still an incredibly popular and powerful communication tool. Blogging can help you market your Android and Android tablet app in several ways. The first and easiest way to utilize blogging is to get to know some bloggers who write about Android and Android tablet apps. These people have already established a following with their blogs and can give you a hand in getting a review of your app or at least giving your app a mention. There are many blogs that do Android and Android tablet app reviews where you can submit your app. It's always best if you have established some type of relationship with the blogger before reaching out to him or her for a review. Obviously, if the blogger knows you, he or she will be more inclined to look at your app ahead of someone else's. An example of an app review site that is a blog is shown in Figure 7.6.

Be sure to search on blog sites that discuss the topic of your particular app, even if they don't typically review Android and Android tablet apps. They might just be interested in discussing your app as an interesting blog post. Remember that most bloggers are usually looking for good topics to blog about. Sometimes even the best bloggers run out of ideas, and you may come along at just the right time with a very interesting app for them to discuss.

Figure 7.6   A blog that functions as an app review site.

The second way to utilize blogs is to create your own. If you don't have a product website for your app, you can use a blog page to set up a site quickly. It is easy to set up a blog to discuss and showcase your apps. You can post videos and graphics to your blogs. Starting up a blog is free and easy; you can go to WordPress (www. wordpress.com), TypePad (www.typepad.com), MovableType (www.movabletype. com), Blogger (www.blogger.com), or one of hundreds of other blog sites.

Once you have your blog set up, you can promote your apps on your blog. Post the press release about your app on your blog. You can integrate your blog into other social media sites such as Facebook and LinkedIn so more people will visit your blog and comment on your posts.

 Note

Having your own blog is a time commitment. You have to enter posts at least a couple of times each week or you won't build up a following for your brand or your apps. Once again, building a following is hard work and takes persistence. If you stop blogging for weeks and months at a time, you won't attract much of a following. It's interesting, but in this time-crunched society, we always look at the posting dates of articles and especially blogs. If we see January 6, 2009 as the last post, we tend to click away, looking for newer content.

Using RSS

RSS, or Real Simple Syndication, can be considered a subset to blogging. RSS feeds help you spread your blogs and help people keep in touch with you whenever you have a new blog post. Using RSS, your readers can filter and aggregate similar content so that they are receiving the content they desire. You will want to provide RSS capability on your blog and your product website so that people can sign up for your blog posts and receive information that is important to them. There are a number of RSS tools a reader can use to aggregate content, such as Google Reader, Google News, Yahoo!News, FeedBurner, and so on.

Using LinkedIn

LinkedIn started out as a site for business professionals to stay connected, and although it has morphed into much more, its primary purpose remains the same. Just like many social media sites, LinkedIn has added lots of features, such as complex search capabilities, advertising, job postings, and groups. Its power for you as an app marketer lies in the fact that there are literally thousands of groups you can review and join to take part in discussions and promote your apps. For example, a recent search of LinkedIn for "Android apps" revealed 28 such groups. An example of such a search is shown in Figure 7.7. They are sorted by group size by default, with the largest groups at the top of the list. A search of "Android developers" reveals 59 groups, some with more than 10,000 members!

Figure 7.7 A search of groups on "Android apps" shows 28 groups.

If you haven't signed up for LinkedIn, you should. This is an opportunity for you to showcase your developer skills or marketing skills and to showcase your apps with a professional community. It will take you about half an hour to do a really nice job of listing all your skills and attributes for this site. After you have registered, you can locate and join Android app groups that allow you to contribute your expertise and inform people of your apps and their availability.

LinkedIn's advanced search functionality also lets you locate people, groups, and companies you may have an interest in contacting. For example, you can search for people using "Android app developers," and LinkedIn will respond with a list of hundreds of developers! Perhaps you are looking for another developer to team up with on a project; this is a great site for doing that.

 Note

It will take some time for you to build up your connections to other people. Many on LinkedIn have earned a badge of respect with more than 500 connections. That's a nice network to have when you are looking for development opportunities or any type of work. What's more, you can post a comment to the "What are you working on?" link.

Using YouTube

One of the most powerful ways to get your message across about your app is through a YouTube video. There are now more than 1 billion YouTube downloads of videos each day. This is because most people would rather watch something about an app than read about it. So, a video is a must when you are trying to market your Android and Android tablet apps. Your video should be posted on your product website and blog. It should also be used when contacting reviewers to attract their attention. Reviewers are so stretched for time that they would rather watch something than read about it. You can post a link to your app's video wherever you have an online presence.

Creating and posting your own YouTube video has never been easier. With just a video camera and your app, you can create a compelling video that will eventually be viewed thousands of times, perhaps millions of times if it catches on. We all probably know about the famous "Will it Blend?" videos posted on YouTube a few years ago. In one video segment the founder of Blendtec grinds up an iPhone (http://www.youtube.com/watch?v=qg1ckCkm8YI) verified in his blender! The video has had more than 8 million views and has created remarkable sales for this company. The video was catchy and provocative, something you need to think through carefully when you create yours. A screen capture of this incredibly successful video is shown in Figure 7.8.

Video Basics

Here are a few basic ideas to help you develop your Android and Android tablet app video:

- Keep the video short! No more than two minutes in length.

- Make your video engaging. Humor, where appropriate, doesn't hurt.

Figure 7.8 YouTube videos can be incredibly powerful to help sell virtually any product, including your Android and Android tablet apps.

- Write out a script to cover what you will say in the video. Shooting the video without a script will look like, well, you shot the video without a script!

- You can do the video with a $300 digital video camera. No need to purchase expensive tools, but the lighting and sound quality must be good.

- Present the video in a "problem/solution/demo" format. State the problem your buyer is having. Then state the solution your app provides. Demonstrate the app in a brief demo.

- In your video, ask the buyer to go to your product web page or blog, as well as to the Android Market, to learn more.

Summary

In this chapter, we have discussed the value of using social media to help you market your Android and Android tablet apps and build your overall brand. Social media marketing is more about having conversations with your community of buyers rather than developing outright leads. Once you have invested time into developing your social media strategy, you can look for opportunities to discuss and showcase your app.

There are many ways to utilize social media to help you market your Android and Android tablet apps. Developing a successful social media strategy takes some time. You can shortcut the time required by partnering with bloggers, Twitter users, and LinkedIn (or other) groups who have already established a presence in your market area.

Timing Your Marketing Activities

For most developers, getting an app's message out will take some time and consistent marketing efforts to make buyers aware of the app. The good news is that so few apps have any marketing at all that your marketing efforts will likely pay off. Even if you apply only some of the marketing methods recommended in this book, you're bound to see improvement in your sales. If one marketing idea doesn't work, you can try something else until you get some positive results.

Some marketing activities should be timed for maximum impact. Other marketing activities are equally effective at any time, as long as they are part of a consistent marketing plan. For example, a press release announcing the launch of your app (or the re-launch of your updated app) should be timed as close as possible to when your app is posted for sale on the Android Market. I'll tell you how you can line up your posting date with your press release date later in this chapter.

Other activities, such as getting articles or blog posts out about your app, getting reviews, seeking partnerships to co-market your app, and so on, can and should be done before and after the launch of your app. These activities must be done as part of your marketing plan. It's ideal to have them coincide with your press releases, but it's usually quite difficult to make all this happen at once. If you can get a press release, app review, and a blogger all talking about your app at the same, you will generate the best outcome.

 Note

Be sure to allow adequate time to get someone to blog about your app. If you want a blogger to write about your app as your app launches, you will need to allow at least a month prior to the launch and press release to get someone lined up. People generally don't return phone calls and emails too quickly, and these things take time to get in place.

As we discussed back in Chapter 1, "Your Android App Marketing Strategy: Grand Slam or Base Hits?," successful marketing involves delivering the right message at the right time to the right audience. If you have effectively segmented your market and you have a clear message to deliver, then you want to look at the timing of your marketing campaigns and activities. Each app will vary as to how important the timing of your marketing needs to be. For example, if you are selling a holiday app, it obviously will have a certain shelf life and you'll need to time your announcement and marketing very carefully.

App Buying Cycles

App buying cycles vary with each customer. Some people buy apps daily for a few days or weeks and then they get busy with other things and don't buy again for a few weeks. Other buyers will make an app purchase (or free download) a couple of times a week. Some people only buy an app monthly. And other app buyers show no pattern at all, only buying and browsing the Android Market every once in awhile. App activity for new buyers of the Android platform is strongest when they first purchase the device and then over time their buying activity tends to taper off.

 Note

In Q1 2010, reported in late January 2010, Google and other Android phones sold 10 million units worldwide. Android has also reported that 100,000 Android phones sold in China, which is just getting started using the phone. So, there are millions of new customers all looking for apps to download, and you have a vast market waiting to buy your apps.

The problem with many apps is that they are downloaded and used only once or twice and then they are not looked at again. Buyers have limited dollars and limited space to store apps. So, they are choosy about the apps they download, even the free ones. After a buyer reaches a saturation point of apps, he or she generally tends to use only a few apps on a regular basis that help with daily activities.

So, even though someone may have downloaded 148 apps, that person will tend to use ten or fewer on a daily basis. The rest of the apps just sit there and aren't used much at all. Occasionally, a buyer will do an inventory of his or her apps and delete ones that are no longer appealing. Apps that are useful and frequently updated will remain on most people's Android.

Is Your App Seasonal?

Some app sales are definitely influenced by seasonal activities such as the weather, sports, holidays, current trends, and so on. As a marketer, you want to make sure you understand the external influences that may impact sales of your app during the year. Timing the delivery of your app becomes more important if your app is seasonal. If you release a Super Bowl app in July, you may not see as many sales as you would if you released it in December or January.

Many Android games are somewhat immune from this issue because they can be played year round and aren't tied to any particular season. Holiday-themed games will definitely see more sales around the particular holiday on which the app is based. Racing games and mind-challenging apps are not tied to any holiday and can be sold all year.

 Note

If you are developing a very seasonal type of app, think about building multiple seasonal apps to cover the entire year. If you build multiple apps you'll have a steadier stream of income. If one app is selling slowly, another app may pick up the slack.

Other utility-type apps will be influenced by the time of year that the app is most likely to be used. Tax-related apps, for example, will have a stronger showing early in the year due to the April 15th tax deadline in the U.S. Other countries will have similar deadlines, and if your app is focused on another country you'll experience the same thing. Financial apps such as banking, personal finance, and so on will do well during the entire year due to their daily use.

Health and lifestyle apps will also do fairly well during the entire year unless the apps recommend activities outdoors that are not suited to the current season.

A learn-to-ski app is going to do best in the winter months when people are thinking about skiing. A camping app is probably going to do better in the spring and summer than in the winter.

Table 8.1 shows a number of different topics and events during the year and how app sales may be impacted. Although not an exhaustive list, it does give you an idea of how some Android apps can be subject to sales fluctuations during the year. This does not mean you should not consider writing such an app. It simply means that you should be aware of seasonality for apps and understand beforehand whether your app might be impacted by these factors.

Table 8.1   The Time of the Year and Specific Events Can Impact Sales for Certain Apps

App Category	Indoors/Outdoors	Subject to Seasonal Influence
Sports	Either	Sometimes
Finance	Indoors	Taxes yes, others no
Food/Cooking/Holiday	Either	Yes
Food/Cooking/General	Either	No
Health and Fitness	Either	Sometimes
Lifestyle	Either	Sometimes
Games	Indoors	Rarely
Social Networking	Indoors	Never
News	Indoors	Never
Navigation	Either	Never
Education	Either	Rarely
Music	Indoors	Sometimes
Photography	Either	Never
Utilities	Either	Never
Business	Indoors	Never
Weather	Either	Never
Travel	Outdoors	Sometimes
Entertainment	Indoors	Sometimes

Hitting the Grand Slam

In Chapter 1 we talked about hitting the grand slam with your app. Your strategy should be to try to hit the grand slam but also keep making base hits. This way you hedge your bets. You may or may not hit the grand slam with your app, but with marketing you're going to have some base hits in terms of consistent sales. Here are some ideas for hitting a grand slam with your app:

- *Identify an idea for an app that has never been done before.* With tens of thousands of apps on the App Store, the chance of you coming up with an app that has never been done is difficult, but not impossible. Sometimes you have to look for an app idea to solve a problem.

  For example, we are starting to see apps that help you address the sheer volume of apps available on the app store. These "recommendation apps," as I like to call them, will make headway here in 2010.

  Some apps are geared toward recommending apps for a specific category or several categories that might contain the same app. These recommender apps help you save time by giving you a list of apps that have been reviewed by the app developer or have gone through a peer review.

- *Sign an exclusive sponsorship deal.* If you have a well-written app that is seeing steady sales, you can search for corporations that are looking for an app that fits their marketing model. Most corporations either build an app or look to partner with a popular app developer to give them a marketing presence on the app store. If your app is extremely well written and has broad appeal, you may be a candidate for such a partnership. Start by evaluating your app to see if it would be a fit for any company that might be interested in building a brand.

- *Gain national and prestigious recognition for your app.* This method can work for almost any app, but actually the apps with a fairly narrow buying audience may have an edge. This is because the editors of publications who would cover your app are probably easier to contact and may be more responsive to doing a story about your app.

  You can contact editors who would be interested in reviewing and writing about your app by going to their websites and looking up their contact information. Landing a review from a key Android magazine would create tremendous buzz for your app. An example of such a review is shown in Figure 8.1.

Figure 8.1 A positive review in a major publication can generate strong traffic for your app.

Timing the Launch of Your App

There are a few things you want to do before choosing a date to announce the availability of your app. For one, you should review the upcoming date as best you can to see what other big announcements might be occurring on that particular date. You can check the News section of Google or Yahoo! to uncover big news events that might be coming up.

 Note

If Google is making a big announcement on the same day, you may want to look at doing your announcement the day before or the day after. At least make your press release go live at 8:00 a.m. London time in an effort to get your news out early from a global standpoint.

Keep in mind that you are trying to get other news agencies to pick up your announcement and do a write-up on it. If there are too many other announcements competing for their time, your announcement may get overlooked. It's best to find a time on the calendar that doesn't have so many big press releases going out.

Submitting Your Android App

When you submit your app to the Android Market, you first need to register with the service using your Google account and agree to the terms of service. Once you are registered, you can upload your application to the service whenever you want, as many times as you want, and then publish it when you are ready. Once published, users can see your application, download it, and rate it using the Market application installed on their Android-powered devices. An example of the Android Market developers site instructions is shown in Figure 8.2.

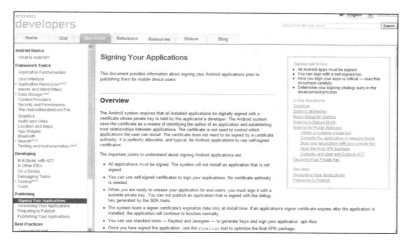

Figure 8.2   You can upload your app make it available on the Android Market at anytime.

 Note

The Google Developers Guide states the following about distributing your app: Requirements enforced by the Android Market server:

1. Your application must be signed with a cryptographic private key whose validity period ends after 22 October 2033.

2. Your application must define both an android:versionCode and an android:versionName attribute in the **<manifest>** element of its manifest. The server uses the android:versionCode as the basis for identifying the application internally and handling updates, and it displays the android:versionName to users as the application's version.

3. Your application must define both an android:icon and an android:label attribute in the <application> element of its manifest.

Summary

In this chapter we have covered the importance of proper timing of your marketing activities. Buyers of apps are influenced by a number of factors, including how recently they have purchased their Android, how many apps they have already downloaded onto their device, and how much money they feel they can afford to spend on apps.

Your app could be subject to seasonal influences if it is based on a holiday or particular event during the year. You may see 65%–80% of your sales during a few months out of the year if your app is designed to help someone with a certain seasonal challenge such as taxes.

Use a press release to announce the availability of your app and try to time your press release to within a few days of the launch of your app. This will help drive momentum for your app and build sales. The press release is only one aspect of your marketing plan. You also need to include marketing campaigns targeted to your specific audience. These campaigns will help drive awareness and sales when executed properly and consistently.

Getting the Word Out About Your App

A press release is one of the most powerful ways to get the word out about your app. A lot of independent developers don't understand that a press release can serve as a launching platform to begin to get the word out about an app. In fact, you shouldn't just consider one press release but many well-timed press releases to help you build momentum.

There are some key points to creating a successful press release. First, the press release must be well written to attract a following and a "pickup," which means getting news agencies, bloggers, and other online outlets to write about and run with the story in their publications.

Writing quality press releases is not for the faint of heart. It takes an experienced writer to capture and convey the key value of your app and interest your busy readers. Certain style elements must be followed in the press release so that it reads like a press release and not like an advertisement.

Second, the press release must be positioned so that it gets into the right hands. Some developers think that with a hastily written press release in hand, they can simply email it around to a few people and like magic the word will get out. However, that is not the case.

A number of online outlets can help you get your press release pushed into the path of prospective readers and news agencies. Some of these press agencies have broad reach into major news organizations, newspapers, and other publications. These PR companies can be highly effective in giving you the muscle you need to get your press release out to the masses via the Internet. Some PR firms charge for their services, and some are free. As is usually the case, you get what you pay for.

In this chapter we will first discuss how to write a press release for maximum impact. Then we will talk about how to deliver your press release to the right outlets to get the coverage you will need. We will also cover some of the most well-known PR firms that help you distribute your press release electronically around the world.

When to Write a Press Release

The first question often asked is, When should I write a press release? The following situations warrant issuing a press release for your app:

- **Newly shipping app**—If you have just placed your app for sale on the Android Market, this is a perfect time to issue a press release. You want to get the word out, and this is a very good way to alert the public and your buying audience that you just posted your app for sale on the Android Market.

- **Updated app**—If you have just updated your app with new features, fixes, or other enhancements you want to let your audience know about, a press release is a great way to announce that your app has been updated.

- **Free app issued**—Perhaps you have just issued a free app to complement your paid app. This is an excellent time to issue a press release announcing your free app. This will drive instant downloads and will absolutely help spur sales of your paid app.

- **Second app in a series**—Perhaps you have written a second app in a group of similar apps. A press release shows a steady drumbeat of activity for your apps and your brand. One developer built eight apps and so each week for eight weeks he did a press release for each one. This kept his apps in the news and helped him to build up his audience base.

- **Download milestone reached**—Perhaps you have achieved a significant number of downloads and you want to let the world know that your app is doing well. Depending on your type of app, you can issue a press release when you have achieved several thousand downloads or more.

- **Place of your app into an Android Market category**—If you are fortunate to have your app place into the "Top Selling" category, you will definitely want to issue a press release announcing the good news.

- **New developer added to your team**—If you are building a small company and a brand, you can issue a press release announcing the addition of a new team member to your company. At the same time you can mention in the press release the apps you develop to remind the readers about your apps.

In short, you can do a press release for many reasons, and you should always be thinking about when you are going to issue your next press release. Marketing is all about keeping your message in front of your audience. If you see your sales slowing for your app, a good way to energize them is to do a press release. If you go to any medium-to-large company's website (Intel, IBM, Google, Adobe, Mobclix, AdMob, and so on), you'll notice it has frequent press releases and the company posts them in the media center of its site.

Google's Android Market site, shown in Figure 9.1, has frequent announcements, many in the form of official press releases. If you search for "Android apps" in the News section of Google.com, you'll see all kinds of hits for the latest news for Android apps, as shown in Figure 9.2. Each time you do a press release, you should post the press release to your own product website. You can easily create a "News" or "Media" tab for your site. Newer press releases can be placed on your home page for a month or two following the issuance of your press release.

Figure 9.1 Google's Android Market website has frequent press releases that are displayed on its website. You should always post your press releases and news items to your own product website as well.

Figure 9.2 A Google news search for "Android Apps" on Google.com will reveal the latest news stories for this selected topic. You can sort by date or relevance.

Do You Have What It Takes?

The first step to writing your press release is to figure out who will write it. Do you have the writing skills necessary to produce persuasive and crisp copy that will move your audience into action? Do you want to learn how to do it? Or should you hire someone to handle this aspect of your marketing plan? Either approach is fine. The important thing is to make sure you end up with a quality press release.

If writing is not your forté, then it's best to find someone who can write the press release for you. Perhaps you know someone who is a good writer and can help you out. There are lots of writers in every city around the world. Preferably you'll want to locate someone who focuses on writing press releases. He or she will be able to produce the writing fairly quickly and in the format required for publication and distribution.

 Note

> How much will you pay to have someone write a press release for you? You should plan to spend somewhere around $250 to $400 to get a professionally written press release. Be sure to ask the person you are considering hiring for some samples of his or her work and for some references. Also ask whether he or she has written Android app or similar press releases before.

If you have decided to take on writing the press release yourself, then read the next sections of this chapter to learn the nuts and bolts of writing a press release. You will want several people to review and proofread your press release before you send it to any online firm for distribution. Online press release sites also have editorial reviews before they allow your press release to be launched. They review it for relevance, appropriateness, formatting, and other criteria. It's a good thing that they review your press release before it goes out. They can often pinpoint errors and offer suggestions to make your press release a better read. They also have certain standards about how and where in the release you can use your website address and other contact information.

You only have a few seconds to attract your reader's attention. You need to figure out what's top in their minds and address that immediately in your headline so that you can attract the attention of the media, bloggers, and others. You must then point out in the first paragraph what your news is and how it will benefit the reader. The rest of your copy is in support of your headline and first paragraph. Boiling out the key elements of your app and why it's so important to the readers will try your writing skills like never before!

Writing Your Press Release

The next step to writing your press release is to define your objectives for writing it. Understanding your goals and audience will help you position your press release for maximum results. Are you trying to get your app noticed by various reviewers or bloggers? Are you trying to build your brand and drive traffic to your website? Perhaps you are trying to generate revenue for your app and you want to create news that will cause readers to go to your product website or purchase your app.

You'll want to write your press release in such a way that you are attracting your target audience. If you haven't read Chapter 4, "Identifying Your Target Audience," you'll want to go back and read that first. This chapter will help you to message your audience in the best way possible.

The beauty of an electronic press release is that you can include web links, video, and graphics in very compelling ways to capture your reader's attention. The online press release can come to life in ways that a printed press release cannot. Depending on the type of app you have written, you will want to consider different options for your announcement. If you are launching a new game app, a video is a great way to get your reader to take a look at how your game is played. At a minimum, you'll always want to include your product web page and a link to the Android Market so people reading your news release will click over immediately to your app on the Android Market and buy it right away. An example of using a video clip (along with web links) in an Android app press release is shown in Figure 9.3.

Figure 9.3   This Android app press release has an embedded video clip showcasing the app and is hosted on YouTube.

The Anatomy of a Press Release

All press releases have some common components: the headline, the body, company information, and contact information. For an Android app press release, you will want to have a headline, body, company website, and a link to your app. An example of an Android app press release is shown in Figure 9.4 and includes all of the previously mentioned components.

Figure 9.4   An example of an Android app press release.

 Note

When using one of the online organizations to launch and distribute your press release, you can write up the press release using Word and then you simply copy and paste into an online form. We will discuss several of the more popular online PR firms at the end of this chapter.

The format for an Android app press release is fairly standard. Once you have created one press release, you can use the same layout for other press releases you may create in the future. The biggest challenge of the press release is not the layout but writing the creative copy to convey your message. This is where the key values you identified in Chapter 3, "Identifying Your App's Unique Value," will come in handy. You will want to use those key value statements in either the headline or the body of your press release. Table 9.1 shows the elements of an Android app press release, along with each section's characteristics.

Table 9.1   Android App Press Release Components and Characteristics

Components	Characteristics
Headline	Eye-catching, 20 words or less
Summary	Builds off headline, two sentences
Body	Supporting content, two to three paragraphs
Contact info	Your website, link to Android Market

Writing Your Headline

Your headline is the first component of your press release and will be displayed at the top of your press release's web page. The headline is where you attract the readers' attention and entice them to read on. This sentence or two must be crisp and provocative. This is your hook to get readers pulled in. If you fail to capture readers with the headline, the chances of them reading on are slim.

You also want to make sure you are using keywords or phrases in your headline that will be picked up by search engines. These keywords will help your press release to be pushed along when prospective buyers perform a search. For example, the phase "new Android game" or "new Android app" works well to help your headline to be picked up by Google, Yahoo!, and others. Here are some examples of not-so-good headlines, each followed by a rewrite to make them into good headlines:

Not-so-good headline:

"Android Developer Announces New Android Game"

Good headline:

"New Highly Interactive Android Game RasterBlaster HS Math Hits Android Market This Week"

Not-so-good headline:

"Scientific Android App Ready to Sell on Android Market This Week"

Good headline:

"Science4School Group Releases New Chemtastic Android App for High School Students on Android Market"

Not-so-good headline:

"New Android App Helps People with Their Bills"

Good headline:

"New MoreMoney Android App Helps People Manage Their Finances and Save Money Instantly"

Hopefully you can see the difference between the headlines in these three examples. You have to approach writing the headline from the standpoint that your reader knows absolutely nothing about your app. Often when writing we take "leaps" in our explanations because our minds tend to fill in the blanks. You must assume that your reader will not fill in any blanks about your app. You must clearly state what you're announcing.

Use the name of your app in your product announcement. If someone does a search for educational games, for example, your app's press release and product website are more likely to show up because you have seeded the search results.

Notice that your headline should not be lengthy. Most headlines are 20 words or less. Again, this will challenge your writing skills to see how crisp you can be in creating a headline that is eye-catching and includes your app's name, your brand's name (if you have one), and some keywords to help those search engines find you.

Your headline must also be a lead in to your summary, which will be discussed in the next section. The headline is the setup for the entire press release. Your readers must be able to grasp immediately the essence of your announcement so that they want to know more about it and will read on, at least to the summary section. If you can get them to read the headline and the summary, they are most likely to read the body of the press release as well.

Summary Copy

The next step in writing a successful Android app press release is to create a powerful summary statement. The summary builds off the headline and is two to three sentences that succinctly cover what your press release is all about. With your headline and summary statement, your readers must be able to grasp all the key information about your app and why this is a newsworthy announcement. If you can get your audience to read these two pieces of information, you are well on your way to having a successful press release.

The summary does not need to repeat the heading, but you can add some additional flavor about your app and why it is a game changer for your readers. For example, you can include the name of your company or brand if you didn't already do it in the headline. You can expand on the headline by adding more detail about the app and its importance to your readers. You want to highlight unique characteristics of your app or explain a new angle on an old problem that your app addresses. In the headline you are announcing to the world that you have a better mousetrap. In the summary you're basically explaining why you have the better mousetrap.

Keep in mind that you also want to include keywords and phrases in the summary statement that you believe will be popular with search engines. Again, write your press release with an eye toward how someone might search for your app and then make sure those keywords are being used in your headline and summary. These keywords include Android, Android apps, game apps, educational apps, lifestyle apps (or any other Android Market category that fits your app), Android Market, smartphones, and mobile phones.

Using a couple of the examples from the previous section, we'll now add summary statements to them:

Headline:

"New Highly Interactive Android Game RasterBlaster HS Math Hits Android Market This Week"

Summary

"RasterCorp expands its lineup of Android games apps by adding a new interactive math game geared toward high school students. RasterBlaster HS Math offers four levels of play incorporated into learning modules for algebra, geometry, and trigonometry."

Headline

"New MoreMoney Android App Helps People Manage Their Finances and Save Money Instantly"

Summary

"MoreMoney takes the hard work out of shopping and budgeting by helping you build your own shopping list with prices automatically imported through barcode scanning. Take the MoreMoney app with you to the grocery store, scan items you typically purchase, and see your total before you get to the checkout line!"

The summary should also serve as a transition to the body of your press release. Again, the headline should link to the summary, which should in turn link to the body of your press release. Remember to give the readers more information than you gave them in the headline. A press release is designed to lead readers down a path of wanting to know more and more information about your app.

Developing the Body Copy

The next component of your press release is the body. This is where you can expand on the comments you made in the headline and the summary as well as provide supporting quotes, sample graphics, web links, and so on, to substantiate your claims. You still want to write this section with the idea that your readers know nothing about your app. But you've piqued their curiosity with the headline and summary, and now they are interested to know more. Keep your writing focused on your primary and secondary messages and don't try to say too much.

 Note

> The body of the press release can be 300–800 words in length, or typically three to five paragraphs. It is, however, better to create a shorter press release than a longer one, especially in the Android app world where brevity is expected. You want to adequately convey your message but not make it so lengthy that a reader gives up on it.

One of the most powerful ways to strengthen and give credibility to a press release is by providing quotes from experts who can vouch for your app. If you are selling a game app, try to get a quote from an expert in your gaming area that will help strengthen your press release. If you are selling a financial app, try to get a quote from a financial expert. If you have a sports app, then get a sport star if you can. You get the idea.

 Note

> If you have trouble getting a quote from an expert in your app's area, then get a quote from the founder of your app's company or the lead developer. If that's you, then you can include your own quote in the press release and relate your number of years of experience doing development work.

Keywords are also very important for the body of your press release. You have the space to include keywords in multiple sentences and paragraphs in the body of the press release. You want to reinforce your message in the body of the press release without going overboard.

After you have provided quotes and supporting information for your press release, you'll want to give your readers a call to action. What is it that you want your readers to do? If you want them to learn more about your app, then be sure to give them your product website address and ask them to visit. You should always include the download link to take readers directly to the Android Market to purchase your app.

Embedded Links

Embedding links in your press release is a very powerful way to drive traffic to your product website and drive sales of your app. You want to position your web links at the right spots in your press release. Keep in mind that many online press release services will designate where you can embed links and limit the number of links you can embed into the copy. So, you need to choose carefully how you'll use your links. If you have a product web page, be sure to provide a link directly to your app's web page. In other words, if your app is not on your home page, be sure to provide the whole link directly to your app. Don't make people search for it on your site.

Also, be sure to include a link in your press release to your app's page on the Android Market so people can go directly to it, read about it, and make a purchase. You want to make it as easy as possible for your readers to grab a copy of your app. Some online press releases will allow you to embed a graphic with an embedded URL. If so, you can use the common Android Market logo shown in Figure 9.5.

Figure 9.5   Use the Android Market logo in a press release that allows graphics to lead the readers directly to your app.

Some online PR services provide additional areas where you can add links to your product website or to the Android Market. Don't overdo your embedded links because your press release may get flagged as spam and ignored by a lot of publications and readers. Some online PR services will also check your press release for too many links prior to allowing it to be launched. They may reject your press release and ask you to remove the links from the body of the announcement.

Attaching Multimedia to Your Press Release

The great thing about doing an electronic press release is that you can use images, video content, PDF files, and web links. These elements help you bring your press release to life, gain the attention of many readers, and increase your search rankings. If you're allowed by the online PR service, always include a graphic of your app's main screen or the app's icon in your press release. You can graphically convey what your app does in a split second with a graphic. Don't waste this opportunity to reach your readers.

 Note

Most online PR services will allow you to attach an image to your press release. Some may charge you more for this option because they know it's definitely a value add. Using a graphic in your press release will display in Google News and Yahoo!News, so it's definitely worth the extra cost. Use JPG format for the image and keep it less than 1MB in size. Your online service will restrict uploads that are much larger than this.

Don't forget the keywords in graphics, too. Be sure to think of appropriate keywords or phrases that you can use to describe your graphic. Always give your graphic a name that includes a keyword such as "Main screen for the new Mega Android App." If your online PR service allows you to write a longer description of the image, be sure to use this space (with keywords) to describe it.

You should also look to add PDF documents where appropriate. For example, you could attach a little document in PDF format that gives further details about your app and shows more screenshots of how your app can be used. Anything that you can add to your press release that will create additional value will increase your readership and make your press release even more visible.

Press Release Signature

One of the last steps is to provide your digital signature. Your readers will want to know who composed the release and how they can contact you with additional questions about your app. If you have hired someone such as a PR firm to write your release, you will want to include that person or firm as the contact. Online PR services will have a section when you submit your release for the appropriate contact information. It's usually called a profile or corporate contact page, and you simply fill in the contact information.

As part of the profile you will also fill out information about your company. If you are an independent developer, you'll want to create a short page about the types of apps you create, how many years of experience you have, and so on. You want your readers to be comfortable contacting you or your contact person. For example, you could say the following:

> "RasterCorp is the creator of innovative educational games for the high school market. With its launch of RasterBlaster HS Math, the company now has five Android apps to help high school students improve their grades and test scores. Founded in 2009, RasterCorp has achieved outstanding success with two of its apps, making it onto the Android Market's New and Noteworthy category. RasterCorp can be reached at www.rastercorp.com."

If you should be contacted about your press release, this is a good thing. Most Android app press releases don't attract a lot of questions, but if yours does, that's great! If your press release is timely and relevant to world events, you are much more likely to receive requests for more information from the media. Answer the questions of those who make a query and they will help you spread the word about your app. Be ready to send the media screenshots, photos, and even promo codes for your app.

Also, be sure to include a web link, as shown in the preceding example, so your readers can reach you. Some online PR services allow you to put your email address in the signature area as well. Always include an email address and phone number so you can be reached easily.

Finally, don't forget to have your online PR service push your press release to bloggers and other forums that might not typically see the release in Google News or Yahoo!News. RSS, or Really Simple Syndication, will help you get your press release to bloggers and other new sites around the world. Most online PR services will allow you to set up your press release for RSS feeds. Don't ignore this simple option to get more mileage out of your press release.

Publishing and Distributing Your Press Release

There are a number of online outlets for publishing and distributing your press release. Two of the more popular sites for Android apps are PR Newswire and PRWeb. Both sites offer excellent service with very good results, although they vary in price and capabilities.

PR Newswire (www.prnewswire.com) offers very solid online PR services with lots of flexibility. Pricing depends on how much coverage and how many options you wish to add. Most Android app press releases will need at least the $600 option to get the best coverage. If you wish to add embedded video to your press release, you will spend more.

PRWeb, another popular site to issue press releases, has the potential to reach millions of readers and tens of thousands of news sites and bloggers. It is an excellent service with great coverage and depth. An example of the PRWeb home page is shown in Figure 9.6.

A number of developers are using PRWeb for their first press release announcing the availability of their apps on the Android Market. They follow this up with additional press releases about their apps using other free press release services on the Internet, which are less expensive. Doing multiple press releases every month or so helps keep your app in front of your buyers and helps you to build your brand.

When to Launch Your Press Release

There are certain times and days of the week that seem to work best for launching press releases. Monday, Tuesday, and Wednesday are good days to launch a press release for your app. This is because most people are looking for news after the weekend and will be interested to read about your announcement. As you move later into the week, people tend to be less interested in reading announcements

Figure 9.6 PRWeb offers a very powerful online PR solution and is geared toward a broader audience for distribution.

because they are preoccupied with work and other issues. Fridays are generally not as good to issue an announcement as earlier days in the week.

You should aim for your press release to hit at midnight of the day before you want to issue your announcement. This will allow those in Europe to pick up the announcement first thing in the morning and start to spread the word. Then, your announcement will be available in the U.S. when people come into work or log on to their computers.

Summary

Writing a press release is an important tool for announcing the availability of your Android app. You can use the press release as the starting point of your marketing efforts. Press releases should be issued whenever you post a new app for sale on the Android Market and whenever you have updates to your apps. If you do not feel you have the experience or skills to write a press release, you should look to hire someone who does. A press release must be written in the right way to attract the attention of journalists and to have it picked up by other news outlets.

Should you consider tackling the process yourself, this chapter discussed the nuts and bolts of writing a press release. All press releases have common elements, including the headline, the summary, the body, and the contact section. Understanding the format of a press release is not difficult. Your challenge will be to pull the key elements of your app's value to the surface and provide a message using those key points. A successful press release will draw your readers in and get them to take action by either forwarding the information on to someone else or buying your app themselves.

Pricing Your App

It has been said that the exercise of pricing is as much an art as it is a science. There is no doubt that pricing is a challenge, especially with Android applications, because the Android Market is so new, relatively speaking. Whenever there is a new market for a good or service, it takes some time before the market achieves a sense of equilibrium. The state of the economy over the past couple years has not helped the situation for developers because people scrutinize their purchases more closely. Even a $0.99 app is scrutinized as the customer decides whether to spend his or her dollar on your app or someone else's. It's also very possible that the low-priced apps have been highly influenced by the fact that Apple's iTunes Store started selling songs for $0.99, which set the stage for their App Store and the Android Market.

Many developers, however, are simply following the herd, pricing their apps low with the hope of gaining acceptance and market share. However, the goal of this chapter is to get you to focus on delivering value instead of just a low price. Many developers are finding that they can't make enough money at $0.99 to break even, let alone realize a profit. Understanding your audience and delivering value can help you price your app appropriately in this cutthroat market.

Regardless of the current economy, Android app developers would do well to carefully examine all aspects of pricing as it pertains to their products, make careful pricing decisions, monitor and measure sales, and make adjustments as needed to maximize their revenue. Keep in mind the purpose of this book is to help you maximize sales for your app through better marketing—and marketing includes the challenging area of pricing.

 Note

> The right price for your Android app is where your profits are maximized. Therefore, the highest price you can charge without reducing your pool of customers is your goal. Knowing the exact price to charge is difficult, but you can get fairly close to the right price based on how steady your sales are and customer feedback via the reviews and comments they make.

You need to consider a number of factors when pricing your Android app. For starters, look at competing apps in your category and then consider the following questions:

- **How much do your competitors charge for a similar app?** Take a look at the Android Market and review how many apps are similar to yours. Have you produced a battleship game that is similar to other battleship apps? For example, a recent search for battleship games on the Android Market revealed at least 15 similar apps.

- **What are the differences between your app and someone else's?** Does yours have more features? Does yours have more levels of play if it's a game? If you are offering a new financial calculator app, does it offer something more than the other calculator apps in the store?

- **How does your app rate against the competition?** Do you feel that your app has better graphics? Better sound? Are there more exciting types of play? Have you confirmed this with your reviewers, friends, followers, and customers?

- **How do you define your app and its market?** If you are selling an app for sales reps only, have you attempted to define approximately how many sales reps are in North America or any specific country? How many of these sales reps might own an Android phone? Having this knowledge will help you make a better decision in the pricing process.

- **How does your app compare to free apps?** If there are many similar free Android apps, you will need to strongly communicate and market the value of your app. Overcoming free is a high hurdle but can be done with the right marketing. See Chapter 14, "Level the Playing Field with a Free App," to learn about the pros and cons to creating a free version of your app.

 Note

Remember the old adage "You get what you pay for." It applies to anything, including Android apps. Many free apps are downloaded and never used.

Additionally, consider the following questions from a cost perspective. These questions will help you get some context on how much you need to recoup:

- **What were the actual development costs or time involved for your Android app?** Knowing your development costs is very important in helping you determine the price of your app, to a degree, as we will discuss later in this chapter.

- **How much would the app cost to develop by another company?** Larger development firms can often create an app less expensively than a small developer because they already have developers and graphic designers on staff and can redirect their efforts to that Android app. If you know someone who works for a development firm, ask him or her how much the firm typically spends to develop an app. Sometimes independent developers have to outsource some of the development for graphics and other complex requirements to outside agencies or other developers.

Competing Against Free Apps

One of the more challenging aspects Android app developers are coming up against from a pricing perspective is competing against free apps. Many developers get discouraged thinking that their apps may not fare so well against competing free apps. However, if your app truly has functionality that goes beyond what a free app can do, you should not worry...as much. In fact, free apps (whether your own or others) might even help drive sales of your app because the users find that "free" will only take them so far, and they have to pay to gain additional functionality. If you think creating a free app is for you, then be sure to read Chapter 14 on how to develop a free version of your app. Consumers want a deal, and the word "free" is programmed into everyone's brains at birth! Nevertheless, we also know that in many cases we get what we pay for.

 Note

Don't be intimidated by free. If you have developed a unique app, use your app's unique features as your marketing angle.

Consumers have also learned that free apps could mean risky software with a clumsy interface that does not really solve their problem. They also know that free may mean lots of advertisements that sometimes get in the way of a useful app. So how can you effectively position your paid app to compete against free apps? The following sections provide a few ideas that will help you out.

Be Found

There are really only two ways to be found: on the Android Market (or other Android app site) and on your own product website. As discussed in greater detail in other parts of this book, you should use care in selecting keywords in your web content to describe your app. You want to make sure you are maximizing your use of keywords that are going to help people locate your app site when they do an Internet search. Make sure your app's icon is catchy and colorful. Icons without a lot of sizzle will be scanned over and ignored during a search on the Android Market.

Make sure your app appears in the top listings of search engine results if possible. Use search engine optimization (SEO) techniques to make sure your website will rank higher than those of competing free applications. This takes time to achieve this ranking, and you must have a website that showcases your app extremely well by utilizing key phrases and keywords for maximum effect. One of the other keys to high search rankings is to get many other sites link to your site. Establish a relationship with other sites that are complementary to yours and exchange links on each other's site. Additionally, a carefully placed article that you have written about your app or a press release announcing your will app will help bloggers and other sites to link to your website, thus raising your website in search engine rankings.

Make Your App Better

This should go without saying, but your app must provide greater functionality, better graphics, and more features than a free app. Many free products are often stripped-down versions and offer minimal functionality. Make sure that your Android app is more robust and feature rich, but without compromising the ease of use or functionality. Include features and functions that are not available in the freeware competitors, and then use these features to promote your product.

Make Your App More Intuitive

Your Android app design and program operation should be intuitive and should not require advanced instruction for the primary functions. Your buyer should be able to operate the basic features of the program immediately after installing it, and without needing to refer to any documentation to figure out how to get started. Consider developing a video on your website to guide the user through the primary features, as well as the more complex ones.

Provide Better Graphics

Initial impressions matter. Use professionally designed graphics, attractive color combinations, and a modern user interface (UI) to distinguish your application from any freeware alternatives. Yes, you are going to spend some money here, but it is worth the expense if you want a successful app. If you are writing a game app, it is a necessity to have catchy graphics.

 Note

Getting your app to stand out against free apps is always possible. Carefully look at the free apps and design your app to take advantage of their weaknesses.

Create Documentation

The one thing that is so often lacking with free applications is any documentation or tutorials. Instructions (beyond the app's in-product instructions) seldom exist at all. Create documentation and tutorials to assist your users in how to use your Android app. You can post this documentation on your product website designed to help market this app. This documentation does not need to be lengthy at all. Just having it provides a value add.

Offer Some Technical Support

No, I don't mean offering 24/7 support or an 800 number! But do offer a way for your customers to reach you if they have a question about your app. Your product website should have an email form they can fill out or a contact email address. Do not rely solely on product reviews from the Android Market. Someone may never make a comment on the Android Market and might send you an email instead.

Developers of "free" Android apps may have little incentive to invest their time providing ongoing technical support for an application that generates no income or revenue. This depends on the objective of the developer, of course. Some developers are trying to build a brand with a free app and so updating their app is very important and they want to get feedback from those who download their app. But, other free apps won't offer much in the way of support. Distinguish your apps and your brand by providing fast responses to any customer complaints or bugs that your user community has identified.

Develop a Reputation for Customer Service

Do not discount the value some customers place on customer service, even with a simple app purchase. Invest some energy into providing superior customer service for any technical issues brought to your attention. It's unfortunate that the Android Market does not allow developers to respond to reviews posted about their apps. Perhaps in time this capability will be added.

If you see a negative comment on the Android Market or someone sends you an email, be sure to respond immediately so he or she knows you're acknowledging and addressing the problem. People who take the time to write to you will also take the time to write a positive or negative review.

Go Viral

Recruit and encourage "fans" of your Android app to promote your products for you. Reward customers who faithfully endorse your application by providing free upgrades or other perks such as giving them an advanced copy of a soon-to-be-released update to your app. Some developers offer prizes for the most referrals received from a particular buyer of your app. This requires some registration capabilities on your site. For example, you can have a button that reads "Refer a Friend" and allows a user of your Android app to send a message to a friend. You can track the referrals and give away a prize at the end of the month.

Some Pricing Misconceptions

So, you have just completed your app and you are trying to figure out the best price to charge. Often, developers think that in order to compete on the Android Market they must price their apps very low, like $0.99. Your thinking may have been influenced by one of the following:

- You see a lot of downward pricing pressure on the Android Market from what you've read and think you had better not price your app too high.

- You think customers will expect you to charge only $0.99 for your app because you believe everyone else is. You succumb to the pricing pressure.

- You think that pricing your app at $0.99 will help your app to make it into the top Android Market sales results. You rationalize that you will make up for the low price in volume sales.

- You see dollar signs looming and think your low price will attract tens of thousands of buyers, even if they have no use for your app.

Caution is recommended *against* adopting any of these mindsets and dropping your price right away. Any one of these thoughts may quickly result in low revenues, no immediate paychecks from Google, and discourage you from creating more apps for the Android Market in the future. Let's review each of these thoughts in a little more detail.

You see downward pricing pressure and think you should follow suit. Yes, it was true that overall average prices were falling on the Android Market. But, more recently prices have seemed to stabilize and some categories have actually seen slightly higher prices, even with games. Because the Android Market was a relatively new storefront, developers and buyers were trying to find that sweet spot where buyers would buy and developers would receive fair compensation for their work. What we are learning over time is that while prices have stabilized for Android apps, many are being sold at two to four times the $0.99 price point and they're seeing steady sales. Base your initial app price on a rational determination of how much time and money you have put into the project, the size of your buying market, and other factors we'll discuss later.

You think customers will expect you to charge only $0.99 for your app. Not so fast. If you truly offer unique functionality for your product, you can certainly charge more for your app as a starting point. Pricing your app at $0.99 is like putting your newly published book in the $5 bargain bin at your local bookstore! Is that where you want your work of art to go first? How will you discount from there? How will you do any promotions or entice users to buy additional apps if you are already at the lowest price point possible?

Next, you think that by entering the market at $0.99 you will easily enter the top 100 in sales and make up for the low price in volume. As more apps are being added every day to the Android Market, your chances of making it into this exclusive club become narrower. You've got to use other means to help buyers find your app on the Android Market.

Note

Let's face facts! The chances of entering the top 100 in sales on the Android Market by pricing your app at $0.99 are getting slimmer by the day as more and more apps are added to the store.

Lastly, you want to see those dollars coming in as soon as you launch your app on the Android Market, so you price it at $0.99. This is a mistake. We all want to make money, but you need to adopt a longer-term vision if you want to be successful selling on the Android Market. Unless you have very deep pockets, like a large game developer, you most likely have little to no brand awareness. Building a brand takes time and big bucks unless you happen to be one of the lucky few to have a best-selling game or other app. This is getting harder and harder, and the reality is that most developers won't make it into that cherished circle through luck alone.

So, what's your best option? You have to level the playing field as best you can, and that's by offering your users a free version of your app. Let your users "try before they buy." You want to establish a following for your app, and one of the best ways to do that is to offer an Android "light" app that allows users to preview the app, test drive it, and get a feel for it before committing monetarily. This is a long-term strategy, and it takes some time.

Offer a Free Version of Your App

We will touch upon building a free app briefly in this section, but please refer to Chapter 14 for more in-depth information on developing a free app. You can use a free app as a way to build a strong following for your paid app. As an independent Android app developer, you can offer a free application in order to compete with the big players on the Android Market. Offering a free app helps your customers gain confidence in your product and allows them to use it without risk. Various studies from analytics companies such as Flurry.com indicate that a free app strategy is a must going forward. Flurry and Pinch Media have merged (http://www.pinchmedia.com/#pinchanalytics). You can see the company's blog at http://blog.flurry.com/, which includes strong research evidence that this strategy works. One blog post states the following:

> "However, even if you're the proud steward of such an uber-brand, remember that free trials drive discovery of your title, helping increase the adoption of your paid version and ranking in the Paid App category. And don't forget that all the previously disadvantaged Indies now have a shot to take away your consumer with their free trial."

In this blog post, Flurry sums up this recommendation by saying that everyone regardless of their success on the Android Market should have a free app. The decision rests with you, of course, and is dependent on how much time you have to create a free app. You can always go back after you've launched your paid app and develop a free app. Or you can offer an app for free to see what type of response you get from it. Both strategies can work to eventually help you achieve sales of your paid apps.

Setting Your App's Price

Now that we've got a few misconceptions out of the way, the question then remains, "How do I price my app?" You've come this far to develop a great app so don't pass up this crucial exercise to make your app as successful as possible in the market. Everyone defines success in his or her own way. Perhaps you want to generate $20,000 a year in additional income from an app that cost you $5,000 to create. You might not be able to live on that income entirely, but it sure doesn't hurt if it's additional income to your regular job.

Or perhaps you have grander ambitions and want to generate $100,000 in app sales for a product that cost you $20,000 to create. If you start at a $0.99 selling price in either example, you would have to generate 28,572 downloads to achieve $20,000, or 142,858 downloads to achieve $100,000 in sales! These are huge numbers of downloads regardless of how successful the app is. Again, starting at a $0.99 sales price, it is going to take forever for you to achieve either breakeven or any profits!

In both examples the breakeven is not factored into the equation. I'm assuming you want to make some money selling your Android app. But, for the record you would need 7,143 downloads at the $0.99 selling price to break even in the first example if the app cost $5,000 to produce. The second app example would require you to realize 28,572 downloads just to break even!

 Note

> You must conduct a breakeven analysis to determine how different price points will affect your breakeven timing. See Chapter 11, "Conducting an App Pricing Analysis," to learn more about how to conduct a pricing analysis for your app.

For these examples, you may have spent less developing your app and so your breakeven may be lower. But, regardless of the cost you need to calculate your breakeven so you at least cover the costs of development and marketing. Let's look at a few strategies often used by developers for pricing their app:

- **Price high initially and measure the results.** Pricing high does not mean you pick a random high price. It means that you choose a price that falls in the high end of the range for your app's category. For example, if you are pricing a game, the range is generally priced between $0.99 on the low end and $1.99 on the high end. So, a high price initially would be $1.99. However, pricing higher in your category means you've got the features to back up your price. You can't just start out with a high price because you want to make more money!

- **Price mid range and measure the results.** Pricing in the mid range means you've looked at your category, measured the lowest price and the highest price, and then selected a price somewhere in the middle for your app. For example, you are selling an app that helps users improve their fitness. This type of app has all kinds of competitors and prices. The price range for this type of app is free to $6.99. So, after some research you feel that your app is worth more than free but less than $6.99. So, you start at a price of $2.99.

- **Price low and make it up on volume.** Most developers do very little in the way of pricing analysis for their app. They simply take the low price at $0.99 and wait to see what happens. For many apps, especially games, this may be the right price. But, again, some research should be done to determine if that's where the starting price should be set.

Regardless of which strategy you end up adopting, you will want to perform a breakeven analysis to know how many apps you will need to sell at different price points to break even. The following pricing discussion makes a few assumptions, as outlined here, for simplicity:

- Nearly all apps on the Android Market fall between $0.99 and $9.99. As you calculate your price, you are most likely going to look at price points in this range.

- We make the assumption that your app will not make it into the top 100 most downloaded apps. This is not being pessimistic, just realistic. You're an independent developer and most likely don't have a huge following for your app yet. In fact, if you are not selling a game app, you might *never* get into the top 100.

- Because you are probably not in the top 100, you will most likely sell at most 100 downloads of your app per day. For our following examples, we will assume 100 sales per day.

Our first example assumes no marketing costs to launch the app. Also, let's assume you have spent $5,000 to develop your business application. You believe you can realistically sell 100 apps per day, so that's what we'll go with for this example.

The results of our breakeven analysis are shown in Table 10.1. They indicate that it will take at least 70 days to break even for an app that costs $5,000 to develop charging $0.99 per download. Doubling the price cuts the breakeven time in half to 35 days. Obviously, as the price goes up for the app, the time needed to break even goes down. However, it's not that simple to kick the price up a couple of bucks to lower your time to break even. This is where you have to review other similar apps to see what you can realistically charge for your app. If your app is clearly out of the pricing range for similar apps, your app will not sell.

Table 10.1   A Basic Breakeven Analysis at Different Price Points for an App That Costs $5,000 to Develop

App Price @ 100 Sales/Day	Gross Sales	After Google Commission	Breakeven Reduction (First Sale)	Days Left to Break Even (~)
$0.99	$100	$70	($4930)	70
$1.99	$200	$140	($4860)	35
$2.99	$300	$210	($4790)	23
$3.99	$400	$280	($4720)	17
$4.99	$500	$350	($4650)	14
$5.99	$600	$420	($4580)	11
$9.99	$1000	$700	($4300)	7

 Note

If you have only incurred your time in app development, you should still calculate the cost of developing your app based on estimated hours spent on the project times an hourly rate.

As you can see by looking at the table, pricing your app at $0.99 will take you more than two months to break even, assuming you spent $5,000 to develop your app. Again, as an independent developer your development costs will vary. But if you haven't spent real dollars you most certainly have spent many long nights writing code! So, you should calculate your hours spent in development and estimate some sort of development cost.

Based on this table, we are of the opinion that it's better to price your app higher first and carefully monitor the results. By this I mean in the $2.99 to $5.99 range (for non-game apps!) so that you've got room to adjust your pricing if needed. If you have developed a game app, the pricing sensitivity is much greater and you will need to be priced in the $0.99 to $1.99 range as a starting point.

If you have done what we call "pre-launch" marketing activities, you will have established a following of early adopters who will gladly pay your entry price. In Chapter 19, "Components of an App Marketing Plan," we discuss how to develop a marketing plan for your app. The marketing plan is ideally implemented at the start of your development project, not at the end, so that you can begin to establish a following for your app prior to its launch.

After breaking even, you can begin to enjoy the fruits of your labors. Table 10.2 shows how much you could make on a daily basis assuming a 20% marketing expense that may bring you 50% more in increased sales.

Table 10.2 Pricing Analysis Showing a 20% Marketing Expense with a Resulting Increase in Sales

App Price @ 150 Sales/Day	Gross Sales	After Google Commission	20% Marketing Expense for App	Take Home Net (~)
$0.99	$150	$105	$30	$75
$1.99	$300	$210	$60	$150
$2.99	$450	$315	$90	$225
$3.99	$600	$420	$120	$300
$4.99	$750	$525	$150	$375
$5.99	$900	$630	$180	$450
$9.99	$1500	$1050	$300	$750

The issue with any pricing assumption is trying to figure out how elastic the pricing model is for Android apps. Over time, elasticity will become more predictable. Some bloggers have said that lowering their price has had some effect on sales but for a limited time. Others have said that lowering the price has had no effect on their sales. Who do you believe? Well, they are both right. It depends on the type of app and variances in mileage. So, the best approach is to experiment at a price point that makes sense for your app based on your research, breakeven analysis, and type of application.

If you are confident that your app is unique and has qualities and features that no similar app provides, price it higher and measure the results. If over a few weeks your sales start to drop off, you can carefully begin to reduce the price and measure the results. If you are doing solid marketing, driving visitors to your site, have created a following through the marketing methods discussed in earlier chapters, then there is no reason why your app (non-game) cannot continue to sell at sustainable levels for many months or possibly years to come.

Some app sellers have also found some success in making limited-time offers where they drop the price for a few days only to spur sales. If you have a certain promotion you want to do around an event, you can often encourage sales by offering a temporary price cut. Let's say you offer a financial calculator that includes special tax features. You may want to reduce your price for a few days around tax time to spur sales and let your app take advantage of this particular time of year.

 Note

> Do not undersell yourself by pricing your app too low to begin. You can always lower your price, but it's harder to raise it.

Summary

There is more to pricing your app than just setting the price at $0.99 and hoping for the best. Developers would do well to carefully review pricing of similar apps before setting their own price. As part of your pricing analysis, try to determine the range of prices for your particular category of Android app. You do this by checking the Android Market and taking note of the range of prices found. Once you have a price in mind, compare your features with the features of similar apps in your price range. This will help you feel more confident about your price.

Pricing your Android app at the higher end of the range for your category will give you the pricing flexibility to lower your price when needed or when you want to do a sales promotion and temporarily drop the price of your app. Do not immediately set your price at $0.99 unless you are confident that all competing apps are priced in the same range.

Some developers have adopted the strategy of giving away their app for free, either to build market share or in hopes that they can later upsell the user to their paid app.

Conducting an App Pricing Analysis

Although you may think it's a little over the top to do a pricing analysis for an Android app, the skills involved will come in handy as you build your brand and start to build multiple apps. A pricing analysis (or cost/benefit analysis) is an exercise you should do prior to developing your app. So many developers (and entrepreneurs) think of an idea for an app and set out to develop it (or contract with someone to develop it) without thinking through what it might cost them. It's easy to get caught up in your life-changing, world-dominating idea for an app, but prudence should be your top priority.

A cost/benefit analysis will help you predict whether you are likely to break even on your app and start to make a profit on it. As an independent developer, a cost/benefit analysis is probably not an exercise you are used to, but it's pretty important to count the costs beforehand so you don't end up in financial trouble down the road. The Android Market is littered with half-baked apps that were very costly to produce and have left the developers with no hope of ever recouping their costs.

Think about it. On the low end you may spend $2,500 to develop your app—and that's really on the low end! If you price your app at $0.99, it will take over 3,500 downloads just to break even on your costs after Google takes its 30% cut. It's also not uncommon for a developer to spend upwards of $30,000 to develop and market an Android app. It will take tens of thousands of downloads to break even in this scenario.

The other important step discussed in this chapter is to perform a breakeven analysis so you know how many downloads you'll need just to recoup your costs. Therefore, it's very important to do a little math before you get started down the development path to make sure your finances can handle the costs you are going to incur. Who knows? You may decide, after doing a little analysis, that building a particular app is not worth the effort and scrap the project until you can find an idea that will work.

 Note

> Game apps, as mentioned before, tend to fall into a tight range of $0.99 to
> $1.99, sometimes $2.99. As you define the market for your type of app,
> you may find that the number of potential buyers is quite limited. In order
> to see a profit from your app, you are going to have to identify a price point
> where you can make some money and the buyer will still be inclined to buy.

The challenge for many developers of non-game apps, which usually don't fall into the $0.99 pricing category, is deciding what they should reasonably charge. Therefore, it helps to have some background on how to go about performing a cost/benefit analysis for the more expensive types of apps. Setting an accurate price is crucial to determining a breakeven point and attempting to do some amount of forecasting.

Cost/Benefit Analysis

A cost/benefit analysis is a process to help you understand the total anticipated costs of your app development project as compared to the total expected financial benefits. This analysis will help you determine if this project is worthwhile for you as an independent developer or your development team. If the results of your analysis show that your financial benefits outweigh the costs, you can proceed with the development of your app with greater confidence.

For simplicity sake, the Android app cost/benefit analysis consists of three components:

- Quantifying the app development costs

- Quantifying the benefits of developing the app

- Performing a cost/benefit comparison to make an informed development decision

Quantifying the App Development Costs

The first part of the app cost/benefit process is to identify and quantify the costs associated with your app development. Your costs will fall into two categories: fixed and variable. Fixed costs include any expenses that are the same every month. If you are an independent developer or a small LLC, you may be renting some office space. You will want to include the monthly rent as a fixed expense for the expected duration of app development. If you have just bought a new laptop for development, you have incurred a fixed expense with that hardware purchase.

Variable costs can include expenses you might incur if you pay a developer by the hour to develop your app. This could range from $50/hour (low end) to $200/hour (high end). Your labor rates could vary depending on how complex your app project is. You may hire a developer and find, to your dismay, that the person does not have all the skills needed to develop your app. So, you end up hiring another, more costly developer.

Another scenario is that the developer has underestimated how much time it will take to complete your app. Instead of the project taking 200 hours to complete, it takes 250 hours. This happens more frequently than you think. In fact, you should add 20% to the total of whatever estimates you receive from developers. You won't be too far off the mark and you'll save yourself the shock of having to come up with more money because you will have anticipated this already.

 Note

If you are hiring an outside developer to create your Android app, you can ask for a fixed bid price. Some developers will work with you on a per-contract basis. Keep in mind that if you want to change/add features to your app down the road (and you certainly will), the contractor will most likely charge you a change fee or add on an additional project fee to accommodate your request.

The following steps will help you quantify the costs you will incur during the app-development stage:

1. Make a list of all monetary costs you think you will incur during the development stage of your app. These expenses include office space, developer payroll, training, travel, hardware, and so on.

2. Make a list of all intangible costs you are likely to incur. This would include your own time if you are developing your app, risks if the app fails, lost time on other apps, and so on. Granted, it is quite difficult to quantify these areas, but some attempt is better than no attempt. Table 11.1 provides an example of the monetary and intangible costs you'll want to include on your list of overall expenses. Keep in mind that this is not an exhaustive list, and you should modify it for your unique circumstances.

Table 11.1   App Development Expense Table for Estimating Costs

App Development Items	Monetary Cost Estimate	Intangible Cost Estimate
Hardware (laptop, desktop PC, networking equipment, and so on)		
Software (development tools, compilers, testing tools, and so on)		
Google developer registration fees		
Self-developed app, contract development costs (by project or hourly)		
Development training courses		
Office rent		
Product website development/web copy costs		
Marketing/advertising costs		
Opportunity cost of creating this app versus another app		
Miscellaneous (printing, postage, domain registration, programming books, and so on)		
Totals		

Once you have a list of your anticipated expenses, you can add numeric values where appropriate. Do your best to estimate intangible costs. This part of the exercise gets a little bit fuzzy, but it's still important to have some numbers down in writing. At the bottom of the table add up the totals for each column.

Note

If you are new to developing Android apps, you'll most likely need to get some training unless you are the type who can learn by reading manuals and then doing. Many people are best served by getting some training from experts who can teach basic (and not-so-basic) coding skills in a few weeks or months.

Android training companies such as BigNerdRanch (*www.bignerdranch. com*) can cost $3,500–$4,750, plus your travel and lodging expenses, but offer face-to-face instruction and will get you started with a solid development foundation.

An example of the expense table with some financial values included is shown in Table 11.2. In this example, the person is a fairly new developer in the Android app space but has a development background and needs some training in this unique space.

Table 11.2   Filled-out App Development Expense Table

App Development Items	Monetary Cost Estimate	Intangible Cost Estimate
Hardware (laptop, desktop PC, networking equipment, and so on)	$2,000 (Dell, HP, or similar + accessories)	
Software (development tools, compilers, testing tools, and so on)		
Google developer registration fees	$25	
Self-developed app, contract development costs (by project or hourly)		Self-developed (250 hours @ 50/hr*): $12,500.00
Development training courses	$3,500 with Big Nerd Ranch or another trainer	Two weeks time (10 hours/week @ $50.00/hr*): $1,000
Office rent	Home office	
Product website development/web copy costs	$2,000	
Marketing/advertising costs	$1,500	
Opportunity cost of creating this app versus another app		No other apps scheduled

Table 11.2   Filled-out App Development Expense Table

App Development Items	Monetary Cost Estimate	Intangible Cost Estimate
Miscellaneous (printing, postage, domain registration, programming books, and so on)	$250	
Totals	**$9,275**	**$13,500**

*Assuming this person has development skills that would be worth $50/hr. This is a cost for his time. Granted, this may be low, but it's impossible to peg this number with any exactness.

As you can see from this simple analysis, you might spend over $9,000 in real dollars to develop your first app. You may have the hardware already and so you could deduct $2,000 the total. Regardless, you would still be at $7,000 or more to develop your first app. If you added in your own time (intangible costs), you can see that you might spend $21,000 to $23,000 in time and actual expenses to develop an Android app. The question for you to ask yourself is whether you still feel that your app can make you enough money to justify your time and expense to get the app created, approved, posted, and marketed to the Android Market.

 Note

Although you can pay a foreign developer to get an app created for $1,000 in just a few weeks, it is highly unlikely that you will see success from such an app. The time-honored phrase "You get what you pay for" applies. Most often these apps are quickly designed and buggy. You're better off going to Vegas over a long weekend with your $1,000 and rolling the dice!

Quantifying the Benefits

Your next step in the cost/benefit analysis is to determine the expected benefits from the creation of your app. This is a little trickier than estimating the costs to build your app, but this step is a crucial part of the cost/benefit equation. Keep in mind that most app developers are looking for monetary benefits from their first app. Therefore, you'll need to spend a little time estimating potential sales of your app. Be sure to refer to other chapters in this book to understand market sizing and appropriate pricing for your app.

Some developers offer a free app as a forerunner to another paid app or to demonstrate their skills and solutions, in an effort to obtain consulting opportunities. In such a case, you wouldn't list a profit benefit for your app. Follow these steps to help you quantify the anticipated monetary and nonmonetary benefits of your app:

1. Create another list, similar to the one you used for costs, of all the monetary benefits that will be realized with the creation of your app (see Table 11.3). First on the list is the overall direct profit you hope to achieve from the sale of your app. Next might be additional investment capital you hope to attract by building a fantastic app. Other benefits might be less tangible, such as decreased production costs, name recognition, and building a solid app development reputation.

Table 11.3   A List of All Monetary and Nonmonetary Benefits You Hope Your App Will Achieve Once Completed

Completion of App	Monetary Benefits	Intangible Benefits
Profit from sale of app*		
Additional investment capital if app does well		
Decreased production expense due to standard, reusable app structure		
Name recognition		
Building a solid app development reputation		
Totals		

*The profit assumption must be made by doing an estimate of your target market size multiplied by your app's per-unit price. For more information on sizing your target market, refer to Chapter 4, "Identifying Your Target Audience."

2. Assign some monetary and nonmonetary values to your list. In the example shown in Table 11.4, the developer has created a productivity app that will be sold for $4.99 on the Android Market. The app is expected to have 5,000 downloads over the next six months based on marketing efforts. Once you have filled in all the details for which you have information, add them up at the bottom of the table. Table 14.4 shows the inputs for both monetary and nonmonetary benefits.

Table 11.4   A List of All Monetary and Nonmonetary Benefits with Numeric Values Assigned

Completion of App	Monetary Benefits	Intangible Benefits
Profit from sale of app	$17,465 (after Google's 30% share).	
Additional investment capital if app does well	None.	
Decreased production expense due to standard, reusable app structure	$3,500.	
Name recognition	Yes.	Yes, not quantifiable.
Building a solid app development reputation	Yes, I anticipate this app will lead to other projects, consulting deals ($10,000).	Yes, I expect this to lead to a stronger reputation in the app development community.
Totals	**$30,965**	

Performing a Cost/Benefit Comparison

With your evaluation of costs and benefits completed, you can now do a cost/benefit comparison, which is fairly easy. You are at a point in your analysis where you can weigh your costs and benefits to determine whether it makes sense to build your app. Your outputs are only as good as your inputs. Your investment in gathering data is commensurate with the quality of your results. You can follow these steps to complete the cost/benefit comparison:

1. Compare your two total values for the monetary benefits first. If the total costs are considerably higher than the expected benefits, you can safely determine that the project should not be undertaken.

2. If the total costs and total benefits are pretty close, you need to go back and reevaluate your assumptions for both the costs and benefits. If after a review you find that your numbers are roughly the same, you can conclude that the project is not worthwhile from a strictly monetary standpoint. If profit is not your primary concern, it may make sense to do the project.

3. If the total monetary and intangible benefits are much greater than the total monetary and nonmonetary costs, the development of the app is worthwhile and will be a good financial and time investment for you.

The results for our example are shown in Table 11.5. As you can tell by looking at the table, the benefits outweigh the costs for building this particular app. A breakeven analysis should also be performed to determine more precisely how long it will take before the app is producing profits.

Table 11.5   The Results of a Sample Cost/Benefit Analysis

Monetary/Nonmonetary Benefits	Monetary/Intangible Costs	Results (Benefits − Cost)
$17,465 (actual profit)	$7,299 (actual costs)	$10,166 (actual net)
$30,965 (profit + potential benefits)	$13,700 (actual costs + intangible costs)	$17,265 (net plus potential benefits)
Benefits > costs (for this example)		Decision: Favorable to build app

 Note

When factoring how much time it will take to produce a profitable app, be sure to include two to three months of extra time for Google to pay. Some developers have complained that Google is slow to pay royalties on apps.

Breakeven Analysis

Performing a true cost/benefit analysis requires you to develop a breakeven point for your app so that you will have an idea of how much time it will take you to recoup your investment. It's not much of an investment if it takes you two years to make your money back. Ideally, you want your app to break even within a month of releasing it to the Android Market. If it takes much longer than that, your app is probably not going to be too profitable for you because it will not return payment soon enough for you to sustain a living or complete other projects.

Once you have determined a price (refer to other pricing chapters), it's quite easy to plug the numbers into the following breakeven formula, which divides the fixed costs by the app's true selling price:

$$\text{Breakeven point} = \frac{\text{fixed costs}}{\text{app selling price (less Google's commission)}}$$

This calculation will let you know how many total apps you'll need to sell to break even. Once you've reached that point, you've recovered all costs associated with producing your app (both variable and fixed).

Note

> For simplicity's sake, we will not include variable costs as a separate item in this example. Once an app is complete, the expenses are considered complete for that version of the app. Because the app can potentially sell unlimited copies, the cost to produce each app after breakeven is basically zero.

After you reach the breakeven point, every additional copy of your app sold will increase your profit by the amount of the app's contribution margin. The app's contribution margin helps reduce overall fixed costs and can be defined as follows:

App contribution margin = app selling price (less Google's commission)

Using an Excel spreadsheet can help you figure out these calculations quite easily and figure out your own breakeven and contribution margin. An example using the $4.99 productivity app is shown in Figure 11.1.

Our $4.99 Android App - Breakeven Analysis	
Fixed Development Costs	$7,299.00
Price of App on App Store	$4.99
Contribution Margin (Apple's Commission Deducted)	$3.49
Breakeven (required paid downloads)	2090
Estimated Time to Breakeven	
100 downloads per day (variable)	21
Monthly revenue after breakeven	$2,189.70

Figure 11.1 An Excel spreadsheet helps to easily calculate a breakeven and contribution margin for the $4.99 app.

Some Caveats

Take a close look at what the breakeven analysis tells you. If the calculation reveals, for example, that you must sell 10,200 apps before you'll start to make money, you need to ask yourself if that seems viable. If you don't think you can sell 10,200 apps in a reasonable amount of time, as determined by your financial situation and expectations, you should think twice about building that app.

If you think selling that many apps is possible but at a lower price point, you should redo your calculation at a lower price point to see what the results look like. You can also look at your application development costs to see if it makes sense to cut the cost of your development through cheaper labor and/or adding fewer features to start out.

Keep in mind that the biggest unknown is your level of demand. A breakeven analysis cannot predict what the demand for your app might be. It is simply a decision-making tool that will help you avoid making some costly mistakes prior to development of your app. The best predictor for your app is the research you do around your target audience and what data points you can glean from communities and blog posts that are discussing apps similar to yours.

Summary

Counting the cost of an app before you start is simply wise. Going through the effort of performing a cost/benefit analysis will help you make a more sound decision about spending your hard-earned money developing and marketing an app that the buying community will want. The Android Market is cluttered with apps that provide no real value to Android users, and the chances of many apps breaking even or turning a profit are slim.

A breakeven analysis will help you determine how many apps you need to sell in order to turn a profit and start seeing money come through the door. A breakeven analysis will not help you predict the number of sales of your app. That information is gathered from other research that you do around your target audience and what buyers actually tell you they want. There is no exact science to this complicated area of pricing and predicting sales of your Android app, but a little up-front cost/benefit analysis can go a long way.

Selling Value over Price

There is an ice cream sundae in New York City that sells for $1,000! It's hard to believe, but the restaurant Serendipity sells its Grand Opulence Sundae for $1,000, and it actually sells one or two of them a month. Who would be crazy enough to spend that kind of money on a sundae? There couldn't possibly be enough ice cream or toppings to make it that expensive. So, it would follow that people are drawn to this sundae for other reasons.

Obviously a few people feel there is value in spending so much money on an ice cream sundae. However, the value goes beyond just a bowl of ice cream. The person is also buying intangible benefits such as prestige, attention, adulation, appreciation, and so on. It's almost a guarantee that whoever buys the Grand Opulence Sundae will not be sitting in a faraway corner of the restaurant. He or she will want friends and family and anyone else to watch the presentation. The desire to purchase this product starts with the restaurant's own description:

"Five scoops of the richest Tahitian vanilla bean ice cream infused with Madagascar vanilla and covered in 23K edible gold leaf. The sundae is drizzled with the world's most expensive chocolate, Amedei Porceleana, and covered with chunks of rare Chuao chocolate, which is from cocoa beans harvested by the Caribbean Sea on Venezuela's coast. The master-piece is suffused with exotic candied fruits from Paris, gold dragets, truffles, and Marzipan cherries. It is topped with a tiny glass bowl of Grand Passion Caviar, an exclusive dessert caviar, made of salt-free American Golden caviar, known for its sparkling golden color. It's sweetened and infused with fresh passion fruit, orange, and Armagnac. The sundae is served in a baccarat Harcourt crystal goblet with an 18K gold spoon to partake in the indulgence served with a petite mother of pearl spoon and topped with a gilded sugar flower by Ron Ben-Israel."

The restaurant has done an amazing job conveying the value of its product and convincing a small number of people to purchase it. The restaurant has sold the value of this product by its description, coupled with the strength of its brand and prestige. Through savvy marketing, it has convinced buyers to suspend their focus on price and think about the excitement and quality of the product. Although you may not have a $1,000 app (there are no apps priced above $200, but there are a few priced fairly high, as shown in Figure 12.1), you're nonetheless going to have to sell the value of your app, especially if it's above $4.99.

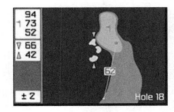

Figure 12.1   One of the Android Market's more expensive apps, Scoreout Caddy, at $34.99, is focused on the golfing market.

Customers are price sensitive on the Android Market, starting at about $4.99. There are a number of reasons why this is the case, including the following:

- **People have come to expect all things Internet to be free.** Because so much information is available at no charge, many buyers think every-thing should be free. It's only recently that online publications (for example, newspapers) are tiptoeing back into the paid subscription model.

- **Apple iTunes set a precedent with $0.99 music.** People who visit iTunes have become accustomed to all prices being set at $0.99. Although many albums are for sale on iTunes for $9.99 and up, most people choose to buy single songs.

- **People don't equate an Android app as having as much capability as a regular PC app.** Over time this perception will change, but some buyers think that a mobile phone means limited app capability, so they instinctively believe that an Android app isn't as powerful as apps provided on other platforms.

- **People don't have unlimited funds.** If someone is looking at an app that is priced at $9.99, they have to forego buying several other apps at a lower price. The average Android Market buyer spends $10–$20 a month, tops, on apps. If you factor in the cost of an Android smartphone, plus the monthly subscription fees, it starts to add up for the average consumer. Therefore, consumers are sensitive about how much more money they will spend for an Android app.

Therefore, if you have an app that is priced in the $9.99 range, you will need to spend some time focusing on selling value. An example of an app that sells in this price range is shown in Figure 12.2. This app is geared toward pilots, allowing them to file a flight plan via their Android. The audience for this type of app is very

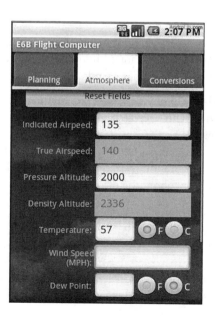

Figure 12.2   A higher priced app is generally focused on a narrow audience, such as pilots who own an Android.

specialized and narrow—all pilots who have an Android. Therefore, the developer of this app cannot possibly make any money selling at $0.99 given the audience size and the uniqueness of the app.

This chapter is focused on selling value. So the two main topics of this chapter are concerned with just that: selling value.

Selling Value

Because you can't have a conversation with your buyer about the price of your app, you may be wondering how you convince someone that the value of your app is worth the asking price. This is really the crux of the issue. Buyers must think that they are getting what they pay for in terms of quality, usefulness, and return on their investment. If you can convince your buyers of at least one of these three points, you are more likely to achieve the sale. You have to let your app, Android Market verbiage, product website, and reputation do the talking.

Selling Quality

One area of Android apps that has done a great job of selling quality is mobile navigation. Mobile GPS apps have really become popular over the past year, and the quality has approached that of regular auto GPS systems. Still, buyers want to be sure they are buying quality when spending $50–$100 on an Android app. The graphics and accuracy of the GPS have to be of the highest quality. Pricing for navigation apps is between $50 and $100 from a number of competing companies. Figure 12.3 shows a navigation app in this category. And, yes, there are a few free and $0.99 apps in this category, but not of the caliber found in the higher price range.

The developer can also help buyers of this app to understand that their Android can function as a turn-by-turn navigation system when they need it, without having to go buy a completely separate navigation system for their car. Any time your app allows the Android to function as another device, the customer is actually saving money by not buying the other device. Be sure to point this out to your buyers, and they will not be as hesitant about the price because you are extending the value of their mobile device.

 Note

Many thought that after Google offered its free turn-by-turn navigation app, prices would continue to sink lower for navigation apps. Although it's true companies such as Garmin and TomTom have had to drop prices dramatically for their apps, the prices for high-end navigation apps have remained fairly constant at the time of this writing.

Figure 12.3 Mobile navigation apps sell on quality and accuracy of their systems, thus keeping their prices far above the regular Android app price.

Selling Usefulness

Any time you can provide an app that saves people time in their business or when dealing with their clients, you have an opportunity to sell your app at a higher price. You can focus your app verbiage on how your app saves users time and makes them more efficient. The more efficient business people are, the more clients they can see daily and the more they can offer in terms of better service. Your app customers will view your app as a valuable tool if it can provide this capability.

There are a number of productivity apps on the Android Market, and some geared to very specific audiences such as doctors, lawyers, financial advisors, dentists, and so on. Figure 12.4, for example, shows an app geared toward physicians that allows them to track their patients. Physicians can wirelessly write prescriptions and patient info to other databases at their office. This helps save doctors time and allows them to provide better service to their patients.

Other apps that fall into the usefulness category include calendaring and organizational apps. For you to charge a higher price than free or $0.99, your app must provide connectivity to other systems or provide a level of functionality not typically found in the less expensive apps. Figure 12.5 shows an example of an app that uploads updates to iCal and Outlook.

Figure 12.4   This app sells for $139.99 and allows physicians to track patients and their health histories, write prescriptions, and transmit data to their main database.

Figure 12.5   Productivity apps can justify a higher price when they connect to/update other common Mac and PC applications.

Selling Return on Investment

One of the most expensive apps on the Android Market is called Pilot My-Cast 8, which is currently listed for $129.95. Yes, that price will get you all the navigation you need. The company justifies the price because it is a very specialized app for a very narrow audience of pilots. Pilots are always looking for the latest electronic gadgets to help them travel more easily and efficiently. When compared against other tools that pilots purchase, this is a small price to pay for so much power in a smartphone device. An example of this application is shown in Figure 12.6.

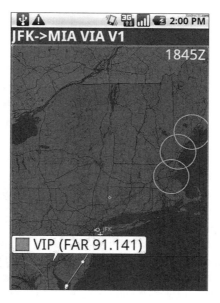

Figure 12.6   The Android Market's most expensive app is Pilot My-Cast 8, which currently sells for $129.95.

If your app sells for more than $10, you can look for ways to communicate to your buyers that your app can save them money. One way to do this is through a case study on your product website or via your Android Market verbiage, where you explain an actual use case for your app, particularly how someone saved money by using your app. Through a case study, you should be able to demonstrate to your readers how your app has saved users money and how long it took them to realize these savings. When reading such a case study, buyers will take comfort in knowing that they will make up their investment in your app with just a few uses. This approach to selling takes away the risk for the buyers to some degree.

Additional Thoughts on Selling Value

Think about how many times you have had a particular problem, and when you found the right solution, price was usually not an issue. You needed that solution and you were willing to pay for it. The same holds true for the more expensive Android apps. Obviously the type of app we are talking about here is one that is geared toward a narrow audience with a specific need. Because you understand the buyers' problem and can provide them with a solution, they are willing to pay for that solution.

 Note

There are really two markets on the Android Market: the flea market and utility market. We all love flea markets and sometimes we are flea market buyers. We browse and walk the aisles of the Android Market looking for something fun. At other times we are utility buyers, looking for a particular app to solve a particular problem.

Here are some things to keep in mind:

- **Differentiate, differentiate, differentiate.** If there is nothing that makes you unique from your competition, you become common. Common means ordinary or not special, and the only way buyers select one common app over another app is price. Take inventory of your development skills, experience, and knowledge. If you have specialized skills in some area, think about developing an app for that skill set. Sure, you are going after a niche market, but it could be a very profitable niche market for you. If you are an expert in certain facets of your business, look to create an app to automate or improve your business. These and other differentiators can make you unique and valuable to the app-buying audience.

- **Dropping your price too low can hurt you.** Depending on the type of app, you may be doing yourself a disservice by pricing the app too low. In some of the previous examples, your customers would question the value of your app if the price is set at practically zero. Most find the old adage holds: They get what they pay for in terms of quality and stability. A higher priced app implies there must be something more to it. Again, this generally does not include game apps, which seem to fall in the $0.99–$2.99 range, with few exceptions.

- **A competitive price adds perceived value.** This chapter is focused on higher priced apps, and if you are selling a higher priced app, do not drop the price so low that you are far and away the cheapest option in your category on the Android Market. It's okay to be a little cheaper, 20% or so, but not 80%.

- **If there are few (or no) Android app competitors, price the app higher.** If you have created an app that could have a strong audience but lacks a lot of similar apps on the Android Market, then look to Mac and PC solutions to see where they are priced. A good Mac or PC app (think Antivirus software for the PC) sells for $24.99 to $39.99 all the time. Your app may be a utility or novel app that helps someone in a certain line of business and can be priced above $20.

Figure 12.7 shows an HVAC app that helps people in the heating and air conditioning trade calculate duct sizes and pipe sizes. This app is currently priced at $23.99, and for an individual in this line of work, this is an acceptable price for this type of tool. I'm sure they've spent a lot more on other tools.

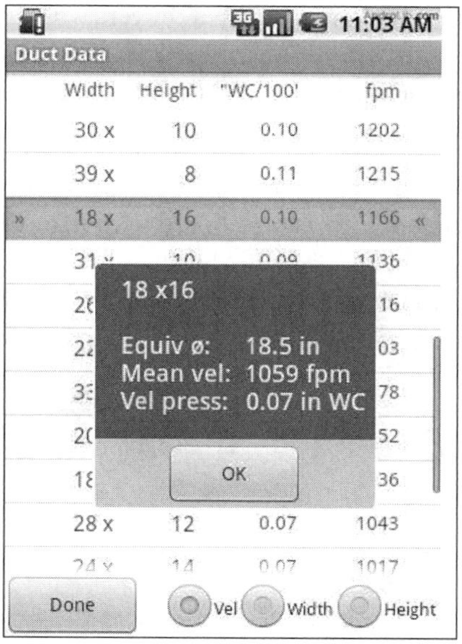

Figure 12.7 If there are very few (or no) apps that do the same thing your app does, you can charge a much higher (but fair) price to a limited audience.

- **Consumers want value and are willing to pay for it.** It may surprise you, but consumers are willing to spend a fair amount for an app that works well and solves their problem. They would rather buy an app that works and spend a little more than buy an app that is junk that doesn't work well or solve their problem.

Summary

If you have developed an app that does not fall in the game category and caters to a narrow audience, you should consider carefully the concept of selling value over price. Many apps will not become blockbuster hits on the Android Market but they serve a very specific audience. You want to maximize your revenue with this smaller audience by selling value over price.

Apps that improve productivity and help solve a problem or save money are candidates for value pricing instead low pricing. The key to selling value is that your web and Android Market content must communicate one or all of these components: quality, usefulness, and return on investment. Buyers will almost always purchase your app if they believe they are getting more from your app than indicated by the price. The mentality for app buyers depends on the type of app being sold.

Someone who is looking to play games or pass the time will be looking for low-priced and free apps. Buyers tend to download an app and use it on average ten times before they forget about it, become bored with it, or delete off their Android. People who are looking to solve a specific business or personal problem will be willing to spend some money on an app. They will also tend to use the app much more frequently, especially if it proves useful for their scenario.

13

Breaking into the Android Market Top Paid Apps

Perhaps the most popular question asked concerning the marketing of an Android app is, How do I get my app in the top paid apps for my category? Developers know that if they can get their apps into the top paid apps, they are certain to see significant numbers of downloads and huge sales volume. This is an accurate assumption and was described as "hitting the grand slam" in the first chapter of this book. Being in the top category in app sales is the Holy Grail for Android app developers.

The challenge, however, is unlocking the mystery of how to break into the top paid apps in sales volume, which by the way, requires at least a thousand downloads per day. There have been rumors that some companies have bought their own apps for a few days to get onto the list, thus creating momentum for their apps.

Although this is possible, it would be fairly expensive to achieve this feat and could only happen with a wealthy developer or large company. I don't recommend this approach.

There is no one single formula for breaking into the top paid (or top 50 or top 10 for that matter). This has been proven by different developers who have told their story of making it into the top paid through articles and blog posts over the past year. So, although I can't pinpoint an exact formula for success, I can give you some common elements that are part of the most successful apps. These things we know must happen to some degree in order to reach orbital velocity.

In this chapter, we will review the key elements of a successful app, which include pricing, promotions, positioning, and integration, to name a few. Doing all these well to the extent possible will increase your chances of building the next best-selling Android app.

Develop a Great App

Far and away the biggest reason an app makes it into the top paid is because it's a great app. Hands down this is the biggest reason, and yet so many developers seem to discount this first recommendation. They say to themselves, "Of course I have a great app. It's the best app to ever hit the Android Market!" Then, they don't give it too much more thought. But, a rash decision to create the perfect app without really thinking it through could be your undoing. Consider the following hard questions before you start development on your app:

- Are people really going to be interested in the app you are going to write?

- Have you floated your idea to a small group of trusted friends or business partners?

- Will someone be willing to pay for the app you are going write?

- Are you so confident in your app that you will bet your whole reputation on releasing it?

- Are you prepared to work nights/weekends/holidays, whatever it takes, to ensure the highest quality app gets produced?

- Are you prepared to take criticism and blunt appraisals about your app?

If you can honestly answer these questions with a "yes," then read on. As they say, you may have what it takes to get your app into the top paid for your app's category.

If you are creating a game, it must be exciting, fun, addictive, and simple. Not an easy feat. Spend some time on the Android Market familiarizing yourself with the best-selling free and paid apps. Spend a few bucks and download the most popular games in your category and really study them to understand why they are so popular. You really have to pick apart the app to understand how it ticks and why it's so appealing to so many people.

Figure 13.1 shows one of the most popular Android game apps—*Robo Defense*—at the time of this writing This app has a few key ingredients to a very successful app. First, it has mass appeal because nearly everyone likes to play games. Second, it has multiple levels of play, which is always a requirement when building a best-selling game. Third, there are a number of games that use the same "tower" concept and the buyers of this game already how this type of game is played. Fourth, the product is well written and has "stickiness," meaning that users enjoy using the app over and over again.

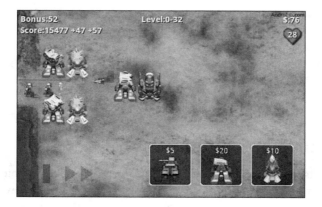

Figure 13.1   The number one selling game app *Robo Defense* has many key ingredients required for a top selling app.

Note

Build your app with an eye toward television. When you are designing and building your app, try to envision your app being selected for a TV commercial. The quality of such an app would have to be of the highest caliber and the usability superb. Setting the bar this high will help position your app with the greatest possibility for success even though it will probably never be showcased in a commercial.

Beat Up Your App Mercilessly

Nobody likes to be told that their baby is ugly, but in the case of Android apps, you've got to get second and third opinions on what users like and don't like about your app. If you have produced a game for teens, you need to get it into the hands of teens prior to launch. Send out an email or post an ad on your website that you're looking for early testers of your app. You can offer them a free version of the app when it ships, a t-shirt, or some other small gift. Google allows developers to provide pre-release versions of their apps to Android users. This will allow you to conduct a fairly substantial beta test of your app prior to launching it on the Android Market.

 Note

> You need a way to solicit feedback about your app. Don't just have your testers give you random comments or tell you what they think. Create a structured survey form on your product website or through a service such as Survey Monkey (www.surveymonkey.com). Ask your beta testers to rank the level of play for your app, ease of use, graphics and sound, and so on. Ask them about ten questions total so they can quickly give you their feedback. You can also leave a space for open comments on the survey to capture their suggestions.

Have Friends in High Places

It never hurts to have lots of friends and family who can help promote your app. You can offer them a free download of your app to give it a try. Always ask them to post a review on the Android Market. Now, what about the ethics of doing this? I am well aware of the reports about some companies creating fake reviews for their own or their clients' apps on the Android Market. This is clearly not appropriate and I am not suggesting that you ever take this approach. I am, however, suggesting that you contact everyone you know, ask them to download the app, test it out, and write an honest (and hopefully positive) review. This is no different than reaching out to a regular reviewer and asking him or her to give you an honest evaluation of your app. If you have created an outstanding app, you won't need to worry about getting a bunch of negative reviews. You will get a few, but that's just the nature of selling any product.

If you are fortunate to know reviewers at different companies, always solicit their help in providing a review for your app. Also, numerous sites have popped up recently that allow you to post your app for review by others. Android Tapp (www.androidtapp.com), for example, allows you to submit your app for review and gain greater exposure to help your sales efforts. An example of the submittal page for Android Tapp is shown in Figure 13.2.

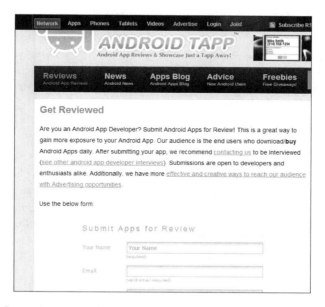

Figure 13.2   Android Tapp allows you to submit your paid app along with five or more promo codes.

 Note

It doesn't hurt to ask your users to write a review for your app. If you offer an instruction page within your app, you can include a request at the bottom of your instructions saying, "We appreciate your feedback. Don't forget to write a review on the Android Market."

Cross-Promote

Cross-promoting your apps is a powerful way to increase sales and move you into the top paid. Once you have one successful app, it's easier to build off that success with your next app. It's similar to an author who publishes a best-selling novel. The next book is much easier to get the same success because he or she is a known quantity at that point. The author has a following of readers and they will most likely buy the next book.

There are numerous ways to cross-promote your app. If you have a PC or Mac app that you have already built, you can utilize that audience to promote your Android app. If you have developed a free version of your app, you can easily cross-promote the paid version in that app. For more information on developing a free app, refer to Chapter 14, "Level the Playing Field with a Free App."

Each time you introduce a new app to the Android Market, be sure to issue a press release. In your press release you will talk about your new app, but you should also mention the other apps you have available. For example, at the end of your press release you can mention your company name and tell the reader you are also the developer of other apps as well.

Price It Right

As mentioned in many sections of this book, you have to do some homework on where to set your price. If you are hoping for a quick win, you've got to sell a game app and your price must be between $0.99 and $1.99. Nearly all games are priced at $0.99. Some name-brand game apps are priced a little higher, but they have a strong following and strong name recognition before launch. Refer to the other chapters in this book that discuss how to price your app.

Integrate Your App with Other Apps

You can build your app to work with a number of very popular apps in the area of social media. Search the Android Market for popular apps around MySpace, Twitter, Facebook, YouTube, and many others. Look for ways to enhance or expand the use of these social networking sites with your Android app.

When someone searches the Android Market for a social networking app, your app will also appear in the search results. For example, when you search the Android Market using "Twitter" as a keyword, you will bring up a number of apps that work with Twitter, such as the app shown in Figure 13.3.

Optimize Your Web and Android Market Copy

Carefully choose the name of your app and think about keywords you might be able to use in your app's name that will be common to users searching the Android Market. Descriptive words such as *Easy*, *Fun*, *Fast*, and *Exciting* are all common terms used in searches. If your app has these types of words, it is more likely to show up in the search results at the top of the list.

Figure 13.3 Creating an app that works with an extremely popular app will help others find your app when they do a keyword search.

 Note

> Google keeps upping the quality of the Android Market search engine.
> When the store was initially launched the search capabilities were fairly
> primitive. But, with each upgrade of the Android Market, the search capa-
> bility seems to improve. Google is becoming sophisticated in properly iden-
> tifying the right apps for the search terms entered.

If your app is connecting to another popular app such as Twitter or Facebook, be
sure to mention the app by name in the body of your copy. This can help your app
to appear when someone does a search for these popular apps. You'll also want to
add keywords to your web copy to assist people in locating your app. It is widely
believed that the more keywords you use in your Android Market copy, the higher
your app will appear in the search rankings. Don't overdo it, but a generous use of
keywords can't hurt.

Develop Your Brand and Promote It Like Crazy

If you plan to develop more than one app (and you should), then you want to think
about building a brand instead of just an app. Many young development companies

are vying for a piece of the spotlight in the app development world and they are working diligently to build a brand. Here are some of the benefits of building a brand:

- A brand allows you to build a bigger following as you reach a larger audience of Android app users across multiple apps.

- A brand helps your company attract venture capital if you achieve success with a bestseller and desire to grow your company into a large-scale business.

- A brand allows you to cross-promote your apps across your user base.

- A brand allows you to concentrate development efforts where needed to efficiently produce your next best-selling app.

The best way to build a brand is to start before the release of your first app. You can develop your brand by designing the look and feel of your product website. Once you have established an identity for your brand, you can include elements of your brand (colors, font styles, graphics, and so on) into each of your apps. The carryover between your website brand and your apps does not need to be 100%, but it should include some elements so that subconsciously the buyers link your site to apps they see on the Android Market from your company. Here are two examples, shown in Figure 13.4 and Figure 13.5, of companies that have created a brand for their apps and are doing very well on the Android Market.

Another way to build your brand is to create a blog and start blogging about Android app development topics. You can build up a following for your brand even before you release any apps to the Android Market. Prior to launch of your first app you can generate buzz about it, which allows you to generate stronger sales when it is released.

Figure 13.4 Coheso has built a brand around a number of diet and carb counting apps.

Figure 13.5   iHandy has built its brand around a number of free and paid apps, giving the company a strong presence in the Android and iPhone Markets.

Reach Out to Google

Getting chosen for one of the New and Noteworthy, What's Hot, or Staff Picks categories is a complete mystery for the outside app developer. I'm not sure there really is a system in place. It may be whatever bubbles up to the top or catches the attention of a Google reviewer. Sometimes all you have to do is ask, right? It doesn't hurt to approach a reviewer at the Android Market and ask him or her to take a special look at your app. Remember the postcard idea? If you can stand out in the crowd to get someone to look at your app, you have a shot at being selected for one of these special categories. It may sound silly, but doing something like sending a postcard puts you in a class of a handful who do anything beyond submitting their apps.

Remember, Google reviewers are much like your buyers. They will be interested in an app that has a compelling value proposition with exciting graphics, an easy-to-understand interface, a broad audience, and stickiness. If your app has some of these characteristics, you're more likely to attract the attention of a Google reviewer—although I have to admit that some of the apps selected for these special categories have not always been the best.

Summary

In this chapter you learned about the common elements present in apps that break into the top paid for their category. Although there is no set formula for a winning app, we know that they are typically games that are easy to learn, fun to play, and don't cost much. Increase your chances of breaking into the top paid categories by building a free app along with a paid app and making sure that your app is outstanding, not average.

Don't quit after a few weeks of posting your app to the Android Market. Sometimes all it takes is the right combination of a great app at the right time with the right exposure. Building a brand is more powerful than building a single app. It takes more time and effort but improves your odds of having that breakout app.

Always seek positive customer and professional reviews. People make purchases based on the positive recommendations of others. The more positive reviews you have, the more your app will be viewed favorably. Don't forget to seek reviews from industry experts outside of the typical Android realm. These experts can give your readers a positive recommendation for your apps and bring lots of credibility to your apps.

Level the Playing Field with a Free App

As long as there are developers creating Android apps, the debate about free apps versus paid apps will probably continue. This is because some people will have success with a paid app and others will generate ad revenue through their free app. Both models can work, and often the success depends on the type of app written and the audience you are marketing to. Some buyers don't mind having ads appear in their free apps and will download lots of free apps and use them for a short period of time, or they will upgrade to paid apps to get additional features that were not available in the free apps.

One thing developers should remember is that a free app can help them level the playing field and build their brand inexpensively. When a large app developer enters the Android Market with a new app, they have the marketing clout and brand recognition that an independent developer does not. They can release a paid app and immediately start to see large downloads because their brand is recognized and trusted. They have already spent perhaps millions of dollars building their brand over many years. They have many followers already.

An independent developer does not have that luxury and must look for other ways to get the word out about his or her app. If you offer a free app along with a paid app, you are covering your bases, building your brand and generating some revenue. You're allowing someone to "try before they buy," which gives the buyer a risk-free opportunity before deciding to obtain the paid version. Even if he or she doesn't buy your paid app, you are building your brand and gaining recognition in a very competitive field. If the buyer likes your app, he or she will be inclined to tell others about it and will also be inclined to look at what other apps you have for download and sale.

 Note

Do not make the mistake of thinking that people are not price sensitive, even at $0.99! With so many apps to choose from on the Android Market, one cannot possibly buy even a fraction of the available apps. Buyers are selective in what they download for free and especially selective in what they purchase.

In this chapter we will review the different approaches to monetizing apps. Take a close look at the type of app you are marketing. Game apps tend to do very well with free and paid versions. Games are generally easier to delineate between free and paid as well. For example, you can limit the levels of play in the free app or the number of weapons in the game. Non-game apps are more difficult to limit on features, but can be done with some thought. An educational app can offer the first set of test questions in the free version, but require purchase of the paid app to obtain all the questions.

Table 14.1 illustrates the different app-development strategies you can consider when building your app marketing plan. Ultimately you will have to decide which approach works best for you and also what your budget will permit you to accomplish. One other point that's worth mentioning is that you can always start out with a paid app and then offer a free version later on to help boost your sales. Many developers have had strong success in reigniting their app sales by going back and introducing a free version with ads later on.

Table 14.1   Multiple Development Strategies You Can Pursue When Creating Your App Marketing Plan

App Development Approach	Pros	Cons
Paid app, standalone	Lower costs and faster time to market.	Many competing apps, limited brand recognition, and slower sales until you build a following.
Free app, standalone	Likely to experience multiple downloads quickly. You can build your brand.	You must rely on ad revenue, which may or may not result in significant revenue.
Free app and paid app	You can build a following, offer in-app purchase inside the free app, and achieve ad revenue and paid app revenue simultaneously.	It's more costly to build and support two slightly different versions of your app.
Paid app, with ads	You can sell the app and gain some ad revenue.	This strategy is not widely used and you are unlikely to achieve significant revenue from either approach.

Build a Standalone Paid App

Most developers who have been around the Android Market for a period of time have chosen to build paid versions of their apps first and then monitor their sales. Even a year ago there were far fewer apps competing for buyers' download dollars, so this strategy could pay off handsomely if you hit upon the right app. If you have a strong brand and a strong following for your apps, you may be able to build a paid app without offering a free version.

For developers of games, this is getting more difficult to achieve. Customers are looking for free first and then maybe they will buy the full app. Even Ethan Nicholas, the iPhone and Android developer of the incredibly successful game *iShoot*, began offering a "Lite" version after he noticed his sales of the paid version start to slow. Offering the free version allowed his sales to resume their upward growth.

Perhaps the best opportunity for standalone paid apps is in the more technical and business-oriented apps categories. The reason for this is that often people are looking for an app to solve a particular problem. If they can find it for free, great. But, if they can't, they are prepared to buy the app. Most app-pricing studies show that the buyer is not price sensitive up to $4.99.

Build a Free App, Build a Following

There are many reasons to build a free app, most notably so that you can build a following for your apps. Perhaps your goal is not to make money right away from your app but to get your name out there in the development world. Building a free app has a number of benefits, including the following, you'll want to consider as you build your company:

- **Build an app to showcase your development skills.** If your goal is to develop apps for other people, you can use a free app to demonstrate your skills to potential clients. You can create a free app that you can post to the Android Market and gain experience building an app. When potential clients want to see a sample of your work, you direct them to the Android Market to download a copy of your app. An app that has many downloads will help convince clients to use you to develop their apps.

- **Build a free app for future sales.** Many developers build free apps first with the intention of charging for these apps after they have built up a following. However, in certain studies of app sales, a free app that gets changed to a paid app often sees a significant decline in sales after the switch.

  Other studies have indicated that even if the app developer moves the app back to free after trying to charge for it, the damage has been done and the number of free downloads is still impacted even though the price is set back to free. It appears that the momentum is broken at that point when a free app is altered in any way.

  It is probably best to develop a free app and leave it as free and then create another app that is paid after you monitor the downloads and level of interest around the free app. This will allow people to download your free app without risk and then purchase your paid app if they like what they see or want to obtain additional functionality.

- **Build a free app to support other products.** Perhaps you are selling another product that can benefit from you building an Android app. You can develop a free app that can either be used to complement your other products or help you to strengthen your brand. One example of this is an app from TMZ. This app shows you the latest news for TMZ. This app has had tens of thousands of downloads and has helped TMZ to strengthen their brand. The TMZ app's main screen is shown in Figure 14.1.

Figure 14.1   The TMZ app is a free app that is used to strengthen the TMZ brand and generate awareness about the shows.

- **You are new to Android development.** If you are new to developing apps, creating a free app might be the best route to take as you get your feet wet. Building a free app takes the pressure off you to make money right away on the app. However, unless you have very deep pockets, you should build your free app as inexpensively as you can without sacrificing quality. Use this as an opportunity to learn the Android Market submittal process and make your mistakes with a free app.

Build a Paid App and a Free App at the Same Time

Many developers are now looking at pursuing a dual strategy of building a paid app and a free version at the same time. This strategy allows you to establish a following for your app from the start, obtaining possibly thousands of downloads of the free version, along with sales of the paid version. Conversion rates from free apps to paid apps are around 1% according to some developers. Therefore, it takes 1,000 free downloads to generate ten paid app sales. Keep in mind that some apps can achieve hundreds of thousands of free downloads, if not millions, so your free app may be able to generate considerable sales of your paid app.

The more free downloads you get, the closer you are to being shown on one of the Top Paid or Top Free download categories on the Android Market. Placement of your app in the top listings in your specific category (Health and Fitness, Lifestyles, and so on) can catapult your sales. Figure 14.2 shows an example of the top paid apps and free apps in the Health category. If you open up the list, the Android Market shows the top apps in that category, both paid and free.

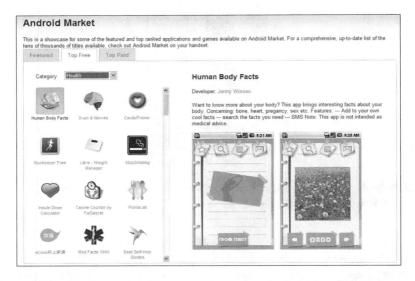

Figure 14.2   Top free and paid apps are shown by selecting tabs off the main page for the Health category of the Android Market.

The challenge to creating a free app and a paid app is that you may have to maintain two apps for the Android Market. This depends on whether you developed the free and paid apps separately over a period of time. If you are going back to develop a free app, you'll have to decide how you want to build your app. Most likely you will take the original paid app and modify the original code to limit its features so that you have a limited-function free app. This is probably the easiest and fastest way to come up with a free app when you already have been selling a paid app.

The other option is to develop both the free app and the paid app at the same time. You develop the app from the ground up, with all the features available, but you disable some of them for the free version. In the free app, you can invite users to purchase the full app and instantly upgrade them to the full-featured version. As shown in Figure 14.3, the developer of this app has created two versions of the app.

In the next example, shown in Figure 14.4, the developer of this app released both the paid and free versions on the same time. The buyer can choose to download the "Lite" version of the app or purchase the paid app instead. If the free version is downloaded, and the user likes the app they can always purchase and download the paid app at any time.

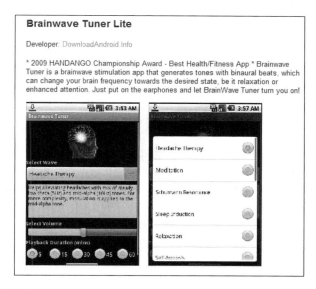

Figure 14.3   This developer released a free version first and then followed up later with a paid version of the app.

Figure 14.4   Both paid and free versions of this app were released on the same day.

Note

Amazingly, a number of free apps on the Android Market don't have an ad for their paid version to prompt the user to upgrade. If you are going to have a free app available, I highly recommend that you prompt the user to upgrade and purchase your paid app.

Many game developers are offering free and paid versions of their games as a matter of course. They update the games at the same time and post to the Android Market at the same time. This is becoming the norm as a marketing strategy for game development on the Android Market and really any smartphone market. If you are a game developer, think seriously about offering both free and paid versions right from the start. Two examples are shown in Figures 14.5 and 14.6.

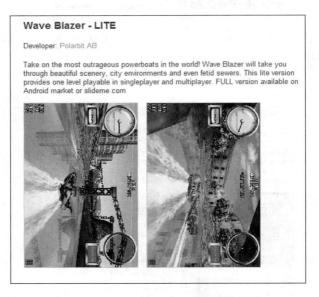

Figure 14.5 Game developers are increasingly offering both free and paid apps right from the start.

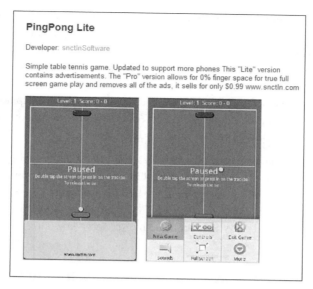

Figure 14.6   Another example of a free app that has helped cross-promote sales of the paid app.

Free Apps with Ads

Some developers have found success by building free apps with ads. Their strategy is to make money by achieving huge downloads for their apps and selling ad space on them. Companies that wish to advertise on the new emerging mobile platform can utilize mobile ad platforms and bid on ad placement just like with Google AdWords. This can be profitable for you as a developer if your apps achieve significant downloads and lots of users click through on ads displayed by your apps. Some developers have achieved considerable success by creating free apps and posting ads in them.

 Note

You will have to do an analysis between what you think ad revenue will generate versus what a paid app will generate. This has been a subject of great debate among developers; some saying there is not enough revenue in ads for the developer and others saying that there is. If you find that your free app is not generating the ad revenue you thought, don't abandon your free strategy. Keep in mind that the other benefits of offering your app for free go beyond just ad revenue.

There are number of different routes you as a developer can take to pursue ads on your apps. Ad network companies provide a small amount of code to install within your apps to enable ads, and there are many ad networks out there competing for your business—companies such as Traffic Marketplace, Google, Yahoo!, VideoEgg, Mojiva, Adtini, Jumptap, Quattro Wireless (acquired by Google), and ValueClick Media, to name just a few. These companies provide an ad marketplace for app developers who want to sell space on their Android apps and major companies who want to sell their products via the mobile platform.

Other companies have created ad exchanges, bringing together competing ad companies for your business and promising 100% fill rates for your app, meaning that any open time slot while your app is in use will display some sort of ad. The websites of three of the most popular ad exchange companies—AdMob (acquired by Google), Mobclix, and AdWhirl (acquired by AdMob)—are shown in Figures 14.7, 14.8, and 14.9.

Figure 14.7 AdMob provides developers and advertisers a method for mobile advertising.

Figure 14.8   Mobclix allows developers and advertisers to provide advertising in their free apps.

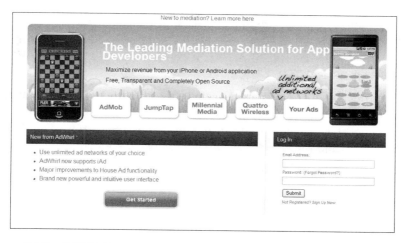

Figure 14.9   AdWhirl is an aggregator of different ad networks and was acquired by AdMob in 2009.

AdMob is a mobile advertising marketplace that connects advertisers with mobile publishers. The company allows advertisers to create ads, choose landing pages, and target their ads with plenty of detail. Ads can be targeted to locations, carriers, phone platforms, and phone manufacturers.

Mobclix is an ad exchange provider for Android apps. Mobclix targets users based on location and the type of app to maximize the money that Android developers can make. Mobclix provides the following:

- More than 20 ad networks
- Advanced analytics
- One-hundred-percent fill rates

From Paid to Free

Some apps start out as paid apps and then over time the developers move them to free. This can occur for a number of reasons, but generally it's because an app is no longer producing sufficient revenue to warrant that it continue for sale. Thus, if you are developing other Android apps, do not simply pull the app from the Android Market. Convert the paid app to a free app by logging in to the Android Market and changing the price to free.

Having a free app will give you the benefits of keeping your name and your app's name on the Android Market. It's better to have someone downloading your app for free than not at all. When you launch your other apps, you already have a following for your brand and you already have a presence on the Android Market. What's more, if you are looking for app freelance work, you can point prospective customers to your work on the Android Market.

Summary

Multiple strategies can be used to monetize your Android apps. The first strategy is to create a single app that is completely free, with ads. Your strategy is to make money by getting people to click through on the ads displayed within your app. Many users will download the app because it's free and they don't mind seeing the ads come across their Android device every 30 seconds.

The next strategy is to create an Android app that serves ads but also includes an option to upgrade the user to the paid version of the app. If you're going to serve up ads on your app, it makes sense to include an option for the user of your app to make an in-app purchase of your app. Some apps do this and others don't. I recommend that you include this option.

The last strategy is to create a paid app along with a corresponding free app. This is the best strategy for most developers because they can build a following and attract customers. In the extremely competitive Android Market, you must do everything you can to stand out from the crowd. Remember to only give away enough functionality in your free app to interest your users in getting the paid app.

15

The App Pricing Rollercoaster

In this chapter we will take a look at the various tactics that can be used when adjusting your app price. Pricing adjustments can make a difference in how many copies of your app are sold. However, many times these pricing adjustments are temporary and lose their impact after a few days. So, you will want to adjust prices carefully and monitor the impact to your sales before making a permanent price adjustment.

The average price of an Android app at the time of this writing is $3.13. The average price of a game app is between $1.30 and $2.60. The question that many developers often have once they've posted their app to the Android Market is when should they adjust their pricing? How long should you wait before making a price adjustment? What if the pricing adjustment has no impact on sales? Then what?

As I have said in other chapters, your pricing should depend on what type of app you are selling. Even if you are selling a game app, you need to price it more or less in line with the prices for other games in that particular category. Table 15.1 shows the range of Android app prices for April 2010 as reported by Distomo. The highest ranked game apps are between $2.11 and $2.99 on the Android Market, as shown in Table 15.2, also provided by Distomo.

Table 15.1   Android App Prices Vary Widely Depending on the App Type, as Reported by Distomo Analytics

Rank	Application	Publisher	Category	Price
1	Beautiful Widgets	LevelUp Studio	News & Weather	$2.04
2	MyBackup Pro	rerware.com	Tools	$4.99
3	ServiceTIME	TPC Solutions, LLC	Productivity	$1.49
4	Weather & Toggle Widget	Android Apps	News & Weather	$1.99
5	NewsRob Pro	Mariano Kamp	News & Weather	$6.83
6	Advanced Task Manager	Arron La	Tools	$0.99
7	Mobile Package Tracker	Minstech	Tools	$1.99
8	WeatherBug Elite	WeatherBug Mobile	News & Weather	$1.99
9	NewsRoom – RSS News	Trileet Inc.	News & Weather	$4.99
10	Touiteur Premium	LevelUp Studio	Social	$2.72

Table 15.2   Highest Ranked Games Apps, as Reported by Distomo Analytics

Rank	App	Publisher	Category	Price
1	Robo Defense	Lupis Labs Software	Arcade & Action	$2.99
2	Jewellust	Smartpix Games	Brain & Puzzle	$2.95
3	Armored Strike Online	Requiem Software Labs, Inc.	Arcade & Action	$3.99
4	Radiant	Hexage.net	Arcade & Action	$2.34
5	GameBoid (GBA Emulator)	yongzh	Arcade & Action	$3.99
6	Fishin' 2 Go (FULL)	CyxB	Arcade & Action	$2.25
7	SNesoid (SNES Emulator)	yongzh	Arcade & Action	$3.98
8	Farm Frenzy	HeroCraft Ltd	Arcade & Action	$4.69
9	aTilt 3D Labyrinth	FridgeCat Software	Arcade & Action	$2.99
10	Abduction! World Attack	Psym Mobile	Casual	$2.11

Once you have selected a price for your app, you should maintain that price for the first few months of sales to get a clear picture of how things are going. Avoid the app pricing rollercoaster where you are constantly raising and lowering the price of your app in an attempt to find the best price. The constant shifting of price does not give you enough time to see how a particular price point is working out. You will not be able to gather any concrete data unless you wait a few weeks to see how a pricing adjustment impacts sales.

This does not mean you can't do a promotion or two to experiment with temporary price drops, but you should plan to keep prices steady for a while to see how sales go and to get a read on the market.

Raising Your Price

Just like when selling almost any software product, it's very difficult to raise prices for an Android app. This is because the buyer becomes used to a certain price, and discovering what others have paid for the same or similar product is fairly easy to do in this connected Internet world. So, even if you add features to your app, you will be hard pressed to raise the price of your current app even if you are completely justified in doing so. Your existing customers will expect you to add more features as you create new versions, while your current customers will get your upgrades at no additional charge anyway.

 Note

> Some will argue that new customers won't know if you raise your app's price, but this is not true. People who write reviews of your apps and those that follow your app—including your competition—will know that the price has been raised and will comment on that in reviews or blogs.

One way to approach a price increase that *can* work to your advantage is to create a separate new app altogether with a higher price point. It's really the same app you already have for sale, but it has additional features. You can call this version of the app "Pro" (for Professional). If you don't already have a free app, you can take your current app and make it the free app. You can call this version of the app "Lite." Then, you can introduce the new higher-priced app to the market. The new price cannot be dramatically higher than the previous price of the old app, however— perhaps a dollar or two more. There is almost no other circumstance where you can easily raise the price of your app without negatively impacting sales.

Lowering Your Price

Lowering your app price is easier than raising it. When you first launch your app on the Android Market, you need to give it some time to determine whether or not the price is working. If, after a few months, you are not seeing steady sales or your sales are starting to drop off, you'll want to look at pricing as a possible option to adjust. Be sure to consider the following questions before determining that you want to lower your price:

- Have sales for your app steadily declined over the past two to three weeks?

- Have you checked competitors' prices? Have they dropped their price?

- Have the leaders in your category of apps dropped their prices?

- Have your reviews indicated that your price is too high? Figure 15.1 shows a reviewer's comments that indicate an app's price is too high.

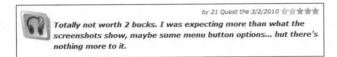

Figure 15.1   Buyer's feedback will always tell you when the price of your app is too high.

- Has an external reviewer from a website indicated he or she likes your app but it's priced too high?

 Note

You can track price drops through email alerts or RSS feeds by going to sites such as www.appbrain.com. You can search by categories, free or paid, and most popular with this site. An example from this site is shown in Figure 15.2.

If you have determined that a price cut is in order, then the next step is to determine how much to lower it. This depends on where your price point is. Some apps are priced at $49.99 and are dropped to $9.99. That's an astounding 80% drop! However, other apps are priced at $1.99 and are dropped to $0.99. That's obviously a 50% drop and will impact your revenue substantially.

Changelog for FlightStats for Android

May 18, 2010	Update	Version 2.1.6
Apr 8, 2010	Update	Version 2.1.5
Mar 17, 2010	Update	Version 2.1.4
Mar 14, 2010	Update	Version 2.1.3
Mar 13, 2010	Update	Version 2.1.2
Mar 11, 2010	Update	Version 2.1.1
Mar 10, 2010	Price Drop	New Price: **$4.99** ($6.99)
Mar 10, 2010	Update	Version 2.1
Jan 12, 2010	More Downloads	5,000-10,000 downloads

Figure 15.2   Use a website to help you track price drops for apps in your category. This will help you gauge where prices are trending for your type of app.

 Note

Always factor the 30% cut that Google takes in your pricing decisions. An app that was priced at $4.99 is giving the developer $3.49 after Google takes its cut. If that same app is priced down to $0.99, Google pays the developer $0.69 after the price drop. That's an 80% decline in any revenues you might have.

Once you have dropped your price, carefully monitor daily sales activity. If your app is priced at the right level, you will see an increase in sales immediately. As you know, there is a great deal of price sensitivity for Android apps. This can be attributed to a couple things. First, the buyer has already spent several hundred dollars on an Android phone and even more on accessories and other add-ons. So, in addition to a monthly phone/Internet bill, the buyer is sensitive about spending more money on additional apps for the device. Second, the global economy over the past couple years has made budgets extremely tight for most typical buyers.

The last piece of advice for pricing is that you have to keep your overall brand strategy in mind. If you intend to build many apps and release them on a fairly frequent basis, your app prices will most likely be on the low end. If you keep prices low and update your app frequently, you can extend the life of your app.

Temporary Price Drops

Temporary price drops do work and can drive traffic to your site. Carefully plan your price drops and make sure you publicize them through your product website and in the Android Market. Follow these three easy steps when planning your temporary price drop:

1. Clearly state the promotion on your site and on the Android Market.

2. Include a timeframe (offer good until a specific date).

3. Provide a clear "call to action." (Buy today to receive your app discount!)

You can do a temporary price drop every other month or so, depending on the type of app you are selling. If you do promotions too frequently you'll condition your buyers to simply wait for the next "sale" and then buy the app.

Value-Add Sales

As discussed in other chapters, some developers offer their apps for free to sell advertising as a means to generate revenue from their apps. Another model that is growing in popularity among mostly game developers is to give away their apps for free but attempt to generate revenue through consistent add-on sales. Developers that used to charge for their game apps have recognized that another way to monetize their app is to use the razor/blades business model, where the seller gives away the razor, but sells the customer blades over and over again.

So, developers give away their app for free and sell add-ons to get the player started. Perhaps you have a music app. Your approach could be to give away the app, but sell the music that goes with the app. The more songs that are sold, the better for you. Another example would be a fishing app that users can download for free. The first couple of fishing locations are free, but if the user wants additional locations, they have to purchase them for $0.99 each, for example. This is a very good approach because it allows the app vendor to sell the customer products over and over again. It is quite likely that many games will adopt this model in the future if they are serious about gaining strong momentum and achieving repeat sales from the same app buyer.

Summary

If possible, always have a pricing strategy before you post your app for sale. Know exactly where you plan to set your app price. Be sure to research your entire category for app prices. If you are selling a game, be sure to look at the categories of games for your specific prices. Reports by research companies such as Distomo can be very helpful in providing the latest app-pricing information.

Keep your price set for the first few months so you can gather sufficient data about how sales are trending. Product reviews will often reveal that your price is right or your price is too high. If your price is too high, you can do a price drop. A price drop is a reason to issue a press release. You should also make it known on your product website and on the Android Market.

Temporary price drops should have an expiration date associated with them to help spur the buyer into action. If a promotion shows that your sales increase dramatically, you may want to consider permanently dropping your price.

16

App Promotions and Cross-Selling

Promotions, plain and simple, provide a marketing strategy to help your customers make a buying decision. Cross-selling is a technique used to sell more products to your existing customers. We're all somewhat familiar with promotions and cross-selling, even if only when we buy products such as cars, furniture, clothing, and electronics. In fact, there aren't too many areas where promotions and cross-selling aren't used. Go out to dinner and you are cross-sold to buy an appetizer or soup or salad with your dinner. Even your neighborhood dentist uses these techniques to sell teeth whitening and other add-on services.

Promotions and cross-selling are so popular because these techniques work! Most consumers like to get a deal on their purchases or win a prize. Many consumers, when prompted, will buy additional products that are complementary to their purchase. Buy a sofa and you're asked if you want stain guard protection. Many will sign up. Buy a TV and you're asked if you want the extended warranty. Again, many will sign up.

In the app world, developers can also use promotions and cross-selling techniques to help sell more Android apps and add-ons to these apps. In the highly competitive Android Market, you need every edge you can find to help maximize your revenue. In this chapter we'll first take a look at promotional marketing and how you can apply this technique to selling your Android apps. In the second half, we'll discuss cross-selling ideas that can help you increase your app sales. Just think about it. If you sell an app for $0.99 and you are able to sell an add-on for an additional $0.99, that's a 100% gain in your sales from that customer.

In this chapter, we will take a look at how to create promotions for your Android apps and how to utilize cross-selling techniques to help increase your app sales.

Promotional Marketing for Android Apps

Promotional marketing attempts to get people to make a buying decision. You can create various incentives to move someone to make an app purchase, including contests, half-off sales, and free downloads. Before you begin an app promotion, review the following questions:

- **What is your reason for the promotion?** Are you just trying to sell more apps or are you trying to build a following? If you are doing a temporary app price reduction, for example, you are trying to bolster app sales. If you offer the app for free for a limited time, you are trying to build a following. Both are valid reasons for doing a promotion.

- **What is your promotion budget?** If you only have $500 to spend on a promotion, you will plan differently than if you have $5,000 to spend. Don't start a promotion until you know exactly what you can comfortably spend. I give you some ideas in Table 16.1 on promotions you can execute, depending on your budget.

Table 16.1   App Promotions Vary Depending On Your Budget

Budget Amount	Promotional Recommendations
No money	Offer the app for free for a limited time or reduce the app price for a limited time. See Chapter 15, "The App Pricing Rollercoaster," for more information on raising and lowering prices.

Table 16.1   App Promotions Vary Depending On Your Budget

Budget Amount	Promotional Recommendations
Up to $500	Here are some contest ideas: • Give away an Android tablet to the winner who makes the most creative use of your app. The contest should run for a couple of months at least. • Give away five $100 gift card prizes to the best entries. The gift cards can be for almost any store. You can also change up the amounts, giving first place a prize of $250, second place $150, and third place $100, or any other option. • Give away savings bonds that have a maturity value of $250 or $500 for the person who makes the best use of your app as judged by your expert panel. You can purchase bonds for less than face value, of course. • Give away app development books, online app development courses, t-shirts, mugs, caps, and so on, to app users who submit how they've used your app (while supplies last, of course).
Up to $1000	Consider all the previous options or consider a contest for a PC (value $999) for the person judged to use your app in the most creative or innovative way, as judged by your outside panel.
Over $1,000	Consider all the previous options or consider a contest for a trip to a certain destination, such as a Google/Android event or another locale. The trip requires the winner to be published on your website, along with a press release and description of how he or she has used your app to create certain content or solve a certain problem.

• **How will you measure the success of your app promotion?** You'll need to set some objectives and then measure them. Perhaps you want to capture 500 email addresses and have 350 customers purchase the app through your promotion.

• **What type of promotion do you think will work best for your app?** If your app is a creative type of app (say, photography), you could sponsor a contest for the funniest photo and have an outside panel of judges choose the best use of your app.

Note

Any contests or sweepstakes offered by a company that require a purchase to enter are illegal in the United States. Check your own country or state government agency to make sure you comply with regulations and laws. Make sure your promotion is in compliance with all laws.

Here are just a few ideas you can employ to increase sales and/or awareness of your app. Keep in mind that you need to choose promotions that are appropriate for your particular app. Some apps may not lend themselves well to doing a contest, but might do well if you mark the price to free for a temporary period of time. Other apps are more appropriate for cross-selling, which is discussed later in this chapter.

- **Contests**—Everyone enjoys winning a contest, even though it doesn't happen too often for most of us. Having a contest allows you to acquire new clients and create awareness about your app. For example, Smule, Inc., an iPhone app development company in California, offered a contest giving away a three-day all-expense-paid trip to San Francisco and to its corporate offices. The contest required you to use one of its apps in creating a video or song. If you wanted to enter the contest, you had to use one of its apps so your creative work could be judged. A screen capture of the contest page is shown in Figure 16.1. This is not a raffle or drawing; it is a contest where your entry is judged. Here is some of the text from the contest's rules. A similar type of contest could be used for your Android apps just as easily. Notice the strong tie-in to using one of the company's apps:

  "Just make sure to Smulify your video somehow. You need to use at least one Smule app in the video—make music with *Ocarina* and *Leaf Trombone*, tell a scary story with *Sonic Vox*, or sing a song with *I Am T-Pain*."

  You will want your contest to run for a few months to give it some time to attract attention and help your app sales to grow. This type of contest could have first, second, and third place winners. The prizes could be in cash, savings bonds, trips, hardware, and so on. However, be sure you understand all tax laws regarding prizes for your country before launching a contest with prizes.

- **Periodic giveaways**—You can also create an ongoing promotion where you select certain entries of your app being used in creative situations. Buyers can go to your website and enter their name and email address with a description of how your app has helped them. You feature the

Figure 16.1   Smule had a contest giving away a free trip to California for the best song or video entry using one of its apps.

best write-ups on your product home page each week. If a buyer's use of your app is selected, you can send him or her a t-shirt or small gift for being selected as this week's best user of your app.

- **Half-off sales**—Half-off sales (or third off, quarter off, and so on) attract buyers' attention and help to spur sales of your app. You can put the verbiage in your Android Market text announcing the sale or you can post a temporary app icon with the sale announcement. The announcement can go for a few days or a few weeks, depending on the sales results. If you have strong results you can extend the promotion by saying, "Back by popular demand," or something like that. If sales do not improve fairly quickly you can set the price back to where it was before the promotion and look to other ideas.

✉ *Note*

Always set a timeframe for your promotion. For example, you can say "Ends at Midnight, June 15th" or "Sale Only This Weekend." This will help your buyers to make a purchase decision more quickly if they know the clock is ticking.

- **Free (for a time)**—Does giving away free samples work? Yes, most definitely! You don't want to give it away forever, of course, but for a limited time. You can specify in your press release or in an announcement on the Android Market and the product website that the app is being given away for free for a limited time. If you have a well-written app, the free users will give you positive word of mouth, which should help your sales.

Table 16.1 gives you some recommendations for promotions you can employ at different budget levels. Again, consider whether or not your app is appropriate for a promotion such as a contest. These are just a few examples of what you can do in the way of promotions. The sky is the limit. Just make sure you stay within the laws of your state or country.

 Note

Whenever you have a contest you'll want to require entrants to provide their name, email address, and phone number to contact the winners. The contest will help you build your company's database of customers for future promotions and app sales.

Cross-Selling

Cross-selling involves offering your buyer another product that is complementary to what you are already selling. In the app world this involves offering app buyers another app or add-on pack to whatever they have already bought. Amazon perfected this approach by displaying other items that similar buyers have purchased along with the item being displayed. This marketing approach has dramatically lifted sales for Amazon across the entire website.

Google, perhaps taking a cue from Amazon, also includes the icons for similar apps purchased through the "View More Applications" link. The Android Market is helping you out by displaying your app along with other apps when someone does a search on the Android Market for a particular type of app. Depending on how many similar apps there are, your app could be displayed frequently when someone does a search for the same type of app.

Every customer is a valuable asset for you. For certain apps, you can create additional add-on packs for your app. For example, Figure 16.2 shows a very popular app that has both a free and a paid version. The free version includes an announcement at the bottom of the app inviting you to purchase and download the paid app instantly through the Android device. This is an example of up-selling the app buyer from a less expensive (free) app to the paid version of the app.

Figure 16.2   The *Shotgun* app invites the user to purchase the paid version to avoid further ads.

Another way to cross-sell is to provide an announcement to purchase other apps within your app. You can provide a separate screen with your other apps to promote within the app your buyer already has. Also, some developers have formed consortiums to help each other sell their app. This is something you would have to arrange between fellow developers because Google does not provide a means to handle this type of transaction from the Android Market payment perspective. However, other means could be employed to track where a purchase originated from. See Chapter 17, "Using Android Analytics," for more information on using analytics to track sales of your apps.

Although not available yet, the Android should enable in-app cross-selling for the developer so their developers can sell more apps. Anywhere that you can post text about your app you should be thinking about cross-selling opportunities. In other words, you have an opportunity to cross-sell on your product website, the Android Market, and the Android device. The biggest factors in influencing the success of the cross-sell will be price and reputation. If your app or brand has established a good reputation, it will also be easier to cross-sell a buyer on additional functionality or add-ons. Always be thinking about how you can market to your existing customers. It's far easier to sell to them than it is to get a new customer. Here are some other ideas to consider as you cross-sell your app:

- **Cross-sell on your product website and within the Android Market.** Use some space on your Android Market text to mention your other apps. At the bottom of your text you can put a note for buyers to check out your other apps as well. Be sure to do the same thing on your website. For each product displayed be sure to show other app icons to the right or left of the screen displaying the other apps you have for sale.

The Android Market also helps you out with cross-selling by showcasing other apps you have for sale on the lower left side of your app's display. This is a big advantage that the Android Market provides to help you cross-sell or up-sell your customers on other apps you have written.

- **Cross-sell to build your brand.** If you are looking for a way to build your brand, you can always sell other items on your website, such as mugs, caps, and t-shirts with your company's logo or app's icon. Are you going to make tons of money doing this? No! But, you will help to build a following for your apps and establish your brand more firmly with your buyers and site visitors.

Up-Selling

The definition of up-selling is moving someone from a less expensive product to a more expensive one. Auto dealers will advertise a less expensive car to get people to visit their showrooms. Once at the dealer's, potential buyers will be shown multiple models of cars. The dealer knows that the chances of them buying the original car that brought them in are slim.

The most common example of up-selling with an Android app is when a user downloads a free app and then converts to the paid version of the app, as mentioned earlier. Your marketing messaging must invite the user to upgrade to your paid app. Do not assume that just because you have a free version of your app that customers will instinctively upgrade to the paid version. They need to be prompted, prodded, coerced, coached, cajoled, and invited to move over to the paid app. You can do this in the following ways:

- Prompt the paid version within a menu screen of your free app.

- Invite users to upgrade at the bottom or top of your free app.

- Tell users that they will no longer have ads if they buy the paid version.

- Explain to users how many more features they will get with the paid version.

- Prompt users periodically within the free app to give the paid version a try.

Note

Do not annoy your customers by bombarding them constantly with invitations to buy your paid app. Just remember to push your paid app where appropriate in the menu page, with an icon they can click to get more information, or at the bottom of the first screen of the free app.

Summary

Promotions and cross-selling should be a part of your overall app marketing plan. You can't afford not to explore these approaches when the competition for apps is so strong. Promotions, when done right, can help you increase your profits and raise your brand awareness. Another benefit of doing promotions is that they can be repeated multiple times, especially if you find success with one type of promotion over another.

Contests can be done as promotions, even on a limited budget. You can sponsor a contest where the user of your app demonstrates how he or she has used your app in a creative way. You can give away cash prizes, hardware, software, t-shirts, hats, mugs, and other items. Contests will drive awareness and downloads for your app.

Using cross-selling and up-selling techniques on your app buyers is another effective approach. You can cross-sell add-on packs for your apps or subscriptions that generate additional or recurring revenue for you. Always attempt to up-sell your buyer from a free version of your app to the paid version. Do not assume that if you have a free app that your user will automatically move to the paid version. He or she must be invited to do so.

17

Using Android Analytics

Don't let the word analytics *scare you off. From an Android marketing perspective, being able to gather information about how your buyers are using your apps is extremely helpful to making adjustments to your marketing plan. Marketing is a dynamic activity. You'll find that some strategies work better to market your app than others. Analytics data helps you make better decisions about what's working and what's not for your particular circumstances.*

In this chapter we will explore the basics of using analytics and how these tools can help you improve your apps and target your sales more closely. Analytics makes use of simple code that you insert into your Android application to collect information about your users' actions. The information is gathered periodically on the local smartphone and then it's transmitted to the company who has licensed the code to you.

You can then view the results for your individual app or in aggregate for multiple similar apps. If a connection is not available at the time of transmission, the analytics software will try again when a connection is established.

Analytics data allows you to make better marketing decisions because you will know who is using your app, when they are using it, and how frequently it gets opened. You can develop more targeted ad campaigns, focus on refining specific features, or identify certain user groups for your app. As long as the information you are gathering is not intrusive to the end user and you are not violating any privacy laws, you'll find this type of data to give you the competitive edge you need in the app world.

 Note

Apps that have access to location data must have the user's consent. The user must opt in for location tracking. Clearly explain this in your terms of service. See the "Analytics and Privacy" section at the end of this chapter for more information about protecting privacy and complying with the law.

Analytics Components

This section outlines the key components and features of app analytics tools. Analytics helps you track how your apps are being used and which features are being used the most. This key information can help you design better products and target your marketing to highlight specific value that your app provides.

Track Your App's Sales

From a pricing perspective, analytics can also help you to assess how your app is being used in the market. For non-game apps you can measure the frequency of use for your app over time and see if it makes sense to drop your price or give your app away for free and pursue an ad revenue model. Analytics provides another data point to help you make a pricing decision.

Track Your App's Location

Another helpful feature of most analytics software is that you can track your app's use by location. This requires the user to opt in to provide this data and therefore does not give a complete picture of usage because not all users will permit it. However, it will give you a general idea of where your app is being used in different parts of the world. This can help you make advertising and product decisions.

For example, if you see that your app is doing really well in the UK, you can dig a little deeper to discover why that's the case. You may want to look at making adjustments to your app.

If you are able to determine where your app is being run *and* which features are being used, you can tailor your advertising efforts either to that geography or to other geographies that might respond in a similar fashion to the same type of marketing.

Track Your App's Usage

As a developer, you can also discover how many times an app is opened during the day. You can identify if your app is used frequently, several times a day, or infrequently, such as once a week or month. A game app, for example, that is used several times a day indicates that the game has that winning formula everyone's looking for. A game that is downloaded and then rarely played is a sure indication that it doesn't have the staying power needed to become a hit. It may cause you, as a developer, to make adjustments to improve the app to drive future success.

Tracking average time used for your app can also help you determine whether your app is going to have longevity in the market. If you feel that the average amount of time your app should be used is 20 minutes and you're seeing it used only ten, you can do further research to figure out why this is happening. It could be an indication that your app is not easily understood or that the users are getting bored with it too quickly. Both cases are cause for concern and can be addressed. Without analytics, you'll never know why someone is abandoning your app.

Analytics can help you track your sales and the number of users for each app. You can then look at how frequently your app is being used and which features are getting the most use. This can be a big benefit for a game developer who wants to know which features are being used the most and which are used the least. This information can inform future development decisions and help determine the focus for subsequent revisions. Some features that don't get much use could be eliminated altogether or replaced with new features. Other features that get used somewhat more frequently could be enhanced. You are essentially gathering product use data that you're not going to get any other way.

Track Specific App Events

Events include almost anything that occurs during the operation of your app. Events can be tracked for frequency, duration, or a combination of factors. A developer can track a feature being used, a button being pressed, or the time to complete a task. If you are selling an educational app, you may want to get some information on how long it takes the typical user to complete an exercise or how long it takes to take a quiz. Developers can also gather valuable information on how long a certain process or task takes a user. For example, an app that handles finances might track how long it takes the typical user to balance his or her checkbook. Understanding this information allows the developer to modify the code, focusing on improving the most-used features.

Event tracking is like having a user panel give you feedback about your app. Rather than a live user panel reviewing your app and providing input, you are gathering the data electronically. Precision apps such as games will benefit from gathering analytics data on how they are being used. Levels of play can be analyzed to see if the player is moving through the game in a normal manner or if some adjustments need to be made. You want your game to be more challenging at each level but not so much that it's impossible to win. Analytics will help you gather crucial data to make just the right adjustments for a game.

Measure App Interface Patterns

Developers can also use analytics data to improve and test user interfaces for their Android apps. For example, you can measure how many times a certain menu page is opened or how many times a particular button is pressed. This data will give a picture of how your app's interface is being used. Perhaps you find that your user is going to a particular screen out of sequence, contrary to what you have pro-grammed. This could prompt you to make changes to the screen flow of your app.

Utilizing analytics also allows you to claim, rightfully, that you are in touch with your customers and willing to listen to their product suggestions. Other than reviews, which are often very limited in the information they provide, this is one of the best ways to gather accurate product use data without employing a costly user panel to review and test the product.

Top Analytics Vendors

Many Android analytics vendors offer quality products. For brevity, here are a few of the more popular vendors. These vendors offer free analytics to the developer community with some feature enhancements available for a fee.

Flurry/Pinch Media

These two companies have merged. Both companies provided analytics software for the Android with some similar features and some differing features. They are plan-ning to merge the feature sets together and deliver enhancements to the combined solution as they have stated in the FAQs of their press release from 12/22/2009:

While Flurry and Pinch Media analytics services shares many similarities in terms of what is tracked, there are meaningful differences between each service. We are currently evaluating the feature-set of each stand-alone service, and will be combining them into a "super-set" of features for all to use in the new, unified service. So whether customers come from the Pinch side or the Flurry side, they will each have access to new features. For example, Flurry uniquely provides support for other platforms like Android as well as a unique click-stream tracking feature called "User Paths." Pinch Media offers unique features including jailbroken phone detection and the ability to evaluate data by cohorts vs. absolute date. In addition to this, the new, unified Flurry service will add more new features, delivering the largest set of relevant features requested by our customer base.

Flurry Analytics Features

Here is a quick rundown of the cost and benefits of Flurry Analytics:

Cost:

- Analytics free to developers; optional (paid) solutions are forthcoming.

Benefits:

- Increase revenue by satisfying users and increasing retention rates.
- Save time and money, focusing on features users care about most.
- Improve decisions—know exactly how, where, when, and by whom an application is used.
- Increase coverage by identifying problem handsets.

A screen with some of the analytics and graphs that Flurry provides is shown in Figure 17.1, whereas Figure 17.2 shows an example of the Pinch Analytics screen. I'm not sure how the combined interface will look at this point. Also, at the time of this writing, Flurry AppCircle ad revenue software was in beta testing.

Mobclix

Mobclix is a mobile application platform that, as part of its solution, delivers analytics data for the Android along with its ad network. Mobclix is one of the largest mobile ad exchange networks and gives developers a sound technology if they decide to pursue an ad-generated business model.

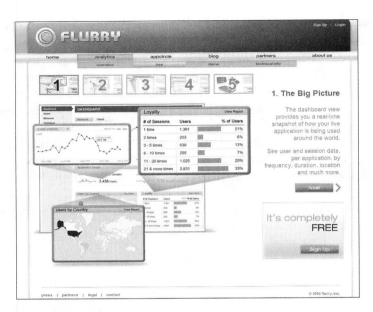

Figure 17.1   Sample analytics from the Flurry Analytics software for the Android.

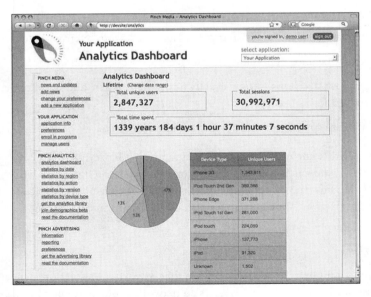

Figure 17.2   Sample analytics from Pinch Analytics software for the Android.

Mobclix Analytics

Here's a quick rundown of the cost and benefits of Mobclix Analytics:

Cost:

- Analytics free to developers.

Benefits:

- Determine how much time someone spends in your app.
- Determine whether users are on Wi-Fi or carrier.
- Determine what version of the Android OS is being used.
- Track the health of your app.
- Find out how often the app fails.
- Employ full event tracking.
- Pop up requests to gather data, with additional opt-out button.
- Get feedback directly from your users with comment plug-ins.

Figure 17.3 shows a section of the Mobclix website that allows you to download its software development kit (SDK) and implement its analytics along with its ad revenue software. The SDK installs in under 15 minutes, so it's quite easy for any developer to implement and realize its benefits.

Analytics and Privacy

Although mobile analytics offers a great mechanism for gathering valuable user data, you do have to be aware of privacy laws and make sure you follow all Google guidelines when gathering data. Always explain in your app what data you will be gathering and how you intend to use the data.

You can explain this information in a terms of service (ToS) document, which should be displayed within your app in English. The user should be required to read and accept the terms of service by checking a box or clicking OK. Always state your intent for gathering such information and how it will be used.

Figure 17.3   Mobclix Analytics can be installed into your app with a simple download of the SDK.

Managing User Privacy Expectations

Although some users may be concerned about their privacy, all data is gathered anonymously. On Pinch Media's own website, the company states that when Pinch Analytics is installed within an application, the following information is sent back on each application run:

- A hardware identifier not connectable to any personal information

- The model of the phone (HTC, Samsung, LG, Droid 2, and so on) and operating system (2.1, 2.2, and so on)

- The application's name and version

- The result of a check to see if the device has been jailbroken

- The result of a check to see if the application has been stolen and the developer hasn't been paid

- The length of time the application was run

- The user's location (if the user explicitly agrees to share it)

- The gender and age of the user (if the application uses Facebook Connect)

None of this information can identify the individual. No names, phone numbers, email addresses, or anything else considered personally identifiable information is ever collected. The information sent from applications, when it arrives at the servers, is quickly converted to aggregated reports—unprocessed data is processed as quickly as possible. The aggregated reports show counts and averages, not anything user specific. For instance, a developer can see the following information:

- The number of distinct users who've accessed the application

- The average length of time the application was used

- The percentage of phones using each operating system

- The percentage of each model of phone (3G, 3GS, and so on)

- A breakdown of user locations by country, state, and major metropolitan area (for example, 20,000 in USA, 700 in New York state, 500 in New York City)

- The percentage of users of each gender

- The percentage of users by "age bucket" (21–29, 30–39, and so on)

Summary

Developers can gain a lot from using analytics software in their apps. This software can undoubtedly help you produce a better app for your customer, make adjustments to marketing and pricing, and plan for future enhancements if you determine your app would be a candidate for using analytics.

Implementing the code for analytics is not difficult, does not cause latency in your app, and is free for the developer. Analytics providers show aggregate data and never divulge any personal IDs or other information about a specific user. However, you need to be sure to inform your users that you are using analytics and seek their consent before transmitting any data.

18

Why Have a Marketing Plan?

Some app developers who are not as familiar with marketing may ask why anyone should spend time developing a marketing plan. The thought of creating a marketing plan conjures up ideas that it must be huge, painful, and lengthy. This is simply not true. A marketing plan needs to be long enough to define a strategy and the components that will give your app a good chance of sales success. It does not need to be composed of binders full of lengthy information. In Chapter 19, "Components of an App Marketing Plan," we discuss the components of an app marketing plan. Don't worry about the length of your plan. Rather, make sure it defines how you are going to achieve success selling your app.

Some developers can cite all kinds of examples of successful apps that don't or didn't have any kind of marketing plan. Although this is true, they are the standout apps that got a lucky break when the Android Market was in its infancy. A marketing plan is going to improve your chances of getting that lucky break. Remember what Thomas Jefferson said about being lucky? "I find that the harder I work, the more luck I seem to have."

The first thing to understand about a marketing plan is that there is a difference between a marketing strategy and a marketing plan. A marketing strategy can be defined as a summary of your company's apps and their position as they relate to your competition. For example, if you are a developer of game apps, you could define your marketing strategy as geared toward a male, teenage audience in the category of racing games. Your marketing plans are the specific actions you intend to take to meet the goals of your marketing strategy. Your marketing plan might include releasing a new racing game app every three months so that you have four apps within the first year of business.

Another marketing strategy could consist of developing the best financial Android app in your category on the Android Market. The marketing plan then could spell out how you intend to make the strategy a reality, such as partnering with a major bank or other financial institution to distribute the app to realize thousands of downloads.

A good marketing plan will help you to improve your odds against more experienced competitors on the Android Market (EA and Sega come to mind) as well as newly emerging ones. The marketing plan enables you to recognize and take action on any trends that other app developers may have overlooked, and to develop and expand your own select group of loyal customers now and into the future.

The plan also means that you have carefully considered how to produce an app that is innovative, unique, and marketable, improving your chances of stable sales and profits, and providing incentive for customers to stick with you for the next release or new app. So, following the popular Top Ten List format, here are the top ten reasons you should create a marketing plan. An explanation of each item is provided in the sections that follow.

1. Focuses on your target market

2. Allocates marketing funds

3. Measures your progress

4. Provides a roadmap for growth

5. Helps you obtain funding

6. Coordinates your app launches

7. Sets realistic sales targets

8. Evaluates your competitors

9. Sets prices and defines promotions

10. Defines a strong value proposition

1. Focuses on Your Target Market

Having a marketing plan will help you focus on your target market and identify any gaps in the market that could provide new or unique opportunities for you. Many developers have an idea for an app in their head and they think they've got it all figured out without taking any time to assess their market. Does the app idea in your head address a few thousand people or does it address hundreds of thousands? Is the idea only going to appeal to a small group of hobbyists or can the idea be global? Just build an app and they will come is often what developers think. A marketing plan will cause you to carefully outline your target market and help you make the decision whether or not to proceed with your idea.

Without a marketing plan, your app may turn out entirely different from where you started. This may be okay if you produce a better app, but in most cases the app ends up being somewhat disjointed and unfocused without a plan. Your customers will immediately recognize this in the app, and the reviews will not be favorable. Start out with a clear idea of who you are developing the app for and what benefits they will gain from using it. Having a written record of this will help you gain a competitive advantage in the app market.

2. Allocates Marketing Funds

A marketing plan will help you identify the most cost-effective ways of reaching your target audience and performing the functions needed to reach that audience. For example, banner ads might work well to advertise your app after you have done some research on how they work and what sites might be the best to take your message to the right audience.

You also save money by cutting out unnecessary expenses and avoiding marketing ideas that aren't going to yield you any results. So many developers approach marketing with a scattered approach, trying one thing and then another without too much success. They end up wasting a lot of money on programs, which could have been avoided if they had spent a little time on a marketing plan. A good plan will allocate funds appropriately for your budget and help you reach your target audience as well as keep your activities and budgets on track.

3. Measures Your Progress

 You've heard the saying, "You can't track what you can't measure." In order to see results from your marketing efforts, you have to be able to measure your progress. Now, some marketing efforts are more difficult to measure than others. You can measure how many people open emails or how many click through to your website based on a particular campaign. But measuring brand awareness is a lot more difficult. You know you've made progress with brand awareness when bloggers are talking about your apps and you're seeing multiple reviews come through.

A marketing plan can help you track your progress from initial development of your app through product launch, along with the various marketing campaigns you employ to sell your Android app. Much of the measurement aspect of a marketing plan will include budgets. You'll set a budget for your app development costs, and you'll set budgets for marketing campaigns. You should measure the amount you spend on a campaign and the number of sales derived from that campaign. Although you won't be able to pinpoint exact sales, your campaigns should yield a noticeable uptick in app sales. If you don't see that uptick in sales after implementing an ad campaign, email campaign, promotional campaign, or other campaign, you'll need to make adjustments to your marketing activities to create better results.

4. Provides a Roadmap for Growth

 If you intend to create multiple apps and build a brand, having a marketing plan is a must. With a marketing plan you can create a roadmap (timeline) for when you want to release each app into the Android Market. Your plan can include a launch calendar, and you can strategically launch each app in succession. Without a calendar to track all your development and launch activities, you will experience confusion in building your brand.

Companies that provide serial types of apps will benefit by having a plan. A serial app could be one that identifies other apps for purchase on the Android Market. For example, you might develop an app that identifies the latest medical apps and provides that list inside the app. You may build an app that aggregates the best finance apps into your app. Your marketing plan will also define marketing approaches you want to take with each app that is released. Your strategy for your first app may be to release it as a free app to gain brand awareness and followers. The next app you release may be a paid app that is a follow-on to the free app. Your entire strategy can be outlined in your marketing plan.

5. Helps You Obtain Funding

Perhaps you have not given much thought to funding your app endeavors. Some developers want to build a formidable company around selling apps on the Android Market and on other mobile phone platforms.

One of the key requirements for businesspeople seeking funding is that they develop a solid business plan—and this would include a marketing plan. A marketing plan is going to help your investors understand the type of apps you are going to develop, who your competitors are, and how you intend to bring your app to market.

The marketing plan provides your outside financiers with the confidence that you know your market and that you know how to achieve your objectives. The key to obtaining funding is demonstrating that you have a solid market for your apps and that you have a clearly defined strategy to meet your sales goals. Having a great idea for an app will not be enough. You'll have to demonstrate that you have the experience and vision to make your apps successful in a very competitive market.

6. Coordinates Your App Launches

A marketing plan is going to help you keep track of all the pieces of your product launch. From your marketing calendar, you can track the following:

- The date your app was submitted for review

- The date (approximately) your app will be released

- Reviewers and bloggers you have contacted to review your app

- The date(s) for your press release(s)

- Articles you have lined up with magazines, newspapers, and other outlets

- Promotions you have planned to launch your app

With your plan you can coordinate the timing of a press release to coincide roughly with the release and posting of your app on the Android Market. If you have a press release that has been correctly written with the right key words, and a few reviews in place, you will see strong pickup in the news about your app, and your website will see a bump in traffic, which will lead to stronger initial sales of your app.

7. Sets Realistic Sales Targets

A marketing plan will help you set realistic sales goals. After you have done a thorough analysis of the scope of your market and your competitors, you are in a position to do more accurate sales forecasting based on your intended promotions. You need to be able to visualize your sales goal in an easy-to-track spreadsheet. Google provides daily, weekly, and monthly sales reports for you to track your progress. These reports can be easily downloaded into an Excel spreadsheet for viewing.

Other companies out there provide tracking services if you want to get very detailed metrics on sales progress for your apps. One of the companies is AppClix (www.appclix.com). This company provides analytics as well as sales trend graphs and other statistical information. AppClix charges a one-time fee for its services but also offers a free trial version of its tool, which can be downloaded from the AppClix website.

8. Evaluates Your Competitors

Your marketing plan will have a section with information on key competitors to your app. Competitive information is crucial in order to develop a better app and to remain competitive in your category. If you have your competitors clearly in focus with a marketing plan, you're more likely to stay up to date on when they release updates and what new features they have added to their apps.

You can utilize a number of websites to monitor when new apps are released into a category where you have an app. One such website is AppBrain (www.appbrain. com), which allows you to create your own app account and an app watch list based on various functions. So, if a new review is posted about an app you're track-ing, you will receive a notification. This is a great tool for automating the tracking of your competitors. The home page of this website is shown in Figure 18.1.

9. Sets Prices and Defines Promotions

Pricing is a big part of marketing an Android app, and you'll want to spend some time writing down detailed notes about how you arrived at your price and what you intend to do over time when making adjustments to pricing your app. Your pricing information should include competitors' pricing and other notes as to why you believe your app will sell for a certain price.

Welcome to AppBrain

Thanks for joining AppBrain! Please install the free app "AppBrain Market Sync" on your phone to sync with this website.

We sent you an email with a link to the app (you can open it on the phone).

Here is how it works:

- Select the apps you would like to have on this website.
- Then start the AppBrain Market Sync app on your phone
- It will then sync and install the apps you selected earlier on the webpage

We would love to hear your feedback. Please don't hesitate to contact us if you have any questions or feature requests.

- **Find your friends on AppBrain and what apps they have**
- **Browse the hottest Android apps**

Getting the app on your phone is easy:

- You can find it by searching for "AppBrain" in the Android market
- Or go to http://www.appbrain.com/install on your Android phone.
- Or scan the QR code below with the barcode scanner app.

Figure 18.1   AppBrain allows you to track new apps and changes, reviews, etc. to new and existing apps on the Android Market.

Your marketing plan will also include promotions that you intend to have during the next 12 months. You may offer a launch special, such as half off to the first 500 customers (or for a limited amount of time). You may want to offer a contest announcing your app and give away an Android tablet to the person who wins your contest.

10. Defines a Strong Value Proposition

Your marketing plan should include a definition of your app's value proposition or key values. Remember this information is what you use to develop your Android Market and website copy and describes what your app does and why it's valuable to the customer. A strong value proposition takes some time and effort to develop. You want to make sure you have this written down as a key point in your marketing plan.

Refer to your value proposition(s) frequently so that you keep your messaging on track as your app progresses from development to finished product, up through the launch. Use your value propositions(s) to support your advertising. This would include banner ads, email blasts, promotions, contests, and so on.

Summary

A marketing plan is essential to growing your Android app business. A marketing plan will force you to carefully consider how to produce an app that is innovative, unique, and marketable. This will improve your chances of stable sales and profits considerably.

A good marketing plan is your blueprint for action. Build your marketing plan with an end goal in mind to develop your brand and grow app sales. Follow the steps in your plan much like a carpenter follows a set of house plans when building a home. A marketing plan is a more sure route to gaining Android Market success then just trying to wing it without any real idea of how you intend to achieve success.

Components of an App Marketing Plan

A marketing plan is your personal roadmap of how you intend to make your app produce a profit once it's released on the Android Market. An Android app marketing plan has some basic components that you should attempt to include in your plan. Not all of these components may apply to your plan based on the type of Android app you are developing. A game app, for example, may have fewer components to its plan than a personal finance app, for example.

Your marketing plan can be simple or extensive, depending on your audience (for example, venture funding or angel investors). If the audience is only you (solo developer), the plan can be quite simple—a couple of pages perhaps. If you are a small firm with a few employees or if you have a few investors, you will need to create a more comprehensive marketing plan. All marketing plans should have the basics, including the sections described in this chapter. These sections would be created in Word and printed so that they can easily be reviewed by your team.

Note

A marketing plan is a strategic summary that demonstrates your understanding of your product, audience, message, and value. A marketing plan
can be an indicator of how successful your app will be when launched to
the Android Market.

Table 19.1 shows the key components of an app marketing plan. The length of the
plan is not important. The information covered in the plan is what counts. After
reviewing the table, we discuss each component in more detail in the following
sections.

Table 19.1   Typical Android App Marketing Plan Components

App Marketing Plan Component	Description (Possible Ideas)
Marketing goals and objectives	Overall objective for your app. Build a brand.
Sales objectives	Gain market share. Achieve huge downloads.
Profit objectives	Break even in one month. Generate a certain amount of money in the first three months.
Pricing objectives	Price high. Reduce price later.
Product objectives	Create game app based on PC version.
Market analysis	How large is my market?
Demographics	Who is my market? Teens? Elderly?
Competition	Who are my top three competitors in this app category?
Consumer analysis	How much do typical consumers spend on this type of app? How often do they buy?
SWOT analysis	What are the strengths, weaknesses, opportunities, and threats to building such an app?
App functionality	What special features will my app have that will blow away the competition?
Promotions	What are the promotions I intend to use to market my app, generate awareness, and increase sales?
Pricing	What is my pricing strategy?
Financials	How much will this app cost to develop and market? What are the dangers to developing this app? What if development time takes longer? (Include key metrics here, such as breakeven charts, revenue projections, and so on.)
Calendar	What are my development, launch, and promotion timelines?

Note

To see a very nice sample marketing plan for Android apps, go to the following link: www.morebusiness.com/templates_worksheets/bplans/printpre.brc

The sample plan shows tables and graphics that will help you visualize many of the financial areas discussed in this chapter.

Marketing Goals and Objectives

To introduce your marketing plan, provide a brief "mission statement" for your business. A mission statement is very simple but clearly communicates your goals to your customers and potential customers—for example, "Develop the best productivity app for pharmaceutical sales reps" or "Develop the most innovative air combat game ever created." Once you have a written mission statement, you can move on to determining your objectives: sales, profit, pricing, and product.

Product Objectives

In this section you want to list your product objectives. What is it that you want your app to accomplish for your buyer?

- Much like what you would be doing for your prices, focus on the wants, needs, and perceptions of your app consumers.

- Show how you will attract more buyers of your app. Determine the decision criteria of customer preference toward your app, such as price, number of features, and so on.

- Indicate the goals you may have for resolving customer complaints concerning your app or fixing bugs.

Your Android App Sales Objectives

This section lists what you have established as your key sales objectives:

- Compare your chances for future sales with past performance, or provide a general estimate of new sales through "guesstimates," as we covered in the chapters of Part III of this book. You'll never get it exact, but you should have a forecast of potential revenue.

- Identify industry-wide challenges and create strategies to overcome them. This will also demonstrate that you have the necessary foresight to allow you to recognize problems in the future. For example, the fact that so many apps are priced at $0.99 is an industry-wide problem in my opinion. What can you do to overcome this low price point?

- Create a goal for how many downloads you would like to achieve on a daily basis. One hundred? Five hundred? One thousand per day? Write down this goal.

Profit Objectives

This section lists what you have established as your profit objectives:

- Include your predictions for profit for the next year for each of the apps you have written. Relate this profit assumption based on the estimated costs to develop your Android app.

- Indicate how you will reinvest some of your profit margin in specific areas of app development, including future releases and marketing activities you might employ.

Pricing Objectives

This section lists what you have established as your pricing objectives:

- Focus on the weaknesses of your competitors by offering better quality at a competitive price. Remember what your own attitudes are toward apps you are familiar with. Remember how you react to low or high prices for poor or marginal quality apps.

- Justifying the pricing for your app while thinking like a customer will give you an advantage. Keep in mind that it's easier to come down in price than go up.

- Survey a sampling of your potential customer group and ask them directly how they feel about competitors' apps and any areas for improvement.

Market Analysis

After completing the objectives section of your plan, you want to create a section for market analysis. This is where you spend some time identifying your market, your competitors, and your chances for success. Going through this exercise will help you evaluate from a more analytical perspective how successful your app might be in the real world.

- Examine whether or not your app has the potential for growth. Be honest with yourself.

- If the market for your app is declining, identify the problems that exist and be able to change the ones you can. Show how you can adapt to changes that you may not control. Think of the *iShoot* example, where the author offered a free "Lite" version of his game and set his sales on fire!

- In a newly emerging and growing market (the best scenario), differentiate yourself from new competitors. Show how you expect to become a dominant game vendor, for example, utilizing the latest technology. Think about the new features coming in version 3 of the Android. Ascertain what new development frontiers are open to you.

- Look for ways to prolong the "life" of your app if you recognize that the market you're getting into is threatened by newly emerging apps. To advance your app in the highly competitive Android Market means finding your "niche," or creating one of your own.

- In your market analysis your focus should be on key areas such as industry-wide sales performance of Android and Android apps. Pinpoint why sales prices (as a whole) may be declining and then carefully consider if you have pricing flexibility with your particular app.

Business Environment

The business environment area of your marketing plan provides information on the demographics for your app. You need to have a clear understanding of your audience so you can create age/gender-appropriate marketing campaigns. You'll spend your marketing funds more wisely and you'll be more accurate in reaching your target audience if you have this information.

Demographics

This section lists what you have established as your demographics for your particular app:

- Describe the population base that exists to support your app sales. Identify the market size for your app as well as the people who make up your app's consumer group—for example, teenagers, young adults, children, females, males.

- Describe the expected response to your advertising and how this will boost sales. Indicate what overall market trends you will be following in order to stay current and "in touch" with your app buyers. What special techniques will you employ to match consumer demands? For example, are you employing social media to drive interest and demand?

Competition

This section lists your most direct competitors:

- Identify your direct competition by naming their apps, describing their capabilities, identifying their share of the market (if you can find this out), and reviewing the weaknesses of their marketing approaches. Perhaps they have done limited marketing and you feel you might have an advantage through better and more consistent marketing.

Consumer Analysis

This section is where you describe your target market and the type of buyer that would most likely buy your app:

- Identify your target market, describing how your app will meet the needs of the buyer better than the competition. List the expectations buyers have for your type of app.

- Identify the segment of the market that will benefit from your app as well as your approach to selling your app to that audience.

- Predict the sales potential that may be realized by tapping into and holding onto your target market and then attracting others through different strategies and approaches. These different approaches can be done at the same time or can be more incremental—obtaining a core audience for your app first and then expanding into the rest of your potential market. Identify the sales potential for each of these target groups.

Strengths, Weaknesses, Opportunities, and Threats (SWOT) Analysis

A SWOT analysis is commonly used in all kinds of marketing, not just software. A SWOT analysis gives companies a more complete view of their products and how they're positioned in the marketplace. A SWOT analysis will help you hone your marketing efforts and spend your limited marketing funds in the best possible areas for maximum sales impact.

Building an app that clearly fills a need to a particular audience allows you to deliver a very concise message to an audience that understands your app's value from the beginning. Not having to convince potential buyers that they need your app is 80% of the battle.

Strengths

This section of the marketing plan is where you list your app's strengths:

- List the strengths of your app, such as number of features, quality of graphics, ease of use, and so on.
- List other assets of your app, such as the following:
  - Innovativeness
  - Camera support
  - Email support
  - Ability to connect to other apps
  - Ability to upload/download data
  - Sound quality
  - Android technology (Accelerometer)
  - Use of other Android graphics capabilities

Weaknesses

This section of the marketing plan is where you list your app's weaknesses. A weakness could simply be a feature that you can't add to the app due to cost or time constraints.

- Describe any areas of weakness in your app. For example, is there a large number of competitors? Is it a difficult app to differentiate?
- List the costs to develop the product that may require a higher price and possibly hinder your sales.
- Recognize the limited impact of a new app on the market—its lack of recognition may be attributed to your inexperience in promoting.

- Recognize that poor performance will mean lower-than-expected profits—which will result in a lot of the money going to reduce your debts rather than contributing to your profitability.

Opportunities

This section of the marketing plan is where you list your app's opportunities. Do you believe your app has the potential to revolutionize how phone calls are made to foreign countries, for example?

- Examine how proper timing, as well as other factors (such as your app's innovativeness), may improve your chances of success.

- Use analytics tools in your app to determine usage patterns (see Flurry.com and Pinch Media).

- Relate your app's focus to a segment of the present market that is being overlooked.

Threats

This section of the marketing plan is where you list your app's threats. What other apps out there could potentially impact your sales?

- List the external threats to your app's success, such as existing and newly emerging competitors, the performance of the overall economy, and your dependency on driving traffic to your personal website and the Android Market.

Marketing Focus

In this section, list the key areas your app will focus on. This type of information includes the basic functions of your app, the type of promotions you intend to use to sell it, and pricing considerations. In other words, if you intend to sell a higher-priced app, your marketing focus should be on greater functionality for the buyer. Someone else may be developing an app that is in the $2.99 range but will have periodic price promotions (discounts) to attract attention and drive sales volume.

Your App's Functionality

This section is where you list your app's functionality and how it's better than any competing app on the market:

- Identify your app by what it is, who will buy it, how much they will pay for it, and how much it will cost for you to produce it. Also indentify why a consumer demand exists for your app and where your app sits in comparison to similar apps now available.

- Describe the marketplace rationale for the differences between your app and a competitor's. Look at quality, price, new ideas/approaches, and how your app appeals to a specific customer base—both existing customers and new customers you hope to attract to the market.

- Be specific about how your app improves upon those apps already existing on the Android Market.

Promotions

In this section of your marketing plan, describe any promotions that you intend to use to market your app:

- Describe the type of promotional methods you will use to spread the word about your app. Identify techniques such as word of mouth, social media, and Internet ads.

- For newspapers and other print mediums, mention if you will be obtaining reviews for your app and in what mediums (for example, professional, recreational, cultural, hobby, special interest, or trade magazines), how often, and the timing of such reviews (seasonal, special issues, and so on).

- Create a list of tradeshows or other forums that might work to showcase your app to your buying audience.

- Explain your use of mediums such as television and radio to conduct interviews where you can discuss your app.

- List promotions through social networks, including Facebook, MySpace, Twitter, and others.

Price

This section of the marketing plan is where you discuss the possible price for your app:

- The price of your app should reflect your overall marketing strategy. Pricing should be competitive as well as a reflection of the quality, costs, and profit margin. Again, I am of the opinion that you should start out higher than $0.99 for most apps.

- List the features of the app to help justify the price, such as six levels of games, complex graphics and charting capabilities, and so on.

- List the strategies you plan to use, such as providing a discount during certain times in order to spur sales of your app and generate some buzz.

Financial Information

In this section you identify the levels of sales you hope to achieve with your apps and how you plan to break even on your apps:

- Show the predicted level of sales with and without the strategies you have outlined in the marketing plan. Show a baseline level of sales and then show the expected increase in sales as they relate to specific marketing techniques you will use.

- Show the market share you hope to attain, based on high, medium, and low estimates for the success of your marketing strategy.

- Forecast the breakeven point for selling your app, in the number of sales in dollars. This will demonstrate your need to realize a certain amount of sales in order to cover your expected costs for the next year. You should forecast for at least one year in advance and at least two years if you are producing multiple apps with your brand.

Marketing Calendar

A marketing calendar will be a crucial part of your marketing plan as you map out the development and marketing aspects of your app. It will keep you focused and driving toward specific dates. Your marketing calendar should answer questions such as the following: How long do you expect your app to take for development? Are there special graphics you need to have developed that might take extra time? What other things might contribute to possible delays in the launch of your app?

You also want to look for opportunities to promote you app around various events during the year, such as complementary product launches, tradeshows, and conferences. You first begin by reviewing a 12-month calendar so that you have a picture of the coming year. Start by considering holidays throughout the year—do any lend themselves as promotional opportunities for your app sales? You can use these holidays as promotional opportunities on your personal website. Next is a list of holidays and promotions to consider:

- **New Year's Day**—Almost all apps can leverage something around New Year's, such as getting organized, making a fresh start, keeping resolutions, and so on.

- **Valentine's Day**—Great time to promote lifestyle apps.

- **St. Patrick's Day**—Fun holiday to promote "green" apps.

- **Memorial Day**—Traditional start-of-summer travel and vacations. Does your app have a play here?

- **Independence Day (Fourth of July)**—Promote patriotic-themed apps or other activities related to the holiday.

- **Labor Day**—Traditional end-of-summer travel and vacations. Travel apps could fit in here.

- **Halloween**—Fun holiday for game apps.

- **Veteran's Day**—Great holiday to support the troops! Offer a percentage of daily app profits as a donation to a veteran's organization.

- **Thanksgiving**—Family, giving thanks, or big meal-themed promotions.

- **Christmas/Hanukkah**—Holiday-related apps. Scheduling and appointment setting apps may fit in here nicely.

Many other holidays may be relevant for your app sales—Easter, Martin Luther King Day, President's Day, Secretary's Day, Grandparent's Day—and on and on. Again, carefully review the calendar and think through the holidays that you could leverage to create a unique promotion for your app. Once you've reviewed the holidays and determined which ones would be good promotional events for your business, take another look through the calendar for annual events that are not necessarily holidays—but are certainly traditions. Here is a list of annual events to consider:

- **Super Bowl**—Guaranteed football parties and an especially great event if your local NFL team is in the Super Bowl (equally, the playoffs leading up to the Super Bowl are great for promotions of local NFL teams). Is your app football related?

- **Mardi Gras**—A fun party-themed promotion. You can even donate a portion of the app's proceeds toward New Orleans rebuilding efforts.

- **March Madness**—Celebrate college basketball's greatest tournament— especially fun to offer promotions if your app is in any way related to college basketball.

- **Tax Day**—Great way to promote a discount for your tax calculator app. No one really likes tax day, so you might as well create a promotion to help lift the burden.

- **World Series**—Similar to Super Bowl promotions—extremely effective if your app is in any way related to baseball; offer discounts for your app or offer a drawing on your website for a pair of baseball tickets to one of the World Series games.

- **Earth Day**—Great day to offer "green" and earth-friendly promotions for your app.

- **Seasons or solstices/equinoxes**—Spring, summer, fall, and winter are great themes for a marketing campaign, as are the summer and winter solstices as well as vernal and autumnal equinoxes. You might have a nature-related app that would work in this category.

- **Mother's Day**—Celebrate mothers by offering a discount or something just for mothers, such as a short-term discount on your app.

- **Father's Day**—Celebrate fathers by offering a discount on your app for fathers.

- **Time Change**—Spring forward and fall back—or whatever your area time change ritual is; you might find something relevant to promote concerning your app around the changing times.

Summary

A marketing plan is a valuable tool to help you align your development and marketing efforts into a single cohesive plan. Most app developers do not consider a marketing plan to be necessary, but it can make the difference between a mediocre app and best-selling one. The plan does not need to be lengthy, but it must include the necessary components to fully cover the app's purpose, development efforts, target audience, launch plans, and financials. If you want to become a big player in the Android Market, spend some time getting organized and create a marketing plan.

Marketing
Essentials

Striking a balance between how much you should spend on marketing and anticipated revenues is a challenge for any product developer. It's especially a challenge for Android app developers because of the low price point and the fact that Google takes a 30% share from all sales. So, the question that's often asked is, how much marketing is needed for profits to be realized?

Think of marketing in terms of driving visitors to two locations to learn about your app: the Android Market and your app product website. You will spend most of your time optimizing your product website, just like any other web-based business. However, you should always look for opportunities to update your content on the Android Market as well.

Thus, the first section of this chapter addresses opportunities for you to update your Android Market content. The second section will help you think through your marketing activities for your app.

Updates to Your App: Write About What's New and Exciting

The following scenarios are opportunities to write about or possibly issue a press release on what's new and exciting concerning your app:

- A new review posted by an external source. (Include the highlights of the review on the Android Market.)

- A download milestone reached. (Include specifics, such as "over 100,000 copies downloaded.")

- Additional app added to your portfolio. (Introduce your new app in your app text.)

- When your app is added to any Android Market category, such as New and Noteworthy, Staff Picks, and What's Hot.

Of course, whenever you have updates that are newsworthy, you should also post them to your product website as well. The business of online selling (of any kind) requires your content to be ever-changing and exciting. If you let the content on the Android Market or on your product website become stale, you will find your customers losing interest in your apps.

Striking a Balance

To strike a balance in your marketing activities, it helps to think in terms of the different phases of your app's progression. You will do some marketing activities prior to its launch. Then you will do some more activities during the app's launch and, finally, you'll follow it up with ongoing activities to help you maintain app sales. Tables 20.1, 20.2, and 20.3 provide recommendations on essential marketing activities during each respective stage of your app sales cycle.

Table 20.1   Essential Marketing Activities Prior to Launch

Marketing Activity	Estimated Cost of Activity
Create app product website.	$500–$2000.
Conduct SEO activities for your site, including keywords, site submissions, and external links.	Usually free. It can take several months for search engines to pick your site up and start to establish your page rank.
Create an app and brand blog.	Free, but does require consistency and time.

Table 20.1   Essential Marketing Activities Prior to Launch

Marketing Activity	Estimated Cost of Activity
Draft a press release.	$250–$400
Identify blog sites and post comments.	Free, but does require consistency and time.
Identify app reviewers and offer them early access to your app.	Free, but does require consistency and time.
Identify nontraditional app reviewers and invite them to review your app.	Free, but requires your time.
Identify companies with whom you can partner that are complementary, not competitive, to your app.	Free, but requires your time.
Contact news media about pre-announcing your app to your audience.	Free, but requires your time.
Determine any promotions you want to have when your app is launched.	Free (planning stage).
Develop a free version of your app.	Costs money and time for you to develop a free version of your app or to hire someone else to develop your app.

Table 20.2   Essential Marketing Activities During Launch

Marketing Activity	Estimated Cost of Activity
Issue press release.	Free on some sites, and $80–$360 with PRWeb.
Contact review sites and distribute promo codes when requested.	Free, but takes lots of time.
Contact bloggers and online publications about your app.	Free, but takes lots of time.
Advertising.	Free (news stories) to unlimited (banner ads and such will cost).
Promotions.	Contests with prizes can cost from $100 to $10,000, depending on the prizes given to the winners of your contests.
Email campaign.	Free, if you have a list already. Email costs 10–18 cents per recipient if you have to rent a list. Possible cost to use an email service to send out the emails. Many services offer a 30- or 60-day free trial, so use that option first before signing up for a monthly fee.

Table 20.2   Essential Marketing Activities During Launch

Marketing Activity	Estimated Cost of Activity
Create blog post about your new app.	Free.
Use Twitter to send out announcements about your new app.	Free.
Conduct SEO activities for your site, including keywords, site submissions, and external links.	Usually free, but it can take several months for search engines to pick your site up and start to establish your page rank.

Table 20.3   Essential Marketing Activities After Launch

Marketing Activity	Estimated Cost of Activity
Monitor pricing and downloads of your app.	Free.
Determine if a temporary price adjustment is needed.	Free.
Make temporary pricing adjustments.	Free to change, but will impact your revenues hopefully in a positive way.
Keep reviewers looking at your app by seeking new reviews.	Free, but requires your time.
Introduce promotions to punch up sales.	May be free or cost money, depending on the promotions you utilize.
Continue working on SEO for your product web page.	Free, but requires your time.
Advertise your app to increase sales.	Costs money (banner ads, product review sites, and so on).
Drop price permanently for your app.	Free to change price, but may impact your revenues and profits either positively or negatively.
Develop a free version of your app.	Costs money and time for you to develop a free version of your app or to hire someone else to develop your app.
Conduct SEO activities for your site, including keywords, site submissions, and external links.	Usually free, but it can take several months for search engines to pick your site up and start to establish your page rank.

Note

The best way to determine how much to spend on your marketing is to do a small trial before launching an all-out marketing campaign. If you plan to do an email campaign about your app, then send out 100 emails first to see what the response is before sending out a blast to 10,000. You'll save money and time by testing what works beforehand.

Summary

Achieving the right marketing balance of activities and cost requires a bit of trial and error. It helps to first break out your marketing activities in pre-launch, launch, and post-launch categories. Many of the marketing activities do not cost you money but will cost you in terms of time. The activities that cost you money should be approached by using a small trial first to measure the results.

For example, place a small banner ad on a popular app game site if you are trying to sell a game app. Then measure the results to see whether this marketing method is effective for your app. If it does help you increase sales, then look to expand the ad's coverage and search out other sites where you might also advertise.

Marketing requires a constant effort. You have to be consistent in order to make people aware of your apps and download them. Some marketing activities work better for one type of app than another. Only you will be able to determine the best marketing mix for your app. Use the marketing activity tables provided in this chapter to help you get started.

21

Twenty-Five Essential Android Marketing Activities

You can use numerous marketing activities to gain exposure and sales for your app. Because the Android Market and Android apps are relatively new in the world of commerce, there is a learning curve in understanding what works and what doesn't for marketing apps through the store and from your own product website.

In this chapter we'll discuss 25 Android marketing activities that are essential to your sales success. Some of these activities we have discussed in more detail in other chapters, but they are brought together here into a single list for easy reference. As you create your marketing plan, you can review this list to ensure that all these activities are being performed at different points in your plan—from pre-launch to post-launch and during your ongoing marketing campaigns. These marketing activities are grouped by category and are not in any specific order.

Delivering Your Android App to the World

This first section provides a list of activities associated with how you introduce your app to the world.

Seek Reviews from Any Site That Matches Your App's Category

Seek reviews by doing the following:

- Submit your app for review in as many places as you can. Try to submit it to at least 30 review sites as soon as your app is launched on the Android Market. Keep an ongoing list of sites and the date you have submitted your review request. This way, you can track who you've sent requests to and when. It is difficult to get attention on review sites because so many app developers and app companies are requesting reviews, but you should still submit to them. It's a numbers game; the more you submit your app, the more likely you'll find a reviewer to write about your app.

- Search on Google and Yahoo! for online magazines and other publications that could be interested in giving your app a review. You should also ask industry-specific magazines for reviews. For example, if you have developed a financial app, look for financial publications that might be interested in giving your app a write-up. See Chapter 6, "Electronic Word of Mouth," for more information.

Showcase Your App on the Android Market

Showcase your app by doing the following:

- Prospective customers often browse within the top apps categories listed in the Android Market—such as "What's Hot" and "New and Noteworthy"—using their computer or directly from their Android. Your app's ranking is determined by the number of downloads—and the more downloads, the more likely you are to get into the Top 100 categories. It does, however, take several thousand downloads per day to take a spot in the Top 100.

- As mentioned before, select a clever and unique app name so that buyers will remember the name and pass it along to others. Having a unique app name for games is crucial to achieving success, whereas having an easy-to-remember name is essential for non-game apps and will help your sales when people search for apps via Google or Yahoo!.

- You should routinely check the Android Market to determine what others are doing in terms of their positioning and messaging. For more information, see Chapter 5, "Building Your App's Total Message."

Use Press Releases Consistently

Publicize your app by doing the following:

- Use press releases to announce the launch of your app and to broadcast any other timely and relevant information to the Android audience. The most effective means is through online PR agencies, which can distribute your press release to all media agencies, including the Internet, blogs, newspapers, and industry trade publications. You should also directly contact editors, news analysts, and other professionals to review your app.

- If possible, have a blogger or reviewer post comments at the same time you issue a press release for your app. The more total exposure you can give your app at the same time, the more likely people will notice and take a look at the app on your product website or on the Android Market.

- See Chapter 9, "Getting the Word Out About Your App," for more information about writing a press release.

Consider Email Marketing

Create email marketing by doing the following:

- Send out an email campaign to potential app buyers. The best list is your own list if you have developed one for other products or apps. You can also purchase lists from list brokers such as infoUSA.com that allow you to filter on very specific categories, including contacts by industry, Standard Industrial Classification (SIC), size, job title, spending, location, and more. You can also purchase millions of consumer email contacts by location, age, income level, hobbies and interests, ethnicity, religion, household occupant information, and so on. As stated before, you should use caution buying email lists because this marketing approach can eat into your profits, especially on a low-priced app.

- Many other agencies (chamber of commerce, business communities located around airparks and in most towns, and so on) have databases of subscriber email addresses and will usually let you have access to their lists if you join their group. Sometimes there are costs to join, so make sure you spend your money wisely on groups that match the demographic for your app.

- Choose online or printed publications whose audiences match your targeted customers. For example, if you are selling an aviation app, you can look at targeting websites or publications catering to pilots. See Chapter 6 for more information.

Create Word of Mouth Buzz

Good old-fashioned word of mouth can help you spread the word about your app. You can create word of mouth by doing the following:

- Tell everyone about your new app, including family, co-workers, friends, and other developers. You can also send an email message to all those people in your address books announcing your new app. If you attend any events such as luncheons, seminars, and forums, be sure to talk about your app to all who will listen.

- Look into attending weekly app meet-ups. These meetings are held in many large cities across the U.S. and Canada so that people can discuss Android app development and share ideas with each other. It's a great way to make new contacts and get ideas on how others are successfully marketing their apps. See Chapter 6 for more information.

Consider Targeted Advertising

Advertising is another way to get the word out about your app. You can create targeted advertising by doing the following:

- If you are concerned about advertising costs, try to find a local television or radio station that might be interested in discussing your app on a show. This way, you'll get free advertising. Keep in mind that not all apps are well suited to TV or radio advertising. Your app must have broad appeal, such as a game, shopping assistant, weather tracker, or navigation tool, to name a few examples.

- For some apps, using good old-fashioned posters may work well. An app that provides train schedules for the Phoenix light rail system, for example, should focus on the ridership for that rail system. It makes sense to look at poster advertising at train stations and in local publications that discuss the trains or are distributed at the stations.

- Banner ads should also be considered. They can be targeted somewhat closely to your app-buying audience. A banner can direct people to either your website or to the Android Market to review your app. See Chapter 6 for more information.

Utilize Analytics for Your Apps

You should look at employing analytics to measure the success of your apps. Analytics tools help you measure how many apps are being sold, how people are using your apps, and where in the world your apps are being used. Analytics is an important marketing tool because it can help you make adjustments to your marketing campaigns as well as add and enhance features your buyers are interested in.

Analytics can be downloaded and used for free from most analytics firms, including AdMob and Flurry/Pinch Media. These firms also provide monetization platforms that can help your free app generate revenue from the placement of ads on the app. See Chapter 17, "Using Android Analytics," for more information.

Android Pricing and Promotions

In this section we'll consider your pricing strategy and promotions. A pricing strategy means that you have some plan in mind for when you will do temporary or permanent price drops. You should always promote your other apps with your apps. Cross-promotion is very powerful because once you have a buying customer they tend to keep buying from you.

Develop a Pricing Strategy

You must have a pricing strategy to find success on the Android Market. Look at other developers and companies to see how they have successfully priced their apps or have done a promotion that has generated large sales. Some companies have found that by doing a three-day promotion over a long weekend they have been able to significantly increase their app sales. For more information on promotion, see Chapter 16, "App Promotions and Cross-Selling."

Promote from Ads Within Other Apps

You can promote your app using interactive ads contained within other Android apps. There are many ways to engage a customer using ads, including click to call, click to see a video, and click to go to the Android Market. You can test different types of ads to see which ones might work the best for you. Also, many ad networks provide in-app advertising options for targeting a very specific audience, such as age group, gender, geography, category, carrier, and device or handset. This way, you can experiment with different ads. For more information see, Chapter 14, "Level the Playing Field with a Free App."

Build an App Product Website

Having your own product website to showcase your apps is a must. The site does not need to be complex or lengthy but must include the essential elements so that you and your apps can be found by someone doing an Internet search. The following items will help you increase your traffic to your site and consequently your app sales.

Increase Your Website Search Engine Optimization (SEO)

To increase your website SEO, follow this strategy:

- Create a product website to showcase your apps. Always include screenshots and describe the features and benefits of your app. Just like with any website, you'll want to optimize the content with keywords and make sure you build a following of other sites that link back to your website. This will improve the search rankings for your site. Always have a "Buy Now" button to link to your app within the Android Market or to another app market where your app will be sold. Promote your app throughout every page of the product website.

- Getting your app noticed also means getting your app product website noticed. If you have just created a new website, you can get it listed in free online directories, such as DMOZ (www.dmoz.com), the Open Directory Project. As stated on the site, DMOZ powers core directory services for some of the most popular portals and search engines on the Web, including AOL Search, Netscape Search, Google, Lycos, HotBot, and hundreds of others.

- Use the Google AdWords keyword tool, research search terms that are most relevant to your app audience, and populate your app description with those terms. Don't go overboard with the use of terms, but make sure you have the relevant ones on every page of your site. Also use the search terms in all your marketing efforts, including social media activities such as blogs, email campaigns, and promotional efforts. See Chapter 5 for more information on creating your product website.

Let Visitors Market Your Site

Use these approaches to have visitors market your site:

- Having a high page rank for your personal website is, in part, about getting external links back to your app product website. You do this by getting visitors to write comments about your site and app on blog posts and on their own websites. Blogging is a great way to help your site get noticed and keep visitors coming to it. Be sure to utilize the AddThis button on your site to promote your apps and website. The AddThis button can be installed on your blog or website pages and allows visitors to share your content with their friends and co-workers who use Facebook, LinkedIn, MySpace, Digg, TypePad, Blogger, WordPress, and other social media sites.

- Be sure to use a "Follow Us" note on your home page. Beneath this you can post links to Facebook, Twitter, YouTube, and other social media sites that link directly to your content on those sites. This will keep your visitors engaged with your apps and development activities. For more information, see Chapter 5.

Social Media Marketing

Social media provides the new tools for advertising and PR. You must become proficient in creating YouTube videos and using LinkedIn, Facebook, Twitter, and others so that you can stay in front of your audience. This section will remind you of those areas of social media that you need to utilize to keep your app sales moving along.

Use YouTube Promotions

Here are some ideas for using YouTube to promote your app:

- Create a YouTube video describing and demonstrating your new app. You can set up an account for free in a matter of seconds on YouTube. In your video, highlight the use of your app and how its features and benefits make it worthwhile. Videos are very powerful because people will tend to watch a video over reading about a subject. So, once you post a video on YouTube, you can have literally thousands of views in a short period of time. People can comment on the video and your app, just like on the Android Market. However, you can also comment back when someone posts a comment. This interaction will help you establish a community of followers for your apps and brand.

- You can also create YouTube ads for your app using a Google AdWords account. As recommended in this book, you should use this approach sparingly and go slowly before spending too much money. Gauge whether your ads are going to work before committing too much money. For more information, see Chapter 7, "Using Social Media in Your App Marketing."

Use LinkedIn Groups

LinkedIn can be a great way to reach an audience of developers and buyers for your app, especially if you have written a business-related app that is geared toward working professionals. Here are some thoughts on creating a LinkedIn promotion:

- You can join up to 50 LinkedIn groups based on your own target audience. A search of groups will reveal perhaps hundreds of groups that you can contact. Be sure to find groups that have many members so that your communication efforts are not in vain. Use the news category to let the group know about your app.

- If you haven't created your own LinkedIn profile, you will need to do that to post to these groups. However, having a profile showcasing your development skills is a huge benefit. You can post announcements on your profile about your app's availability, and you can alert your contacts concerning updates and other news about your brand. See Chapter 7 for more information about LinkedIn.

Use Blog Promotions

As discussed in Chapter 7, you'll want to post an announcement about your new app to your blog. You can create a blog if you don't already have one, but remember that blogging is a commitment and you must post comments at least weekly in order to be followed with any regularity. You can use WordPress or Blogger—they're free and simple to use. There are many ways to link and use your blog posts to spread the word about your app. For example, you can post your blogs to your LinkedIn profile. You can also send out a Twitter message (a Tweet) with a link to your blog post.

Create a Facebook Fan Page

Create a Facebook Fan page to showcase your new app and develop your brand. A number of popular game apps are using Facebook fan pages and have generated huge followings. Facebook fan pages are easy to set up and don't cost you a dime.

Your app page can be found in the search engines as well, which is going to help people find you. Additionally, when a visitor joins your fan page, the update is broadcast to all members of that person's group. Thus, he or she is helping you to spread the word about your app. For more information on creating a Facebook Fan page, refer to Chapter 7.

Employ Digg Articles and Videos

You can spread the word about your app article or video online at Digg.com. Digg will post your submission immediately in "Upcoming Stories," where other Digg members can find it. If the readers like your article, they will "Digg" it, meaning they will give it their approval. Once a submission reaches a large number of Diggs, your post can become one of the most read and it jumps to the home page in its category, where even more people will read it. Be prepared to post many articles to this site before one of them takes off. It's a lot of work but could be well worth it when you app get noticed in a very big way. See Chapter 7 to learn more social media techniques.

Visit Forums and Post Comments

Many developers are already members of forums and discussion groups where they can post comments about Android development topics. You can also identify new forums that meet your target audience criteria for your app and start a dialogue about apps in your category and other relevant topics. You can participate in discussions and talk about your apps, as appropriate, once you have established yourself as a regular. Be sure to follow each forum's protocol, as discussed in earlier chapters. This will help you build awareness for your brand and for your app. See Chapter 6 for more details.

Other App Marketing Activities

Finally, here are a few other marketing activities to help you achieve greater success.

Create Trial and Paid App Versions

Offer a free trial version with an option to obtain more functionality in the paid version, as discussed in previous chapters. A free app is going to drive downloads and awareness for your brand and app. The biggest challenge for your success is developing enough functionality in your free app to be compelling, yet not so much that your audience doesn't feel the need to purchase your paid app. For more information on developing a free version of your app, see Chapter 14.

Use App Launch Sponsorship

Secure a launch sponsor and co-promote. Examples include FRAM Oil utilizing the Gas Cubby app to co-promote its brand. Within your pre-launch marketing materials, promote and provide clear instructions for those who might be interested in being a launch sponsor. Explain the benefits they'll receive in terms of publicity exposure, placement within the app, and other perks. See Chapter 13, "Breaking into the Android Market Top Paid Apps," to learn more.

Continuously Feature Improvements

You must think about new features. Here are some thoughts:

- Add new features to your app frequently, such as every couple months. Just reposting your app will energize sales for a time. Feature upgrades allow you to do another press release and garner fresh interest on the Android Market. Along with feature improvements, you should monitor your app's reviews on the market and act upon insightful new feature requests to keep customers coming back and to lure new ones into the fold.

- When your app is developed, utilize mobile analytics so that you can learn about how your app is used as well as see referring sources and app performance characteristics. Within your app, you can request that your users send you feedback with your company's private email address. Also encourage your users to post positive reviews on the Android Market if they like the app. For more information on mobile analytics, see Chapter 17, "Using Android Analytics," and Chapter 2, "What Makes for a Winning App?"

Collaborate with Other People

Here are a couple ideas for how to leverage collaboration:

- There are many ways to collaborate with other vendors. Seek companies and entrepreneurs who would be willing to talk about your app in their product pitches, meetings, and sales conferences. For example, look for industry conferences where your app might be appropriate to that audience and contact speakers who might be willing to mention your app.

- Some developers are teaming together to create a consortium and a brand. If you are a small independent developer with limited time to create multiple apps, you can look into finding other developers who are interested in building a brand. Android meet-ups are a great place to locate other developers who are interested in co-branding and co-marketing their apps.

Seek Non-App Review Sites for Your App

Seek out other venues to get reviews of your app. For example, if you have an app that helps people learn how to garden, look for online and print publications focused on gardening and make a few inquiries to see if they would be interested in reviewing your app for an article. You'll be surprised how many publications will be interested in doing such a story. The reason is simple: Publications are always looking for topics that would be of interest to their readers.

The Android carries the "cool factor," and for those readers outside of the traditional tech world, the Android and Android apps that are germane to their pursuits carry strong interest. You will probably have to arrange a call to demo the app for the editor or writer of the publication if this person doesn't have an Android, but it is well worth the effort and you can circumvent the long lines at the traditional review sites.

Exchange Ad Space

You can use a download exchange such as AdMob to exchange ad space with other apps. AdMob handles all the placement of your ad within other apps' ads. In return, you exchange ad space on your app. This implies that you are building a free app. This functionality will allow new users to discover your app from inside hundreds of other apps, which will help drive downloads and hopefully sales of the paid version of your app. For more information on this process, see Chapter 14.

Create an Icon Worth Remembering

Carefully evaluate your app's icon to ensure that the graphic describes your app and conveys the value of your app. This is easier than it sounds but requires you to spend some serious time on the creation of this key graphic. If you are concerned that your logo may not convey what your app does, you may want to consider developing another graphic or adding text to the graphic that provides the app's name. Seek the advice of friends who can review the icon and give you some honest feedback.

Determine Your App's Unique Value

In the Android app world, you have to identify the unique functionality of your app and communicate that value to your audience. The trick to creating a powerful and unique selling proposition is to boil down in a few words an identifying message that embodies your app's unique value. Your unique selling proposition must answer the question, why should anyone buy your app over all the other similar apps in the Android Market? For more information, refer to Chapter 3, "Identifying Your App's Unique Value."

Summary

Use the list in this chapter to help you formulate your pre-launch and post-launch marketing activities for your Android apps. These activities are viewed to be some of the most important marketing activities you can perform to get your app off to a solid start when it's posted to the Android Market. As you develop your marketing plan, group your activities into pre-launch, post-launch, and ongoing activities. Many of these recommended activities are free or inexpensive, costing you only your time to develop them.

22

Implementing Your Plan

Perhaps one of the most challenging aspects of marketing an Android app on the Android Market is that you must implement your plan with a sustained effort over time to realize positive results. The most effective marketing campaign is an integrated one that combines multiple marketing touch points by leveraging a carefully developed, consistent app message.

This chapter covers the implementation steps and managing your marketing activities.

Implementation Steps

You can achieve greater results by including many different marketing methods to reach your audience—social media, word of mouth, email, product reviews, banner ads, and so on. The following steps will help you to implement a marketing campaign:

1. Determine the goals for the campaign—what results do you hope to achieve? Before you launch an app campaign, it is important to determine what the overall goals for each Android app marketing campaign will be, so that as the plan is implemented you can measure it and thus have some measure of success. We'll touch upon just a few objectives that you might pursue with your marketing campaigns.

2. Direct traffic to your app's product website. Keep in mind that you have all the control over your product website. You can develop search engine optimization (SEO) programs to drive traffic to your website. You can utilize banner ads and email campaigns to direct traffic to your product web pages. You have much more flexibility in what you can post to your own website than you do on the Android Market.

3. Increase app sales on the Android Market. This is obvious, but you want to have a goal to increase sales by a certain amount so you have something to measure and track against. If you are only seeing ten downloads a day, then set a goal to realize 20 downloads a day, and so on.

4. Establish a brand. Establishing a brand takes time and effort but is necessary and important to building long-term success. You establish a brand by being in front of your target audience. This is done by developing a common look for your apps and icons as well as developing a website that also carries the same look of your brand. Measuring brand awareness is more difficult, but your initial goal should be to simply establish your brand.

5. Bring back old customers to look at your newest app. Although you won't know who your customers actually are from Android Market sales unless you've persuaded them to register on your product site, you can conduct campaigns that will bring some of them back to try out your new app. This can be done through banner ads, email campaigns, and blog posts. You can mention that you are the creator of a best-selling app that they used to enjoy.

Your campaign goals can vary from meeting basic expectations to reaching for very lofty revenue aspirations. The key behind setting goals is to be realistic, based on your overall budget and your timeframe. You will only set yourself up for disappointment if you set a goal to be achieved in two days that realistically could take more than two months to produce the results you have in mind. You will be equally disappointed if you expect huge sales but have a very limited marketing budget. Here are some sample goals you might pursue with your marketing campaigns:

- Establish your app as the hottest new entrant in the Android Market's Lifestyle category.

- Increase online ordering conversion rates from your personal website.

- Increase overall leads while minimizing the cost to obtain new leads.

- Successfully cross-sell to your existing app customer base.

- Establish measurement criteria.

✉ Note

Always have a clearly defined goal in mind prior to launching a campaign. Not all campaigns have the same purpose. Your overall goal is to drive app sales, but in some cases you are also trying to build awareness for your brand and attempting to get your name recognized in the Android Market.

The next step is to determine how you will measure your desired goals. If your goal is to increase Android app sales, you will measure the success by reviewing the number of sales coming in after each campaign. Measure sales before you start the campaign and then during the campaign to compare the difference.

You'll most likely want to associate these measurements to a specific campaign so that you can determine the pieces of the overall plan that were most effective in reaching a set goal. This allows you to refine the marketing plan over time in order to make it as successful as possible. Here are some examples of measurements you'll want to evaluate for your own Android apps:

- Determine the number of app sales on the Android Market.

- Develop a strong lead response to your messaging—ensure the success of all lead-generation programs.

- Review revenue associated by campaign to determine if a sales increase can be attributed to your marketing plan.

- Gather prospects to target for your campaign.

Perform a thorough review of your target audience. Do you have a database with customers who have purchased an app from you previously? As I have mentioned before, always include a registration option on your product website so that visitors can be notified by email of your latest apps and upgrades.

Other developers will have email databases from previous products launched. Maybe you have a PC game that you are now launching as an Android app. If you've sold to a PC audience, you will want to notify them of the availability of your new Android app. Gather all the leads that should be targeted for the campaign and use a clean email list (meaning the names have been scrubbed for duplicates and invalid addresses). The following list explains some steps you should take to track the impact of your marketing activities:

1. Track your results and measure your marketing ROI (return on investment). One of the most important tasks is tracking the successes and failures for each marketing initiative, campaign, and so on. You will better understand the most effective ways to promote your app to your audience, which in turn allows you to maximize your marketing dollars. Learn how to track results.

2. Build tracking mechanisms into your marketing pieces if possible:

   a. Send users to a landing page on your website and track hits using Google Analytics.

   b. Add mechanisms to your product website to track unique hits for each page and links within your site. Understand where website traffic is coming from and what visitors are viewing when they get to your site.

3. Analyze leads and sources by revenue:

   a. Track sales by lead source.

   b. Compare total app sales from Google's stats to conversions from your product website.

   You will be able to identify whether your website is producing more sales than the Android Market by itself. If your website is converting less than the Android Market is on its own, you need to work to improve your website hits and conversion rates.

 Note

You can't improve what you can't measure. Always gather data on the success of each campaign so that you can fine-tune going forward.

Managing Your App Marketing Activities

To reiterate, you need to manage your marketing activities. Use your marketing plan to write down what you want to accomplish and when. Your marketing plan will help you to chart and track your initiatives. You can also use your marketing plan as a tool to review how many marketing projects you've implemented and their levels of success. You could also use a checklist to keep track of what you need to do and when to implement an Android marketing activity.

You should also set up an accountability system. This can be part of your app marketing plan, where you keep track of initiatives. Or you can set up a simple Excel spreadsheet that lists the app name, date, action, cost, target completion date, date completed, and results. By managing your app marketing activities and being accountable for them, you'll be well on your way to actually putting the marketing strategies in motion. An example of such an accountability system is shown in Table 22.1.

Table 22.1   Marketing Campaign Tracking Spreadsheet

App Name	Date	Action	Cost	Target Completion	Completion Date	Results
MyFirstApp	8/27/10	Banner ad	$179.99	9/27/10	9/30/10	Sales increased to 125 downloads per day.
MySecondApp						

Successfully implementing an Android marketing activity requires you to do the following:

- **Focus**—You must focus on the marketing task at hand and the end results (such as more downloads of your app).

- **Implement**—Make sure you do everything that is planned for your app and leave nothing out of your plan.

- **Manage**—Make sure all who are involved in the campaign are working to accomplish all tasks.

- **Delegate**—Do what you know how to do best and outsource the rest. If you are not skilled in writing email copy and doing a campaign, then hire someone to do it.

Implementation is the key to your app marketing success. Implement some kind of marketing effort each and every day, no matter how small, and you'll be that much closer than your competitor to getting that app sale. In order to properly implement your marketing plan, you must do the following:

- **Always check your progress.** Know what's working in your campaigns and what isn't. If you do a status check every day, it will help you stay on top of programs that need work and those that are working.

- **Always try new things.** Never sit on your hands when your app sales are not picking up. The Android Market and the app market are always changing, and so should you.

- **Avoid jumping ship too soon.** Give your plan time to work. So many developers give up after a month or so. If it's not working, don't give up. Work with your development team and marketing consultant, and let them help you succeed.

- **Ask for feedback.** Ask your customers to comment on your apps and how you are doing solving their challenges. Ask team members if they are pleased with how the "plan" is going and how it could be improved.

Summary

Implementing your marketing campaigns is where the real proof of your efforts will be seen. Use your marketing plan and marketing calendar to track and measure your app campaign progress. Set some goals that you want to accomplish for each campaign.

Measure your app sales prior to your campaign and then after the campaign has been implemented. Be sure to give the campaign sufficient time to achieve the desired outcome. If you are not seeing the desired results, make some adjustments to the campaign and try it again.

23

Android Apps for Corporate Marketing

Developers of other products outside the Android world are now looking at mobile platforms as a way to reach millions of tech-savvy users with their product messages. Companies are using Android apps to reignite their brand or to extend functionality from an existing cloud-based app to the mobile platform. Companies looking to extend their brands will provide either free or paid versions of their apps, although most of them will be free. The idea with a free app is to promote awareness of the brand across millions of Android users.

In this chapter we will look at how corporations can use Android apps to help sell more products or enhance brand awareness. Each company must review whether it makes sense to develop an app because there is a commitment of time and financial resources if you decide to move forward.

NBA basketball is a great example of a franchise that has been very successful promoting its basketball app to hundreds of thousands of users. The app helps users find NBA scores, review stats, and track their favorite teams. However, the apps also get people to remember the brand in a very powerful manner whenever they watch or go to a game. Brand awareness is strengthened in a fairly inexpensive way, plus the NBA gets lots of free publicity for its brand.

The other option for corporations is to create an app as an extension to their existing web products. Banks, for example, will create a home banking app that is complementary to their web-based banking access. The Android app may not have all the functionality of the web-based access, but will provide the most common features, such as the ability to check account balances and transfer funds. In these examples, companies are offering the app as an additional customer service option.

 Note

Some companies may charge for their extended apps, but most give them away for free, with the idea that only existing subscribers or account holders of their products will use these apps. Kraft Foods has seen tremendous success with its iFood Assistant app, which currently sells for $0.99 on the Android Market. The app provides over 7,000 recipes (with Kraft ingredients, of course) and a store locator.

Other apps taking advantage of the mobile platform (and are not necessarily paid apps) include commerce apps from companies such as eBay and Amazon, email apps such as Constant Contact, social networking apps for Facebook and MySpace, travel apps (from Hotels.com, for example), and many others. Here are some other reasons why companies should look at the Android platform as a new way to reach their audience:

- The Android mobile platform provides new and exciting ways to interact with company brands and reach an untapped audience.

- The mobile platform lets users connect with their favorite content in their own way and within their timeframe. Once users are connected to a company's app, that company has a huge advantage over its competitors.

- Companies can leverage their brands to create new interactive experiences that utilize the power of Android technologies, including the camera, GPS, and accelerometer.

Is an Android App Right for Your Company?

I would argue that most companies should create an Android app—to either promote their brand or extend existing services to their customers. However, this advice comes with a caveat: The company must have the resources and the wherewithal to keep the app relevant and significant in the eyes of its customers.

 Note

Using Android as a branding tool has had mixed results for a number of companies as they have launched their apps. Using the app as a customer acquisition tool has seen limited success. Using the app as a way to reinforce a brand has seen better results. It takes some clever thinking to identify ways to make an app relevant for a brand, which is a crucial part of an app's success. Your company must produce an app that goes beyond the simple "store locator" functionality that many apps provide.

For example, a company selling paint might devise a color palette that shows pictures of rooms and walls with any paint color the user selects. The paint samples could include an entire inventory of the company's paints and color recommendations. A paint company could have an app on the Android Market that allows the user to snap a photo of an item and compare its color to the company's inventory of paint colors. Building an app is a long-term commitment, and companies need to evaluate carefully whether they have the internal resources to maintain the app and support it (along with the usual customer issues). Providing an app is a big endeavor, requiring a dedicated internal team to ensure the project's success. The following points should be considered before you embark on app creation:

- What is your user demographic? Do you have a way to poll your users to identify how many of them are currently using an Android? Recent reports show that about 10% of the U.S. mobile user community has an Android.

- Do you understand how your customers are using mobile devices? The Android has more features and capabilities than a lot of other mobile devices.

- How will you measure the success of your app? Do you intend to implement analytics into your app to measure beyond downloads?

- What is your budget for this project? Designing and building a free app can easily cost $50,000, if not much more when you factor in a small team to design, code, and support the app.

- What is your timeframe for releasing the app? Will it coincide with other campaigns you are rolling out?

- How will you promote your app and make its availability known?

Build an App to Extend/Reignite the Brand

Some companies are looking at Android apps to help them improve their brand reputation. With its emerging growth, Android is a good tool to promote your brand. The reason is clear. What other medium can you think of that has such a powerful adoption by its users than a smartphone? The user demographic have their Androids with them almost constantly. Young people are online more hours per day than they watch TV. If you can get someone to download your app and use it on a regular basis, you are able to reinforce your brand consistently. An Android app is typically used for about three to seven minutes each time it is accessed. No other medium has had this type of reach before.

Rather than attempting to generate a revenue stream, these brands use apps to create a branded mobile experience that drives usage of the apps. This usage helps reinforce the brand and indirectly drive sales. The intention is not to generate income from the app but rather awareness. Very few brands can't benefit from an Android app if it's designed properly. For example, Sears was able to create a shopping app that helps reinforce its brand, as shown in Figure 23.1. The app facilitates sales of products from your Android phone and builds a strong link between the user and Sears stores where you pick up your purchased merchandise. Therefore, users may be more likely to shop at Sears stores than go elsewhere.

Another company that has created a free app that provides some useful functionality is Walgreens. This app allows you to fill prescriptions, order photos, and view the latest sale items—a great combination of features. So, in addition to building customer loyalty, the company is providing some useful functionality at the same time. The app is shown in Figure 23.1.

Perhaps the granddaddy of branding using an app is Google with their Google Earth app. Google Earth allows users to explore the world from the palm of their own hands. Google has had more than a million downloads of its app, making it one of the most downloaded free apps in the history of the Android Market. Figure 23.3 shows the infamous app. The most popular branded apps for 2010 are listed in Table 23.1. This list will give you a feel for the variety of branded apps that have achieved success—and perhaps prompt a few ideas of your own.

Figure 23.1 Sears has an app that allows you to browse and buy using your phone and helps reinforce customer loyalty.

Table 23.1	Some of the Top Most Popular Branded Apps for 2010
App Name	App Function
Starbucks Mobile Card	Find the local Starbucks in your area quickly and easily.
Dominos Pizza	Use your Android to order your favorite Dominos pizza. Includes all menu items.
Ebay	The app features voice search, alerts, advanced search functionality, leaving feedback, and paying with PayPal. With this app, eBay is open for business, anytime.
Kraft iFood Assistant 2.0	iFood Assistant, powered by Kraft, brings you simple food ideas with over 7,000 recipes.

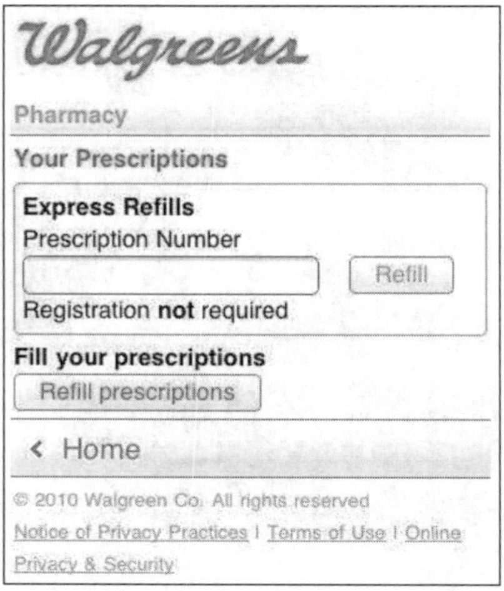

Figure 23.2   The Walgreens App helps the company build greater brand awareness and customer loyalty while providing the ability to fill prescriptions and order photos.

Figure 23.3   The Google Earth app has seen over a million downloads.

Apps to Extend a Web-Based Product's Use

Another option companies can use is to develop an app that is an extension of an existing product or service. These types of apps typically provide a scaled-down version of the main web-based service. They often lack all the features of the original app because the app is new or because the original web service is much more complex than an Android app can support. These types of apps offer a lot of the functionality for traders, but not all of it. Complex option trades are currently not available in many mobile apps, but features that the majority of the audience needs are included.

Any company that offers computing on the Web, where users access a site for account information, placement of orders, or other online tasks, will want to look carefully at extending this functionality to an Android app. It will become vital to provide such apps as more and more users move to mobile technology to accomplish their daily activities. Companies that fail to recognize this trend in mobile technology will find themselves behind the curve and could be at a disadvantage from a competitive standpoint.

Providing a mobile app to extend your web-based technology is also about customer service. Your customers will be pleased when you provide technology that meets their needs and makes their lives easier. Your app can help you retain customers who might otherwise move to another bank, broker, or tool. You can bet your competitors will tout their app as an advantage to their solution over yours.

Some of the most popular apps that help extend functionality are discussed in the following sections. These are just a few examples of some of the most popular apps. Each of these apps requires a user to already have a login and password for his or her existing accounts. The apps are of no value to someone who doesn't already use the companies' products.

 Note

As you evaluate the following apps, look for how your product may benefit from an Android app. An app will help you extend access to your existing web-based tools. Your first version can provide just the essentials from your web-based app. Identify the key features that you believe must be in the Android app and determine if the cost of development is acceptable and the need is there for such an app. Be thinking about how your app can benefit customers and noncustomers alike.

Summary

Companies across the globe are starting to realize that they need to take their product message to their users, wherever they are. As their users are moving toward mobile platforms, smart marketers are looking for ways to leverage this new and exciting technology. Android users provide an "always connected" opportunity where they invite certain forms of advertising—advertising that is clever and at the same time useful.

Many companies are finding that building an Android app can help them extend their brand reach, increase customer interaction, and increase loyalty. They usually don't charge for the app because they can obtain tens of thousands of downloads for a free app and keep their name in front of the users. Companies are shifting some of their ad budget to building an Android app instead of spending it elsewhere.

Other companies are using mobile technology to extend the usefulness of existing web-based tools. These apps are used in banking, commerce, social networking, and many other areas to create extensions of existing services to the mobile platform. It's almost a necessity to provide a mobile-based app as part of regular online access. Companies that embrace mobile technology will experience greater customer satisfaction and retention than those who wait to implement a mobile app. In the not-too-distant future, having a mobile app available will be a prerequisite for many customers when choosing a vendor.

Competitive
Worksheet

The worksheet here will help you organize information about your local competitors. This is a good exercise for any app developer, to have a running list of features in competing apps. A completed worksheet will provide you with the following benefits:

- Gain a greater understanding of your competitors.

- Understand your competitors' key messages and how you might revise yours if needed.

- Identify areas of competitor strengths and weaknesses so you can more fully target your message and marketing campaigns.

- Compare pricing to help you understand where you fit in the local consumer's mind.

Complete the worksheet presented in Table A.1 to assist in highlighting the areas to focus on in sizing up your competition—such as features, key messages, strengths, weaknesses, price, target audience, and any other appropriate areas you want to add.

Table A.1 Competitive Worksheet

Competing App Name	Website	Key Features	Key Messages	Target Audience	Noteworthy Reviews	Strengths	Weaknesses	Price

Indirect Competitors

Competitor Name	Website	Key Features	Key Messages	Target Audience	Noteworthy Reviews	Strengths	Weaknesses	Price

Index

B

C

D

M

S

Biz-Tech Series

Straightforward Strategies and Tactics for Business Today

The **Que Biz-Tech series** is designed for the legions of executives and marketers out there trying to come to grips with emerging technologies that can make or break their business. These books help the reader know what's important, what isn't, and provide deep inside know-how for entering the brave new world of business technology, covering topics such as mobile marketing, microblogging, and iPhone and iPad app marketing.

- Straightforward strategies and tactics for companies who are either using or will be using a new technology/product or way of thinking/ doing business

- Written by well-known industry experts in their respective fields— and designed to be an open platform for the author to teach a topic in the way he or she believes the audience will learn best

- Covers new technologies that companies must embrace to remain competitive in the marketplace and shows them how to maximize those technologies for profit

- Written with the marketing and business user in mind—these books meld solid technical know-how with corporate-savvy advice for improving the bottom line

 Visit **quepublishing.com/biztech** to learn more about the **Que Biz-Tech series**

Jeffrey Hughes

Android™ Apps
Secrets to Selling Your Android App
Marketing

FREE Online Edition

Your purchase of **Android™ Apps Marketing** includes access to a free online edition for 45 days through the Safari Books Online subscription service. Nearly every Que book is available online through Safari Books Online, along with more than 5,000 other technical books and videos from publishers such as Addison-Wesley Professional, Cisco Press, Exam Cram, IBM Press, O'Reilly, Prentice Hall, and Sams.

SAFARI BOOKS ONLINE allows you to search for a specific answer, cut and paste code, download chapters, and stay current with emerging technologies.

Activate your FREE Online Edition at
www.informit.com/safarifree

> **STEP 1:** Enter the coupon code: MCXXAZG.

> **STEP 2:** New Safari users, complete the brief registration form.
> Safari subscribers, just log in.

If you have difficulty registering on Safari or accessing the online edition, please e-mail customer-service@safaribooksonline.com

  Addison Wesley   Adobe Press   ALPHA   Cisco Press   FT Press   IBM Press   lynda.com   Microsoft Press   New Riders

  O'REILLY   Peachpit Press   PRENTICE HALL   Redbooks   SAMS   SAS Publishing   Sun   WILEY